A GUIDE BOOK OF FLYING EAGLE AND INDIAN HEAD CENTS

James B. Longacre
Designer of the Flying Eagle and Indian Head Cents

Portrait by Charles Daughtrey

The Official RED BOOK®

A GUIDE BOOK OF
FLYING EAGLE
AND
INDIAN HEAD CENTS

Complete Source for History, Grading, and Prices

Richard Snow

Foreword by
Tom DeLorey

Introduction by
Q. David Bowers

Whitman Publishing, LLC
PUBLISHING SINCE 1934
Atlanta, Georgia

www.whitman**books**.com

© 2007 by Whitman Publishing, LLC

3101 Clairmont Road, Suite C, Atlanta GA 30329

The WCG™ pricing grid used throughout this publication is patent pending. THE OFFICIAL RED BOOK is a trademark of Whitman Publishing, LLC.

Correspondence concerning this book may be directed to the publisher, at the address above.

ISBN: 079481783-1

Printed in China

Disclaimer: Expert opinion should be sought in any significant numismatic purchase. This book is presented as a guide only. No warranty or representation of any kind is made concerning the completeness of the information presented. The author, a professional numismatist, regularly buys, sells, and sometimes holds certain of the items discussed in this book.

Caveat: The price estimates given are subject to variation and differences of opinion. Before making decisions to buy or sell, consult the latest information. Past performance of the rare coin market or any coin or series within that market is not necessarily an indication of future performance, as the future is unknown. Such factors as changing demand, popularity, grading interpretations, strength of the overall coin market, and economic conditions will continue to be influences.

Advertisements within this book: Whitman Publishing, LLC does not endorse, warrant, or guarantee any of the products or services of its advertisers. All warranties and guarantees are the sole responsibility of the advertiser.

About the cover: These two coins from the Stewart Blay Collection are among the rarities in the Flying Eagle and Indian Head cent series. The 1856 Flying Eagle cent was a pattern coin, struck to show congressmen what a new, small-format cent would look like (earlier "large cents" were 45% wider and more than twice as heavy). The 1877 Indian Head cent is the rarest in that series. Of the nearly one million minted, Rick Snow estimates only about 500 remain in Mint State.

About the frontispiece: Charles Daughtrey is an artist, photographer, and numismatic author who specializes in Lincoln cents. His *Portrait of James Barton Longacre* (pencil on Bristol board, 2006) is the third in a series of tributes to U.S. Mint designers and their coins. More of Daughtrey's limited-edition numismatic artwork can be seen at his web site, www.cdaughtrey.com.

Other books in **The Official** RED BOOK® series include: *A Guide Book of Morgan Silver Dollars*; *A Guide Book of Double Eagle Gold Coins*; *A Guide Book of United States Type Coins*; *A Guide Book of Modern United States Proof Coin Sets*; *A Guide Book of Shield and Liberty Head Nickels*; *A Guide Book of Buffalo and Jefferson Nickels*; *A Guide Book of Flying Eagle and Indian Head Cents*; *A Guide Book of Washington and State Quarters*; *A Guide Book of United States Commemorative Coins*; *A Guide Book of Barber Silver Coins*; and *A Guide Book of Liberty Seated Silver Coins*.

For a complete catalog of numismatic reference books, supplies, and storage products, visit Whitman Publishing online at www.whitman**books**.com.

CONTENTS

FOREWORD

S ome people will forever be associated with a particular numismatic field, no matter who writes what on that field in the future. Think of Overton with early halves, Judd with patterns, Friedberg with paper money, and Davenport with European crowns. Think of Bolender. Browning. Ahwash. Valentine. Think of Sheldon. Newcomb. Cohen. Though others may have taken certain of these authors' fields to new and glorious heights, they were the pioneers.

The world of the future will always associate Flying Eagle and Indian Head cents with Rick Snow, just as he owns the field now. The two unique designs, long collected as one series simply because there weren't enough dates in the former to justify an album of its own, are now a brave new collecting world, with a complete date-and-mintmark set a challenge to complete in decent condition, and the hundreds of significant varieties in the field the challenge of a lifetime to collect.

When I started collecting U.S. coins more than 45 years ago, there were, for all intents and purposes, just five collectible varieties in these two designs. According to the 1960 Red Book, these were the 1858 Large and Small Letters hub varieties, the 1864 With and Without L hub varieties, the 1873 Open and Close 3 date punch varieties, the 1886 hub varieties that are distinguished by the positions of the lettering relative to the feathers, and the so-called 1869/68 overdate (that didn't really exist, but was just a mis-attributed 1869/69). I only ever found two or three Indian Head cents while looking through many rolls of Lincolns, but they were technically still in circulation, and a great thrill for a ten-year-old to find.

However, the numismatic world of 1960 consisted mainly of adults who had grown up seeing Indian Head cents in their pocket change as a normal occurrence, and they refused to take them seriously. There is an old saying that familiarity breeds contempt, and Brahmins of that generation dismissed the Indians as too commonplace for a serious numismatist, just as I used to have trouble taking Franklin halves seriously because, for a while as a kid with a paper route, I could still get new ones every year at the bank.

Flying Eagle cents were in a unique situation. They were long gone from circulation by 1960, but the rare 1856 date kept them alive in the minds of collectors, who unfortunately were handicapped by the lack of solid information about them. Were the coins Proof or were they Uncirculated? How many of them were made in 1856, and how many of them were restrikes? If the mintage was so low, whatever it actually was, why were there so many different die varieties of them?

Part of the problem with the Flying Eagle cent series was that there were so few different dates of them that they didn't even merit their own page in the albums, much less ever having a book written about them. The best that a collector could hope to find on them was their eventual inclusion in Breen's book on Proofs and his great *Encyclopedia*, both of which were sometimes prone to error. Rick wrote the book on Flying Eagle cents, and several other books.

Unlike our predecessors, Rick took the Flying Eagle and Indian Head cents seriously, and dragged them kicking and screaming into respectability by the two-pronged method of good old-fashioned research and, most important, publishing what he learned. I have seen collectors spend 30 years learning everything they could about a series, all the while carefully hiding what they knew lest anybody else know it as well. Rick is not like that. He has always been freely willing to share what he knows, and through this open exchange of knowledge has learned more himself than he could ever have learned in ten lifetimes. This he shares with you.

This book will not bury you in information about the 47 different die varieties of 1907 cents. That will be found in Rick's other books, for collectors such as myself who do care about finding the 48th variety. We cherrypickers eagerly await the next volume of that series, which has been put on hold while he prepared this volume. This book will, however, tell you what classic major varieties you should be looking for, such as the 1873 Doubled Die Obverse coins with their boldly doubled LIBERTY, and the three 1857 cents with clash marks from dies intended for quarters, halves, and $20 gold pieces! It will also tell you how to identify recently discovered treasures such as the 1871 and 1872 cents with the reverse hub of 1864, long thought to have been retired in 1870. Collecting isn't always about making money, but it is nice to know that something you own is special.

◆

I cannot think of Indian Head cents without remembering the passage from chapter four of Harper Lee's *To Kill A Mockingbird*, where Scout and her brother Jem find two "slicked up" (ouch) Indian Head cents wrapped in chewing-gum tinfoil in a knot-hole in a live oak tree in front of the Radley place. The all-knowing older brother explains the importance of the coins to his kid sister in a voice tinged with awe:

> "Well, Indian-heads—well, they come from the Indians. They're real strong magic, they make you have good luck. Not like fried chicken when you're not lookin' for it, but things like long life 'n' good health, 'n' passin' six-weeks tests … these are real valuable to somebody. I'm gonna put 'em in my trunk."

Many years ago I purchased James B. Longacre's original wax models for the $3 gold piece from collector Max Brail of Michigan, who sold them to me because he wanted them to have a good home with a numismatist who would appreciate them. When the time came for me to sell them, I chose Rick to sell them to because the wreath used for the reverse design was also used for the Flying Eagle cent, and I could think of no numismatist more worthy to own them. He understands the magic.

Tom DeLorey
Chicago, Illinois

ABOUT THE AUTHOR

Rick Snow

Rick Snow's interest in coins started in 1972 while he was in grade school in Whippany, New Jersey. The coin-collecting bug bit Rick quite hard: soon he was president of the Morristown Coin Club and started dealing in coins to augment his collecting allowance. In 1976 Rick joined the American Numismatic Association, becoming Life Member #2878. From 1977 through 1981, he worked for a coin shop in Rockaway, New Jersey, but left numismatics when the coin market slowed after the silver and gold boom busted.

In 1987 Rick reentered numismatics, becoming senior numismatist for Allstate Coin Co. in Tucson, Arizona. It was here that he started accumulating information on Flying Eagle and Indian Head cents, focusing initially on the 1856 Flying Eagle and 1858 pattern cents. At the time there was little information on Flying Eagle and Indian Head cents besides Walter Breen's landmark *Encyclopedia of U.S. and Colonial Coinage.* Drawing initially on Breen's work, Rick accumulated much new information regarding these coins. To disseminate it, Rick, together with Larry R. Steve, founded the Flying Eagle and Indian Cent Collectors Society (the Fly-In Club) in 1991. Rick served as first president of the club, and, later, as editor of its journal, *Longacre's Ledger.*

In 1992 Rick left Allstate Coin Co. and founded his own coin dealership, Eagle Eye Rare Coins, with a specialty interest in Flying Eagle and Indian Head cents. That same year, his first book, *Flying Eagle and Indian Cents,* was published, and the resulting collector interest overwhelmed his one-man operation. In July 1993 he moved to Seattle to make Eagle Eye a partnership with longtime collector Brian Wagner. In 1996 Eagle Eye bought and distributed the Alan Epstein Collection, which ranks as the finest Flying Eagle and Indian Head cent collection yet assembled.

In 1994 Rick and Brian started issuing the *Pink Sheet Value Guide,* a reference that sought to answer collector confusions over inconsistent grading in the marketplace, color designations (Brown, Red-Brown, and Red), valuations, and other factors specific to Flying Eagle and Indian Head cents. The *Pink Sheet* has been published ever since, and is used by dealers and collectors alike to stay informed about these coins.

In 2000, Rick became the sole owner of Eagle Eye Rare Coins and moved the company back to Tucson, Arizona, where it is located today.

Rick belongs to numerous regional coin clubs. His involvement in the ANA includes serving as a contributing editor to *Numismatist,* member and chairman of the Consumer Protection Committee, and course instructor at the annual Summer Seminar. Rick is an attributer for the Fly-In Club and he also attributes doubled dies for CONECA (the Combined Organizations of Numismatic Error Collectors of America). He has contributed pricing and content to the *Guide Book of United States Coins* (the "Red Book"), the *Handbook of United States Coins* (the "Blue Book"), and *Numismatic News Marketplace.* His book *Flying Eagle and Indian Cents* won a Numismatic Literary Guild "Best Specialized Book–U.S." award, and its numbering system for varieties is widely used in the hobby.

Rick enjoys hiking in Arizona's mountains and traveling. Besides Flying Eagle and Indian Head cents, his numismatic interests include coins of the early United States and colonial times as those of the Civil War era. Rick's main joys are his lovely wife, Maki, and two fine sons, Kenny and Mike.

PREFACE

The hobby has been due for a new reference on Flying Eagle and Indian Head cents for some time. These attractive little coins have been warming up in recent years, and they show no signs of cooling off. Many writers have shared their research, theories, and insight in magazines and newspaper articles, but it's been a decade since a book-length study has been made on Flying Eagle and Indian Head cents. Much of the recent published research has been Rick Snow's—not surprising, given his well-known love for these beautiful and historic coins. Now he shares his insight in *A Guide Book of Flying Eagle and Indian Head Cents*.

This is a reference for the newcomer to these series—the collector who wants a detailed but engagingly readable education in history, rarity levels, popular varieties, and market values. It's also a book for the longtime collector who wants a single-source overview: a guide not to be read once and shelved, but to be kept handy for frequent visits and consultations.

To create this book, Rick Snow has drawn on 20+ years of experience as a full-time dealer specializing in Flying Eagle and Indian Head cents, plus years of study as a groundbreaking numismatic researcher. Rick has seen and handled all the coins in these series, he has attributed and cataloged them in other references, and, as a founding member and officer of the Flying Eagle and Indian Cent Collectors Society (and editor of its journal, *Longacre's Ledger*), he has been at the center of the hobby for more than a decade. His expertise in this field has made Rick the "go-to" correspondent when a new variety is discovered, when questions arise among other experts, and when nuances of grading or attribution are in dispute.

A multi-part introduction by Q. David Bowers—one of the premier numismatic researchers of all time—describes the design, mintage, and distribution of these early small cents, and gives advice on collecting and grading. Rick then studies the coins themselves, year by year, as individual pieces and within the context of their series. Historical essays and illustrations offer "snapshots" of each year the coins were minted, to put them into cultural perspective. Mintages are drawn from historical records; prices from the author's long experience in the market; and population reports from the leading third-party grading firms. The main part of the book is illustrated with full-color photographs of Mint State coins from the famous Stewart Blay collection, along with enlargements of overdates, clashes, repunched dates, and other varieties. Appendices expand on the life and times of Mint designer James B. Longacre, counterfeit and altered coins, and the market price histories of both series.

These diverse elements—technical and artistic, historical and current, market-driven and hobbyist—combine to make *A Guide Book of Flying Eagle and Indian Head Cents* a valuable addition to any numismatist's bookshelf.

Dennis Tucker
Publisher, Whitman Publishing, LLC
Atlanta, Georgia

CREDITS AND ACKNOWLEDGEMENTS

This book is the culmination of many years of work by many dedicated numismatists. My own interest in Flying Eagle and Indian Head cents started with the publication of **Walter Breen's** *Complete Encyclopedia of U.S. and Colonial Coins*. Early research into this series included help from **Elvira Clain-Stefanelli** at the Smithsonian Institution. **Robert G. Stewart**, senior curator of the National Portrait Gallery, helped with access to the James Longacre collection, including Longacre's sketchbooks and diary. **Dr. Harriett Longacre Phelps** helped with many previously unknown aspects of Longacre's life and information on the family's history. **Andrew Longacre Jr.** furnished the life portraits of James and Eliza Longacre in Appendix A.

Much of this work is built on my 1992 book, *Flying Eagle and Indian Cents*, which was assisted greatly by the photo file of **Christopher Pilliod**. **Larry R. Steve** helped with gathering information through the Fly-In Club. Larry's 1995 book with **Kevin J. Flynn**, *Flying Eagle and Indian Cent Die Varieties*, added much-needed depth to the Flying Eagle and Indian Head cent variety field.

Q. David Bowers helped greatly over the years with this project. When Dave wrote the *Buyer's and Enthusiast's Guide to Flying Eagle and Indian Cents* in 1996, I was relieved of the pressure of writing another book and contributed all my notes to that project. Now, Dave has graciously returned the favor with his continuous help and suggestions.

The fabulous collection of **Stewart Blay** was used for nearly all the full-coin photographs. Photography was done by **Thomas Mulvaney**.

The active participation of the membership of the Fly-In Club was a great help, notably: **William Affanato, Ralph Bergholtz, Larry Briggs, Dr. Eugene Bruder, John Cantwell, Tim Cartwright, Xan Chamberlain, Dr. George Conger, Dr. Ira Davidoff, Marvin Erickson, Dr. Sheldon Freed, Dr. Thomas Fore, Lee Gong, Quent Hansen, Doug Hill, Kenneth Hill, Paul Houck, Alan Kreuzer, Sam Lukes, Mark McWherter, Alan Meghrig, Ron Neuman, Lynn Ourso, Bob Pedlosky, Vernon Sebby, Ronald A. Sirna, Dr. Stanley Spurgeon, Dr. Thomas Turrissini, Mark Van Deusen, William O. Walker, Mark Watson, Alan Williams**, and **Jerry Wysong**. I'm sure there are many others who contributed greatly but I've failed to mention; to those I'd also like to give a heartfelt "Thank you."

Mike Ellis (of Oklahoma), and **Dr. Tim Larson** both reviewed early transcripts of this text. **Kenneth Bressett**, editor of Whitman's *Guide Book of United States Coins* (the "Red Book"), offered suggestions.

Numismatic expertise was given generously by **John Dannreuther, Julian Leidman, Bill Fivaz, J.T. Stanton, Thomas K. DeLorey, Jack Beymer, R.W. Julian, Saul Teichman, Andrew Lustig**, and **P. Scott Rubin**.

The staff of **Whitman Publishing, LLC**, a very talented group, have my thanks. **American Numismatic Rarities** provided a coin photograph. **Miguel Colón Ortiz** contributed historical essays and images. **Dalmatian Press, LLC**, provided an illustration. **Charles Daughtrey** illustrated the frontispiece. **H.E. Harris & Co.** provided a postage stamp image. **Steve Hayden** and **Steven Tanenbaum** provided Civil War token images.

I'd like to give very heartfelt thanks to **Brian Wagner** for all his help over the years. The late **Elliott Goldman**, of Allstate Coins, was very instrumental in getting access to the richness of talent that abounds in this hobby.

YESTERDAY AND TODAY

To complement my study of Flying Eagle and Indian Head cent dates and die varieties, I have invited my long-time friend Q. David Bowers to contribute an introduction to this book. He describes how these coins were designed, minted, and distributed, and offers advice for collecting them today. Dave has included new research material and updated information from his best-selling 1996 work *A Buyer's and Enthusiast's Guide to Flying Eagle and Indian Cents.*

—Richard Snow

Flying Eagle cents, minted for circulation only in 1857 and 1858, and Indian Head cents, produced from 1859 to 1909, were once the most popular, most widely circulated, most plentiful coins in everyday American life. Just about every kid had a pocketful of "Indian pennies," and older folks used them as well. One-cent pieces could do a lot of things: several of them could buy a newspaper, or candy, or a streetcar ride, or entertainment—such as from a Mutoscope arcade machine.

100 years ago, every pocket held a few.

Drop a cent into the slot, turn the crank, and you would be dazzled by an automobile racing around a track, or a boxing match, or a striptease. Indian Head cents were anywhere and everywhere.

In 1909 the curtain fell. The new Lincoln cent was introduced on August 2. By this time, Flying Eagle cents had long disappeared from circulation. Within a few decades, Indian Head cents would become at first scarce in pocket change, then unusual, and by the early 1950s, startling to find.

Although many numismatists collected these coins during the era in which they were issued, most interest arose in the 1930s. In that decade, popular albums were marketed in quantity, including "penny boards" by J.K. Post, of Neenah, Wisconsin, in 1934—soon to become Whitman Publishing Company. Wayte Raymond's *Standard Catalogue of United States Coins* was launched in the same year. In 1935 the *Numismatic Scrapbook Magazine* made its debut. The

hobby of collecting coins was in full swing, and Americans looked to the common cents of yesteryear.

A One-Cent Trip Down Memory Lane

The song "The Old Oaken Bucket" begins with, "How dear to my heart are the scenes of my childhood / When fond recollection presents them to view." Similarly, "Old Folks at Home," "When You and I Were Young Maggie," and other melodies evoke scenes of days gone by, of sweet sixteen, remembrance of things past. Somehow, the "good old days" always seem to have been simpler. In the 1930s an Indian Head cent taken from pocket change—a well-worn coin of 1871 or a fairly sharp one of 1907—with its warm, brown color, was enjoyable to view. These coins were little messengers from days gone by. Collecting them was easy enough to do, with inexpensive holders and albums. With some pleasant hunting, within a week or two most of a complete run of dates could be found. The dates in the 1860s might be worn nearly smooth, the 1877 might be missing and ditto for the 1909 San Francisco Mint coin, but most of the others could be found. In neat little rows in an album—1859, 1860, 1861, 1862, 1863, and onward—such a set was nice to own.

Today, each Flying Eagle and Indian Head cent in existence has its own story hidden between its obverse and reverse surfaces. If only it could speak!

A glittering Proof 1859 Indian Head cent might relate that Joseph J. Mickley gazed down upon it in 1860, and that T. Harrison Garrett admired it in his upstairs study in Evergreen House in Baltimore in 1880. Or, another sparkling little 1859 Proof cent might relate that J.M. Clapp took time from his activities in the oil fields of north central Pennsylvania in early October 1896, to read a slim catalog received in the mail from dealer Charles Steigerwalt, and to post a bid for this piece offered in the Henry Blair Collection auction held on October 14.

A well-worn 1879 Indian Head cent worth just a few dollars probably traveled in most states of the Union in its time, was spent hundreds of times for penny candy, saw the inside of a piggy bank or two or three, was dropped in many gum and amusement machines, and was prized many times as part of a kid's allowance—perhaps even more than a numismatist prizes it today. One can just imagine a freckle-faced, pigtailed little girl running down the street to the store to get rid of this small but quite valuable coin as fast as possible! What treasures it could buy!

Flying Eagle and Indian Head cents were the most egalitarian of all American coins in their day. Anyone could own one—and did. In 1863, when all silver and gold coins were being hoarded and the two-cent, nickel three-cent, and nickel five-cent denominations had not yet been made, the cent was the only United States coin in circulation. Remarkable!

Doubtless, today there are Indian Head cents on the ocean floor in the hull of the *Titanic*, others under the sand on the beach at Coney Island, some moldering in the sod of the Gettysburg battlefield, and still more in attics and dresser drawers. Hundreds of millions of worn Indian Head cents were withdrawn by the Treasury Department and melted. More than likely, of the 1,849,560,942 originally coined from 1859 to 1909, probably no more than about 2% to 3% are in collectors' hands today, or, say, about 37 million to 55 million, most of which are of the later dates in the series (1879 to 1909). Of course this is just an estimate.

Tens of millions of copper-nickel Flying Eagle cents (1857 and 1858) and Indian Head cents (1859 to 1864) have never been redeemed by the Treasury Department, and hundreds of millions of bronze Indian Head cents (1864 to 1909) are presently unaccounted for. Most will probably forever remain that way and, quite likely, were destroyed long ago.

Now, about some coins from that 2% to 3% that *you* might enjoy owning.

COLLECTING FLYING EAGLE AND INDIAN HEAD CENTS TODAY

Today, such coins can no longer be found in pocket change. Even an old-time piggy bank is apt to be filled with Lincoln, not Indian Head, cents. Accordingly, your source is the numismatic marketplace. By the time you buy this reference, you probably already own a copy of *A Guide Book of United States Coins* (popularly known as the Red Book). If not, it is a good idea to buy or borrow one. The *Guide Book* sets the context for these cents among other denominations of their era and gives a lot of basic information about all types of coins and how to collect them.

Flying Eagle and Indian Head cents have become a specialty—the two types are usually collected together—and today thousands of numismatists seek them. The great rarity in the set—if you can call it a *rarity*, for at least two thousand exist today—is the 1856 Flying Eagle cent, not a regular circulating issue, but a pattern coin. Because it looks just like the first regular issue, 1857, and has been collected for such a long time, by tradition it has been adopted into the series. Among Indian Head cents the key issue is the 1877, by virtue of its mintage of 852,500, low for the series (in comparison, more than 108 *million* were made of the 1907 cent). The 1864 bronze cent with the initial L on the headdress ribbon (for the Mint's chief engraver, James B. Longacre, who designed it) is scarce, as are the 1871, 1872, and 1909-S, among others. Interestingly, although 309,000 were minted of the 1909-S, it is easier to find than the 1877. The reason is that by 1909 many more people were collecting and saving coins than in 1877.

Many sources beckon as you build a collection. Coin shops are a great source and permit you to look over an extensive inventory. Shops are a great place to acquire accessories such as books, albums, and magnifiers. Two different magnifiers are ideal: one with two 4x lenses that can be used together and have a wide field of view; plus a smaller, stronger glass to see details of dates and other aspects.

Coin conventions and shows are held regularly. Periodicals such as the weekly newspapers *Coin World* and *Numismatic News*, and monthly magazines, including *Coins* and *COINage*, often available at newsstands, publicize show and convention schedules. It is always wise to doublecheck before traveling a long distance, as sometimes shows are cancelled. At a coin show you can browse to your heart's content, "talk coins" with collectors and dealers, and get many ideas.

The Internet offers thousands of Flying Eagle and Indian Head cents for sale. However, unless they are offered by an established numismatic firm with good professional credentials, there are many traps. Once you become experienced, then feel free to look into a "beautiful 1872 cent I found from an old estate; I don't know much about coins, but it looks nice" type of coin. Until then, deal with professionals.

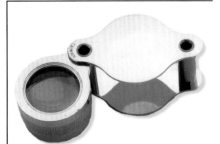

Magnifier (Loupe)
An H.E. Harris magnifier (or *loupe*, pronounced "loop") is a common sight at coin shows. These magnifiers fold into their chrome cases to protect the lens, which is usually 10x to 16x or greater strength.

If you adopt Flying Eagle and Indian Head cents as a serious specialty and pursue many of the scarce and rare items described by Richard Snow in this book, then public and Internet auctions (again, on the Internet, be cautious of non-professionals) offer many opportunities.

DETERMINING VALUE

The price of an Indian Head cent depends on several factors, including its rarity, its condition (the amount of wear it has received), its eye appeal, and its popularity. As to popularity, the basic different dates in the series are all popular, as are the two San Francisco Mint cents, the 1908-S and the 1909-S. Within the dates there are many interesting *die varieties*, explained in detail in this book. These sideline varieties have different degrees of popularity. An 1872 cent with the word LIBERTY doubled in the headdress is a "gotta get one!" coin for many collectors, while a repunched date on an 1869 cent plays to a smaller audience.

The rarity or number of coins available is an important factor in valuation. A rare 1877 cent sells for much more than any of the common cents of the 1890s and 1900s.

Small Details, Big Differences
An 1857 Flying Eagle cent in MS-63 will fetch a price 15 to 20 times that of the same coin in Fine condition.

The grade is one of the most important factors in a coin's price. Today, most collectors and dealers use the 70-point *Official American Numismatic Association Grading Standards for United States Coins* (laid out in a book of the same name, available from all dealers). The details for Flying Eagle and Indian Head cents are given separately in this book, but a brief outline is appropriate here.

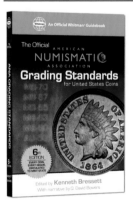

The Official ANA Grading Standards for United States Coins
"The official ANA grading system is used by dealers, collectors, and investors throughout the world," notes numismatic researcher Bill Fivaz. "It is an indispensable aid to properly grading your U.S. coins— the very foundation of smart buying, selling, and collecting."

Each grade has a number and a brief descriptor. A coin graded Good-4 (or G-4) is worn nearly smooth, but with its date and much of its lettering still readable. An Extremely Fine–40 (EF-40) coin has only light wear and all of its lettering is sharp. Uncirculated or "new" coins, called Mint State, are graded from MS-60 to MS-70. The low end of the Mint State range, MS-60, describes a coin that is nicked or has other handling marks, not from general circulation, but from storage in a bag, or otherwise being loose with other coins. An MS-70 coin is in a state of absolute perfection.

All Flying Eagle cents and Indian Head cents from 1857 to 1863 were made in copper-nickel alloy (88% copper and 12% nickel) and have a light golden appearance. Beginning partway through 1864, bronze alloy (95% copper, 5% tin and zinc) was used. Bronze cents tone naturally over a period of time from mint "red" (actually more orange) to deep brown. A bronze cent with original mint red color is abbreviated RD, such as MS-65 RD, meaning that the grade is Mint State-65 and the color is red. One with a mixture of red and brown, and with significant amounts of each, is called red and brown, abbreviated RB, while one that is brown is noted as BN.

Often a small difference in grade and color can make a large difference in price. This will become very understandable as you review catalog listings and various offerings of coins for sale. Since the 1980s more than 100 commercial grading or certification services have been established (most of which have disappeared from the market). These firms charge a fee to give their opinion of a coin's grade and to mark it on a sealed plastic holder (called a *slab*). Today the leading services are, alphabetically, ANACS (descended from the American Numismatic Association Certification Service), ICG (Independent Coin Grading), NGC (Numismatic Guaranty Corporation), and PCGS (Professional Coin Grading Service).

Grading is a matter of opinion, and expert opinions can and do vary. Even the same certification service can view the same coin on two different occasions and assign different grades to it each time. It is best to buy the *coin*, not the label on a certified holder. A numismatist friend who has been a long-time collector can advise you in this regard, as can a trusted dealer.

Eye appeal can vary widely, even among certified coins. One MS-65 RD cent of 1898 might have some annoying stains, while another might be beautiful and pristine. Generally, avoid any coin that does not look "pretty" when viewed under low-power magnification.

ENJOYING YOUR COLLECTION

No one is obligated to collect Flying Eagle and Indian Head cents. The reason to assemble a set is to enjoy the pursuit. The thrill of the hunt, the friendship of other collectors, and the coins themselves are all part of the game. Forming a set may well take the best part of a year. For some of the rarer issues in higher grades the quest is more challenging, and several years or more are needed. Ditto if you become interested in die varieties in addition to the regular dates.

It's a curious fact that many if not most coin collectors receive pleasure from seeking and buying coins, but do not enjoy their coins once they own them.

How can you *enjoy* a coin once you own it? For starters, use the magnifying glasses just mentioned.

Examining a Flying Eagle or Indian Head cent carefully under magnification can often yield much information and perhaps create a puzzle or two. A good way to appreciate die differences is to take an early coin in a given series and compare it to a later one in the series. For example, under magnification compare an 1860 Indian Head cent (the first year with the oak-wreath-and-shield reverse design) with one from the last year in the series, 1909. You will see differences in die relief and details and much else. Or, pick a dozen different Indian Head cents at random and look at their date numerals under a glass. Some have the date in a straight line, others curved. On some the date is small and tightly spaced, on others large and wide. As examples, the 1871 has the date in widely spaced digits curved along the bottom border, and the very next year, 1872, has small numerals, close together, and in a straight line.

Don't be in a hurry. Take your time. Look and then look again. Repunched dates, planchet defects, die breaks, die finish lines, and much more await you. These features are all discussed in the pages of this book. Among Indian Head cents there were so many different dies used that without doubt many presently unknown interesting varieties await discovery, perhaps by you!

Further, each Flying Eagle and Indian Head cent has its own Mint history (how it was struck, what alloy was used, etc.) and numismatic history (market trends, hoards, prices, etc.). The Flying Eagle and Indian Head Cent Collectors Society ("Fly-In Club") publishes *Longacre's Ledger* and is a meeting place for specialists.

If you can bring all of these aspects together—the studying under magnification of a coin's surface, knowledge of its ties with American history, and its Mint and numismatic background—each coin in your collection will come *alive*. It will no longer be simply a date in a specific grade with a market price, but it will be an object of history, art, and admiration. Don't forget the nostalgia part either—Flying Eagle and Indian Head cents as a link to history.

Flying Eagle Cent (1856–1858)
Designer James B. Longacre; weight 4.67 grams; composition 88% copper, 12% nickel; diameter 19 mm; plain edge. All coined at the Philadelphia Mint.

Indian Head Cent, Copper-Nickel, Laurel Wreath Reverse (1859)
Designer James B. Longacre; weight 4.67 grams; composition 88% copper, 12% nickel; diameter 19 mm; plain edge. All coined at the Philadelphia Mint.

Indian Head Cent, Copper-Nickel, Oak Wreath With Shield Reverse (1860–1864)
Designer James B. Longacre; weight 4.67 grams; composition 88% copper, 12% nickel; diameter 19 mm; plain edge. All coined at the Philadelphia Mint.

Indian Head Cent, Bronze (1864–1909)
Designer James B. Longacre; weight 3.11 grams; composition 95% copper, 5% tin and zinc; diameter 19 mm; plain edge. Mints: Philadelphia, San Francisco.

HISTORY OF THE FLYING EAGLE CENT

The government expressed concern in 1849 that Treasury Department profits from copper coinage had fallen sharply. This was an important consideration. While silver and gold coins of the era had nearly their full face values' worth of metal content and were minted as a service to depositors of precious metals, one-cent pieces were a profit center. They cost far less than a cent to produce, and the profit, called *seignorage*, translated directly to the Mint's bottom line.

In an effort to find a replacement for the 10.89-gram copper "large" cent, which was considered cumbersome to handle and too expensive to produce, the Mint experimented with reduced-diameter and lower-weight cents as early as 1850, with several "annular" (ring-shaped) designs in various metals.

The idea of a smaller-format cent was hardly new; in 1837 Dr. Lewis Feuchtwanger had spent much time and effort trying to interest Congress in adapting "Feuchtwanger's composition"—a type of "German silver" made of nickel, copper, and zinc, with a silvery appearance—to make coins. He gave each member a printed notice about his cent and its advantages and attached an example of the coin. The alloy was said to have been "clean, white and durable material, of specific value, from which coins and all articles can be advantageously manufactured as are now wrought out of silver."[1]

Feuchtwanger Tokens
The inventor's "Feuchtwanger's Composition" tokens, struck in 1837, would later circulate during the coin shortages of the early 1840s. (Shown enlarged 1.5x)

His proposal rejected by Congress, Feuchtwanger took matters into his own hands and caused many thousands of small-diameter tokens to be privately struck. These bore on the obverse the depiction of an eagle killing a snake, while the reverse featured a wreath and the inscriptions FEUCHTWANGER'S COMPOSITION and ONE CENT. He also produced several varieties of THREE CENTS tokens.

In 1851 and early 1852 the price of copper subsided somewhat, and within the Treasury Department urgency for a new cent was diminished. Later in 1852 and in 1853 the price rose again—at one point to 42¢ per pound. The Mint estimated that when the price was greater than 40¢ per pound (which was enough metal to make 42-2/3 one-cent pieces), a loss was sustained if the costs of manufacturing were added to the

James B. Longacre (Chief Engraver, U.S. Mint, 1844–1869)
Longacre portrayed himself in this watercolor portrait, circa the 1840s. In addition to designing the Flying Eagle and Indian Head cents, his work is seen in the two-cent piece, silver and nickel three-cent pieces, the Shield nickel, several patterns, and various gold coins.

calculation. In 1853 some patterns were struck in a nickel-copper composition utilizing an 1853 quarter eagle obverse die with a pattern reverse. These pieces appeared silvery, in the manner of 1837 Feuchtwanger cents.

Momentum for a new-style cent increased sharply in 1854 and 1855 when really serious investigation began. Some of the pattern cents of these two years used an adaptation of Christian Gobrecht's flying eagle design created in 1838 for use on half dollars. Other 1854 and 1855 pattern cents featured Liberty Head designs. One particularly notable variant was made by mechanically copying the obverse of an 1854 Liberty Seated dollar (the crossbar and diagonal of the 4 did not copy, and the date appeared as *1851*).

In spring 1856, James Booth, the Mint's melter and refiner, concluded that a mixture of 88 parts copper and 12 parts nickel would be ideal for a new cent. This alloy became known as *copper-nickel*. Booth suggested that a weight of 72 grains would be convenient, as this was equivalent to 80 pieces to the troy pound (although the avoirdupois, rather than troy measure, was usually employed for base metals). The resultant coins were to be of small diameter and fairly thick, to eliminate any quick-glance confusion with silver coins.

On July 11, 1856, Mint Director James Ross Snowden recommended the new format. Chief Engraver James B. Longacre was instructed to prepare patterns. Nickel came from a private mine at Lancaster Gap, Pennsylvania, the owners of which obligingly furnished free samples of the copper-nickel alloy to the Mint, from which patterns were struck. In 1863 Joseph Wharton became the owner of the mine. Afterward he used his political influence to create new denominations in nickel alloy: the three-cent and five-cent pieces of 1865 and 1866.

THE NEW DESIGN

Longacre's obverse design for the small-diameter copper-nickel cent depicted an eagle flying to the left, with UNITED STATES OF AMERICA around and the date below. Longacre adopted the eagle motif created by Christian Gobrecht 20 years earlier and used on the 1836 silver dollar. The national bird featured is said to have been modeled from a real eagle, Peter, once a mascot at the Mint.

The reverse motif of the new cent was not original either, but was a copy of the "agricultural" wreath containing, as usually stated, "wheat, corn, cotton, and tobacco," devised earlier by Longacre for use on the 1854 gold $1 and $3 coins. In modern literature the cotton leaves are often referred to as *maple* leaves, as the more closely resemble the latter in a botanical sense; besides, few numismatists are aware of what a cotton leaf looks like.[2] However, cotton leaf is correct. The wreath composition, beginning at the ribbon, seems to be: tobacco, wheat, corn, cotton, and a corn ear, the last hardly true to nature.[3]

While the reincarnation of Peter on the Flying Eagle cent and the re-use of an old wreath created a design admired by numismatists and others, it remains a puzzle why original motifs were not used on such a momentous change in the most utilitarian of all American coin denominations.

However, at the time the "lowly" cent received very little attention in either the Engraving Department or the director's office at the Mint, despite its status as a profit-maker. This denomination was more or less taken for granted. When experiments in new and artistic motifs were undertaken, likely as not they were in precious metal denominations. Similarly, annual issues of the *Mint Report* typically devoted a great deal of space to silver and gold coins, but said very little about one-cent pieces. There were exceptions, of course.

Moreover, Chief Engraver Longacre was known for the slow pace at which he performed his work. Perhaps Snowden thought it would simplify matters if new motifs did not have to be created. Similarly and at a later time, Longacre copied his own designs and those of others to create several other issues including imitating the face of Miss Liberty (from the 1849 $20 and 1854 $3 gold pieces) for use on the Indian Head cent, copying the shield on the 1864 two-cent piece for the obverse of the 1866 Shield nickel, and borrowing the 1859 cent laurel-wreath reverse for use on the 1865 nickel three-cent piece.

Some of the new artistic work on various coins, patterns, and medals was eventually (after October 1857) given to Assistant Engraver Anthony C. Paquet, whose contribution to the small-cent field is just now beginning to be recognized for its true importance.

SAINT-GAUDENS AND THE FLYING EAGLE CENT

On January 13, 1905, Mint Director George E. Roberts wrote to Augustus Saint-Gaudens, America's greatest living sculptor, asking if he would be interested in redesigning the American coinage. On January 20, 1905, the artist said he would like to explore the matter further in March during a visit to Washington, DC.[4]

Eventually, President Theodore Roosevelt commissioned Saint-Gaudens to create new motifs for all denominations from the cent to the $20 gold piece. Working in his home-studio (now a National Historic Site) in Cornish, New Hampshire, he created motifs for the $10 and $20 gold coins before succumbing to cancer on August 3, 1907.

During the course of his work, on June 28, 1906, Saint-Gaudens wrote to President Roosevelt stating he was working on designs for a replacement of the Indian Head cent, in the process paying tribute to what he considered to be the high point in historical American coinage:

> Now I am attacking the cent. It may interest you to know that on the "Liberty" side of the cent I am using a flying eagle, a modification of the device which was used on the cent of 1857. I had not seen that coin for many years, and was so impressed by it that I thought if carried out with some modifications, nothing better could be done. It is by all odds the best design on any American coin.

Saint-Gaudens died before he completed his coinage motifs for various denominations. As it turned out, his flying eagle was indeed used for coinage, but not on the cent. Today it is familiar as the reverse of the $20 gold coins minted from 1907 to 1933.

Augustus Saint-Gaudens
The artist is shown on this commemorative plaque by James Earle Fraser.

VERMEULE AND THE FLYING EAGLE DESIGN

In his book *Numismatic Art in America* (1971), Cornelius Vermeule of the Boston Museum of Fine Arts commented on Gobrecht's design (as seen on early silver dollars and later adapted for the copper-nickel cent):

> The famous flying eagle…is one of the greatest symphonies of die design and cutting to be performed on any flan at any period in the history of western civilization. This is cold observation, not mere national pride.
>
> Only the most sensitive, most penetrating photograph can bring out the bold yet subtle relief and foreshortening of the bird as he flies across our vision from right front to left rear. Feathers, wing tips, beak, and curled talon are presented with a naturalistic power and precision as advanced in American numismatic art as was Benedetto Pistrucci's 1818 portrait of aged George III [on British coinage]….
>
> This vision of the national bird on the wing was as magnificent a presentation in depth, detail, and silhouette as the human mind could conceive and the human hand translate into the mechanics of coining processes….

In view of the admiration that Saint-Gaudens, Vermeule, and others had for Longacre's "recycled" design borrowed from Gobrecht, and the enthusiasm collectors have for Flying Eagle cents today, perhaps it is all for the best that some other motif was not created in the 1850s at the Mint when experiments to eliminate the cumbersome large copper cent were conducted.

A few comments concerning Peter, the putative model for the Flying Eagle cent, and the engraver, Christian Gobrecht, who first translated the motif to coin form, may be of interest, followed by notes about James B. Longacre, who adapted Gobrecht's design for the 1856 Flying Eagle cent:

"PETER" THE EAGLE

The *American Journal of Numismatics*, Vol. 27, 1893, p. 85, reprinted this from *Harper's Young People* (similar accounts also appeared elsewhere):

> On the dollars of 1836, 1838 and 1839, and the nickel cent coins in 1856 is the portrait of an American eagle which was for many years a familiar sight in the streets of Philadelphia. "Peter," one of the finest eagles ever captured alive, was the pet of the Philadelphia Mint, and was generally known as the "Mint bird." Not only did he have free access to every part of the Mint, going without hindrance into the treasure vaults where even the treasurer of the United States would not go alone, but he used his own pleasure in going about the city, fly-ing over the houses, sometimes perching upon lamp posts in the streets. Everybody knew him, and even the street boys treated him with respect.
>
> The government provided his daily fare, and he was as much a part of the Mint establishment as the superintendent or the chief coiner. He was kindly treated and had no fear of anybody or anything,

and he might be in the Mint yet if he had not sat down to rest upon one of the great flywheels. The wheel started without warning, and Peter was caught in the machinery. One of his wings was broken, and he died a few days later. The superintendent had his body beautifully mounted, with his wings spread to their fullest extent; and to this day Peter stands in a glass case in the Mint cabinet. A portrait of him as he stands in the case was put upon the coins named.

In stuffed form Peter was exhibited widely including at the Treasury exhibit at the World's Columbian Exposition in Chicago in 1893. Today the bird is on view in the lobby of the Philadelphia Mint on Independence Square.

Artist Titian Peale, son of artist and museum proprietor Charles Willson Peale, was asked by Mint Director Robert Maskell Patterson to create drawings of a "lifelike" flying eagle motif for use on coinage, a departure from the perched and heraldic eagles in use for many years.

Whether Peter was actually the model for Peale and Gobrecht may never be known with certainty, but it may have been this unfortunate bird that was mentioned in a letter dated April 9, 1836, from Mint Director Robert Maskell Patterson to Secretary of the Treasury Levi Woodbury, here quoted in part. At the time, sketches were being prepared for new coinage motifs:

> The die[5] for the reverse is not yet commenced, but I send you the drawings which we propose to follow—the pen sketch being that which we prefer. The drawing is true to nature, for it is taken from the eagle itself—a bird, recently killed, having been prepared and placed in the attitude which we had selected. The eagle is flying, and like the country of which it is the emblem, its course onward and upward....
>
> It was my intention to begin the new coinage with the dollar, but it has occurred to me that it might be more proper, and more agreeable to the government, that it should be begun with the indemnity gold.[6] Besides, it would really be a pity that six millions worth of gold coins should be spread over the country with that thing on the reverse which courtesy may call an eagle, but which nature and art refuse to recognize....

The preceding indicates that Gobrecht's flying eagle was recommended for use on gold coins rather than the silver dollar, Patterson strongly disliking the perched eagle design on current gold coins (which were of the denominations $2.50 and $5). Considering that Director Patterson liked the flying eagle, and that he served as director until July 1851, it is curious that the motif was used only ephemerally on American coinage under his watch. It is further curious that "that thing on the reverse" which Patterson detested was used on the reverse of the new Liberty Seated quarter (1838), half dollar (1839), and silver dollar (1840).

Christian Gobrecht

Christian Gobrecht (born December 23, 1785, died July 23, 1844) was an accomplished clockmaker, reed organ builder, medal-ruling machine inventor (1817), engraver of rolls for printing designs on calico, speaking doll or automaton maker, and (most important to his career) bank-note engraver and medalist.

Born in Hanover, York County, Pennsylvania, Gobrecht showed an aptitude for things mechanical by an early age. After serving an apprenticeship in clock making in Manheim (Lancaster County, Pennsylvania) he moved to Baltimore (where in 1810 he engraved an excellent portrait of George Washington for J. Kingston's *New American Biographical Dictionary*), then in 1811

Christian Gobrecht's Dollar Design
The engraver's flying eagle would later appear on the copper-nickel cent.

relocated to Philadelphia, where he engaged in bank note plate engraving. By 1816 he was on the staff of Murray, Draper, Fairman & Company, of Philadelphia, where he prepared vignettes for currency plates ordered by various private banks. Gobrecht's signature on vignettes of this era is not known, but this is not necessarily unusual as most such works of art by various engravers were very small and not signed.

Gobrecht came to the Mint in September 1835 to work as "second engraver" (not "assistant") on the staff while William Kneass held the chief engravership. Kneass had suffered a stroke in late August, and never fully recovered. By that time Gobrecht had done contract work for the Mint for more than a decade, including the production of letter and number punches. He assumed his work at the Mint with a running start, and set about creating dies from sketches prepared by Thomas Sully and Titian Peale for what we know today as the Liberty Seated coinage. After Kneass's death (August 27, 1840), Gobrecht was appointed chief engraver on December 21, 1840, although in fact Kneass had done very little work after his stroke.

Following the production of pattern silver dollars, Gobrecht's flying eagle design was used only briefly on circulating coinage for a limited number of silver dollars dated 1836 and 1839, comprising fewer than 2,000 coins totally. It was also used in modified form (with ruffed neck feathers and somewhat "lumpier" body) on pattern half dollars dated 1838 and 1839. However, when Liberty Seated half dollars in 1839 and silver dollars in 1840 were made in large numbers for circulation, Gobrecht's flying eagle motif was abandoned in favor of a traditional perched-eagle design for the reverse.

Years later in 1854, a decade after Gobrecht's death, the flying eagle from his pattern half dollars of 1838 and 1839 reappeared on copper pattern cents of this date and, shortly thereafter, on pattern 1855 cents as well. However, Peter's most famous and enduring reincarnation was on the copper-nickel, small-diameter Flying Eagle cents dated 1856, 1857, and 1858.

JAMES BARTON LONGACRE

Born on August 11, 1794, in Delaware County, Pennsylvania, to Peter and Sarah Barton Longacre, James Barton Longacre was chief engraver at the Philadelphia Mint from 1844 to 1869.

Young Longacre served for a short time as an apprentice to James F. Watson of Philadelphia, then continued his apprenticeship with George Murray, prolific banknote engraver of Murray, Draper & Fairman, who at one time also employed Christian Gobrecht.

Longacre set out on his own in 1819 and engraved metal plates for bank notes and book illustrations, including for a work on signers of the Declaration of Independence and another on stage personalities, but particularly for the *National Portrait Gallery of Distinguished Americans*, of which the first of four volumes was dated 1834. This last work was published in multiple large print runs, was widely circulated, and brought great fame to Longacre and others whose work was included.

Longacre was appointed as chief engraver at the Mint on September 16, 1844, to succeed the late Christian Gobrecht. While Gobrecht had been a medalist and coin engraver of high repute, Longacre's experience in the medium of struck pieces was limited or non-existent. Certain numismatic historians (e.g., Walter Breen) have ascribed many repunching blunders to him and have called him incompetent as a coin designer and engraver.[7] Nevertheless, the coins he designed serviced a very long span of American history. Longacre remained chief engraver until his death on January 1, 1869.

While numismatists—especially readers of the present text—may consider Longacre's memory dear for the 1856 Flying Eagle and 1859 Indian Head cents, he is also remembered for the 1864 two-cent piece, 1851 and later silver three-cent designs, the 1865 nickel three-cent piece, the 1866 Shield nickel, 1849 and later gold dollars, the 1854 $3 gold piece, and the 1850 double eagle, as well as many patterns, not the least of which are the beautiful Indian Princess pattern silver coins of 1870 and 1871, the latter issued after his death.

For a more in-depth study of James Barton Longacre, see appendix A.

ANTHONY C. PAQUET

Anthony C. Paquet was born in the German city of Hamburg, on the Elbe River, in 1814, probably the son of Touissaint François Paquet, a bronzeworker in that city. He came to America in 1848, and in the mid-1850s had an engraving shop in New York City. Unfortunately, there seems to be virtually nothing in present numismatic literature to identify tokens, medals, or any other metallic items he may have created prior to coming to the Mint.

Paquet did contract work for the Mint in early 1857, and on October 20 of that year joined the Mint staff as an assistant engraver. He remained in that post through early 1864, after which he returned to the private sector, but continued to do important commissions for the government, including two designs for Indian Peace medals. A pattern 1877 half dollar is by his hand.

Paquet furnished the letter punches for certain patterns and possibly for regular-issue coins as well, one recorded shipment arriving in late May 1857, although he could have done earlier work as well. Apparently, the same engraver made up punches for various denominations including the dime, quarter dollar, and half dollar. However, these fonts were not used at the time for circulating coinage.

His coinage work at the Mint included numerous patterns as well as several regular-issue dies, among the latter being the short-lived modified obverse for the 1859 Liberty Seated half dime (Philadelphia Mint only) and the equally short-lived "Paquet reverse" for the 1861 $20 gold coins, the latter made at the Philadelphia and San Francisco mints.

Paquet died in 1882.

THE FAMOUS 1856 FLYING EAGLE CENT

By the mid-1850s American children and adults had grown up with the old copper "large" cents that had been in circulation ever since their introduction in 1793. The change in 1857 to the lightweight, small-diameter, lightly hued copper-nickel cent would require some education, Mint officials figured.

Accordingly, beginning in late November 1856, approximately 1,000 or more 1856-dated pattern Flying Eagle cents were struck for distribution to newspaper editors, congressmen, and others of influence, with some coins held in reserve for distribution to numismatists. Included in the dispersal were one to each senator and representative, four to President Franklin Pierce, about 200 to the Committee on Coinage, Weights and Measures, and other pieces to Treasury Department officials.[8] However, it seem apparent that any congressman who wanted a few extra pieces had no trouble getting them. Exactly how many promotional pieces of the 1856-dated Flying Eagle cent were struck in 1856 and early 1857 is not known, and it could have been far in excess of 1,000 coins.

Reverse Designs of the 1861 $20 Gold Piece
The regular design is at left; Paquet's is at right. The most readily noticeable difference is in the lettering style.

These initial specimens of the 1856 Flying Eagle cent were of the circulation-strike format, not Proof, and were intended to be similar in finish to what the average citizen would see when mass production of the new coin began. The "advertising campaign" was a success, and the Act of February 21, 1857, was signed into law, making the copper-nickel Flying Eagle cent a reality.

COLLECTORS TAKE NOTICE

Word of the curious, interesting, new, little 1856 Flying Eagle cents spread, and these coins began to have a premium value among the small but rapidly growing community of coin collectors. Specimens soon traded for 50¢ to $1 each when they could be found, which was not often. By 1859, Edward D. Cogan sold a copper-nickel specimen for $2. As $2 was more than a day's pay for many people in the late 1850s, this was indeed a significant premium.

Franklin Pierce
The president received four specimens of the 1856 Flying Eagle cent.

Around the same time the Mint was busily engaged in restriking rarities for collectors. In 1859, Director James Ross Snowden announced that he could supply scarce coins to numismatists who had George Washington tokens and medals to trade for them. Snowden had been director since June 4, 1853 (and would continue until he was replaced by the new president, Abraham Lincoln, in spring 1861).[9] Under his administration facilities for what became known the Mint Medal Department were set up on March 7, 1855, to provide a dedicated area for the production of Proof coins, medals, and, as it came to pass, restrikes. Beginning in 1859, Snowden, William E. DuBois, and other Mint officials kept busy augmenting the Washington Cabinet section of the Mint Collection (this display would be dedicated on February 22, 1860).

Snowden offered such numismatic delicacies as recognized rarities, Proofs, patterns, and low-mintage coins in exchange for Washington medals and other desired items. Such trades were pleasing to Mint officials and collectors alike. By this process and by selected purchases, the Washington display was increased from a nucleus of "four or five specimens" to 138 pieces by February 1860.[10]

In addition to the *few* rarities Snowden and his close associates may have made for trading for Washington pieces, thousands of other patterns, Proofs, restrikes and other coins were made and sold secretly—with no entries made in Mint records. This activity commenced with vigor in spring 1859 and continued under later directors until early 1885. All involved kept a code of silence. Occasionally, disinformation was issued by Mint spokesman W.E. Dubois.

Whatever the unrecorded circumstances may have been, during the late 1850s and early 1860s—probably from about 1858 and continuing through the early years of the Civil War—additional 1856-dated Flying Eagle cents were struck, but apparently from original obverse dies (there is no evidence that new dies were made after early 1857). The year a particular reverse die was made—1856, 1857, or 1858—made no difference as reverses bore no dates and superficially looked alike. While three of the reverse dies used to coin 1856-dated cents seem to be contemporary with 1856, a fourth is of a style first used in 1858.

At the time, it was felt by collectors that Proof was a *better* finish than Uncirculated (Mint State). Thus, all of the restrike 1856 cents were made with prooflike or even full Proof surfaces by resurfacing existing dies. However, the surface of these Proofs was not quite as deeply mirrored as would be the Proofs of the later dates 1857 and 1858.

Exactly how many Proof 1856 Flying Eagle cents were restruck is not known. A fair estimate might be 1,500 to 2,500 coins. Today, Proof 1856 Flying Eagle cents are much more plentiful than are frosty-surface Mint State coins, the latter being originals from the distribution in 1856 and early 1857 to congressmen and others. Clouding the situation are the fact that many Proof coins have been certified as Mint State and that in any event for many specimens there is no sharp delineation as to what constitutes a Mint State coin and what defines a Proof. Thus, population reports are of little help to the specialist seeking information.

As time went on, the 1856 Flying Eagle cent became one of the most popular of all United States coins. Although it is a pattern—as the design was not official until February 21, 1857—the 1856 has been "adopted" into the regular series.

COINAGE IN TRANSITION

In the meantime the coinage of the soon-to-be-old-style copper large cents continued with vigor in 1856, and in January 1857, some 333,456 additional large cents were struck. Most of the latter were held back at the Mint and later melted.

The Act of February 21, 1857, abolished the large cent and provided for the production of the new format: cents made of 88% copper and 12% nickel, weighing 72 grains (with the tolerance in weight to be no greater than 4 grains per coin). Although not specified by law, the diameter was ultimately set at 3/4 of an inch (thus laying four coins end to end is a handy way to measure three inches, a convenience if a ruler is not at hand).[11]

The design of the new cent was not specified, but would be whatever the director of the Mint wanted, so long as approval was secured from the secretary of the Treasury. Accordingly, the Flying Eagle cent was created within the Mint with no congressional or other vote needed. While in its draft stages there was a provision that the new cents

Similar Wreaths
The reverse of the Flying Eagle cent bears a resemblance to that of the $3 gold piece (first minted in 1854). Both were designed by James Longacre.

be legal tender up to a total of 10¢ per transaction, this proviso did not appear in the final version. This was hardly novel, as the old-style cents were not legal tender either (the Mint Act of April 2, 1792, regulating the coinage, gave legal tender status to silver and gold coins only). As cents were not legal tender, anyone including government officials could refuse to accept them!

SNOWDEN MAKES PLANS

Director of the Mint James Ross Snowden wrote to Secretary of the Treasury James Guthrie on February 20, 1857, seeking approval of the new cent and explaining its features:

> In anticipation of the approval by the President of the bill entitled "An Act relating to foreign coins and to the coinage of cents at the Mint," and for the purpose of submitting to you at as early a period as possible after it may be signed the question of fixing the "shape and device" for the new cent, I make this communication.
>
> Heretofore, from time to time, I have had the honor to communicate with you in reference to the adoption of the most suitable alloy and the proper weight of the coin. These have been established in the bill in accordance with our views. I have to submit for your approval the selection of dies to be used in the coinage, and I recommend an adoption of the dies from which the enclosed specimens have been struck.

The obverse is a flying eagle with the legend "United States of America" and the date of the piece. The reverse is simply a wreath compiled of the principal staple production of our country, enclosing the denomination. The propriety, simplicity and symmetry of this arrangement I think is apparent on inspection of the coin.

The wreath is similar in design to the three-dollar gold coin, but the greater thickness of the cent enabled it to be brought out in higher and more perfect relief, and it fills more completely the face of the coin. The devices and general appearance of the cent, its thickness and smooth edge, render it so dissimilar as to prevent its being mistaken for any other denominations. The last named characteristic will enable persons...where there is an absence of light, to ascertain the denomination.

The weight of the piece is 72 grains or 3 pennyweights, equal to three twentieths of an ounce troy. The diameter is fifteen twentieths or 3/4 of an inch, and the thickness of the planchet is sixty-five thousandths of an inch. It will be seen that the relative proportions are most obviously variant from the other coins. Retaining nearly the thickness of the old copper cent, its diameter is but one twentieth of an inch greater than the dime. This familiarity of the portion is also relied upon as an important safeguard against mistaking it for other coins issued from the Mint.

I may add that I have caused some dies to be prepared, and if the "shape and devices" meet with your approval we will be able to commence the issue of a new cent at an early day, that is to say as soon as we can procure and prepare the materials necessary for the coinage.

I also take this opportunity to ask for instructions as to the "purchase of the materials necessary for the coinage of the cent," in accordance with the 5th section of the bill. The copper and nickel for these coins must be the best quality and free from other metals. I suggest that they be purchased in an open market on the most advantageous [terms] that they can be obtained in like manner as we have before purchased material for the copper cent. A superior quality of nickel mined and manufactured in the United States is obtainable in any desired quantity at the lowest market rate which will enable us to proceed with the coinage without delay.

I have the honor to be with great respect your faithful servant
James Snowden
Director of the Mint[12]

While this letter was being considered, the Coinage Act of February 21, 1857, became a reality and provided for the redemption of certain old coins and the issuance of the new copper-nickel cents.

On February 24, Secretary Guthrie wrote to Director Snowden to approve the new cent, but also to suggest a change:

I have now to ask your attention to the edge of the piece, and to suggest the propriety of such attention in the die, as will render it less sharp.

To Guthrie's letter the director replied in part:

> I have noticed the remarks contained in your letter of yesterday approving the dies for the cent coinage, and will...have the coin changed in the manner as suggested.

Presumably, the unwanted sharp feature was simply a wire rim—or "fin" as it was called at the Mint—and no true alteration of the rim, dentils, or other design features took place.

Flying Eagle cents were struck in quantity beginning in April 1857, and were stockpiled for several weeks awaiting their initial release.

NEW CENTS FOR OLD COINS

A fascinating account of what happened when the new Flying Eagle cent made its debut was printed in *The Bankers' Magazine and Statistical Register*, August 1857, and was extracted from an article in *The Philadelphia Bulletin*. The time was May 25, 1857, and the place was Philadelphia:

> Every man and boy in the crowd had his package of coin with them. Some had their rouleaux of Spanish coin done up in bits of newspaper wrapped in handkerchiefs, while others had carpet bags, baskets and other carrying contrivances, filled with coppers—"very cheap and filling," like boarding-house fare.
>
> The officiating priest in the temple of mammon had anticipated this grand rush and crush, and every possible preparation was made in anticipation of it. Conspicuous among these arrangements was the erection of a neat wooden building in the yard [interior courtyard] of the Mint, a special accommodation of the great crowd of money-changers. This temporary structure was furnished with two open windows which faced the south. Over one of these windows were inscribed the words CENTS FOR CENTS, and over the other CENTS FOR SILVER. Inside the little office were scales and other apparatus for weighing and testing coin, a goodly pile of bags containing the newly-struck compound of nickel and copper, and a detachment of weighers, clerks, etc.
>
> The bags containing the "nicks" were neat little canvas arrangements, each of which held 500 of the diminutive little strangers, and each of which bore upon the outside the pleasant inscription "$5." Just as the State House bell had finished striking 9 o'clock the doors of the Mint were thrown open, and in rushed the eager crowd—paper parcels, well-filled handkerchiefs, carpet bags, baskets and all. But those who thought there was to be a grand scramble, and that the boldest pusher would be first served, reckoned without their host. The invading throng was arranged into lines which lead to the respective windows; those who bore silver had the post of honor assigned them and went to the right, while those who bore nothing but vulgar copper [old half cents and large cents] were constrained to take the left.
>
> These lines soon grew to be of unconscionable length, and to economize space they were wound around and around like the convulsions

of a snake of a whimsical turn of mind. The clerks and the weighers exerted themselves to the utmost to meet the demands of all comers, and to deal out the little canvas bags to all who were entitled to receive them; the crowd grew apace, and we estimated that at one time there could not have been less than 1,000 persons in the zigzag lines, weighed down with small change, and waiting patiently for their turn.

Those who were served rushed into the street with their money-bags, and many of them were immediately surrounded by an outside crowd, who were willing to buy out in small lots and in advance on first cost. We saw quite a number of persons on the steps of the Mint dealing out the new favorites in advance of from 30% to 100%, and some of the outside purchasers even huckstered out the coin again in smaller lots at a still heavier advance. The great majority of those who came out "made tracks" with their bags of money, and not an omnibus [horse-drawn enclosed carriage for public transportation] went eastward past the Mint for several hours that did not, like the California steamers, carry "specie"13 in the hands of the passengers."

Those who made their way homeward a-foot attracted the attention of passersby by their display of specie bags, and we doubt much whether, in the history of the Mint, there was ever so great a rush inside the building, or so animated a scene outside of it. It was, in effect, at once a funeral of the old coppers and of the ancient Spanish coins, and the giving of a practical working existence to the new cents.

In a few weeks the coin will be plentiful enough at par, the Spanish coins will go out at the hands of the brokers just as they already have disappeared from ordinary circulation, and as regard for the old cents there will be "nary red" to be seen, except such as will be found in the cabinets of coin collectors.

On May 25, 1857, the day that the 1857 Flying Eagle cent made its debut, Mint Director Snowden wrote to Secretary of the Treasury Guthrie:

The demand for them is enormous.... We had on hand this morning $30,000 worth, that is 3,000,000 pieces. Nearly all of this amount will be paid out today. The coinage will go forward, however, at the rate of 100,000 or more pieces per day and the demand will be met as well as we can.

A "Review" of the New Cent

Not everyone loved the new Flying Eagle cent. This scathing commentary appeared in *Life Illustrated*, New York, June 27, 1857, reprinted from a recent issue of the *Albany Journal:*

The new cent coin wins opinions anything but golden. Its color—like copper counterfeiting pinchbeck and blushing at being caught in the cheat—is the ground of objection with some. Others revile the ambiguous figure which the Mint officers interpret to mean a flying eagle, but which, to the uninstructed, resembles a table napkin, or pen wiper got up for sale at a fancy fair.

The latest objection we have noticed is that children swallow it, with great consequent irritation of the stomach and bowels, from the corrosive nature of the metals of which it is composed.

There is just one good thing in the new cent. It weighs precisely the hundredth part of a pound. People inclined to decimals may turn it to some good purpose as a convenient mode of determining fractional weights; sixpence worth is an ounce; three of them can be sent by mail for three cents more.

Those of our readers who desire to see what the new cent ought to have been in color and material, can step into the State Library and admire the beautiful collection of bronze medals of the French kings, presented by Napoleon the Little. They are nearly black. A cent of this hue could not be mistaken for a half-eagle, or a dime, while the present abortion is of a compromise tint between the two. Our Mint is the more inexcusable, because the French have, within the last three years, replaced their old and cumbrous copper coinage by one of bronze, in which the defect of weight was compensated not so much by superior value in the material as by artistic taste and elegance in the devices and execution. Their example was before us for instruction and imitation.

Who cares whether a penny is worth the hundredth part of a dollar, or only the one hundred and fiftieth? Not a soul. It is mere counter change, not designed for keeping. But our Mint is scrupulous on this. Honesty, which has deserted pretty nearly every other civil department of the federal government, still keeps a lingering foothold there. And thus it comes that an administration which sticks at no outrage upon Liberty—whose effigy is banished from the cent—insists upon mixing preposterous German silver with its copper, to the end that the purchaser of a penny may get his dirty penny's worth. So did the Pharisees pay tithes of mint, anise, and cumin, while neglecting the weightier matters of the law.

REDEMPTION OF SILVER

In exchange for the new copper-nickel cents the Mint and two other Treasury branches redeemed outstanding large cents from circulation and also took in worn Spanish-American silver coins, as noted above. The silver denominations consisted nearly entirely of 1/2-real, 1-real, and 2-real pieces (the larger 4- and 8-reales coins were rarely encountered; reales were also called "bits"), primarily made at the Mexico City Mint. Director Snowden had estimated that about $3 million worth of these foreign silver coins were in circulation by early 1857. Most were severely worn, often to the point of virtual smoothness.

Up to this point, these Spanish-American silver coins had been received at Treasury offices, post offices, and government land agencies at these discounted rates:

1/16th dollar or half bit: $0.05
1/8th dollar or one bit: $0.10
1/4th dollar or two bits: $0.20

These redemptions were permitted for two years from the passage of the Act of February 21, 1857, but an extension was later granted, and coins were exchanged until the Act of June 25, 1860, ended the practice.

To facilitate their exchange for new one-cent pieces, the government raised the rate to par with United States coins, subject to several rules to prevent severely worn coins from being turned in.[14] Redemptions took place at the Philadelphia Mint, New Orleans Mint, and the New York Assay Office.

Spanish Dollar
Mostly minted in Mexico City, these silver coins circulated in the British colonies and, later, in the United States, up to the 1850s.

> 1/16th dollar or half bit: $0.0625
> 1/8th dollar or one bit: $0.125
> 1/4th dollar or two bits: $0.25

Although the accounting was sloppy, and figures varied among reports, the *Mint Report* for the fiscal year ending June 30, 1862, gave these totals redeemed as of two years earlier, by June 30, 1860: 1/16 dollars: $114,182; 1/8 dollars: $249,330; and 1/4 dollars: $440,858. The total of $804,380 was equivalent to 80,438,000 one-cent pieces.

COINAGE FOR CIRCULATION

By most accounts, the new small-diameter Flying Eagle cents were a great success. More than 17 million were made for circulation in 1857, followed by more than 24 million in 1858. The old-style large copper cents became an anachronism within the following decade.[15]

However, the Mint was not satisfied with the design. Parts of the relatively large Flying Eagle motif on the obverse were opposite in the coining press from the heavy agricultural wreath on the reverse, and the demand was made at the moment of striking for metal to flow into deep orifices which could not be completely filled under normal die spacing and production conditions. The result was that some coins showed weaknesses, particularly at the eagle's head and tail.

In 1857 Mint Director Snowden suggested that the head of Christopher Columbus replace the eagle on the cent. Chief Engraver Longacre replied on July 17 that the idea was certainly entitled to consideration. However, since earlier objections had been raised against the use of George Washington's portrait on United States coinage, the portrait of Columbus would probably meet with the same problem.

Pattern copper-nickel cents were made in 1858 with a very small or "skinny" eagle on the obverse, thus obviating the metal flow problem, but this motif (which Richard Snow has elsewhere fancifully described as "a quail in the throes of death"[16] and Mint Director Snowden called an "eagle volant"[17]) was not deemed satisfactory. The lettering around the obverse border was fairly heavy in its vertical elements, somewhat similar to that associated with the work of Anthony C. Paquet on other denominations of the era, and was entirely unlike the "Small Letters" or "Large Letters" fonts used on regular issue 1858 Flying Eagle cents.

In the same year pattern Indian Head cents were produced by James B. Longacre. These had an Indian Head motif in the center of the obverse. The face of the new Miss Liberty was copied from Lon-gacre's 1854 $3 gold piece (and is

Columbus and Washington
Rejected from the nation's circulating coinage in the 1850s, they would later appear on commemoratives (the 1893 World's Columbian Exposition half dollar and the 1900 Lafayette dollar).

related somewhat to his 1849 gold $1 and $20 designs), now outfitted with a ceremonial headdress.

On the reverse—designed by James B. Longacre or, alternatively, Anthony C. Paquet—a low-relief laurel wreath was used instead of the heavy agricultural wreath. The words ONE CENT were in shallow relief as well. This solved the metal-flow and striking problem.

Months after patterns had been made, Director Snowden wrote to the Treasury Department, November 4, 1858, stating that the present Flying Eagle cent coinage was not very acceptable to the general population, partly as the public was now used to seeing birds drawn from nature and not the "heraldic eagle which bears but little resemblance to the bald eagle." Snowden went on to say that the new experimental dies were in lower relief and have "an ideal head of America—the sweeping plumes of the North American Indian giving it the character of America," and that there was "a plain laurel wreath" on the reverse enclosing the denomination ONE CENT. Snowden requested that coinage commence as of January 1, 1859, as changes should not be made mid-year.[18]

Exit the Flying Eagle cent.

Judd 192   Judd 193

Judd 201   Judd 212

Judd 214   Judd 220

Various Pattern Cents of 1858

"Pattern cents of the year 1858 form a playground for numismatists, and in time, most of them can be collected.... Specialists with a technical turn of mind can investigate certain die variations and states...." (*United States Pattern Coins*, ninth ed., 2005)

HISTORY OF THE INDIAN HEAD CENT

THE NEW CENT DESIGNED AND COINED

Mint Director Snowden described the new cent motif as "an Indian head with a falling crown of feathers."[19] Quite probably patterns of this format were available by spring 1858, for on April 12 a Mr. Howard wrote to Director Snowden:

> I have learned that a new pattern piece for the cent has been struck off at the Mint, having upon the obverse a head resembling that of the three dollar piece, and on the reverse a shield at the top of the olive and oak wreath.
>
> I beg leave to inquire of you if you will use your efforts to procure me one specimen only. For which I will give you any price you choose to ask if it is not over five dollars.[20]

Knowledge was certainly widespread by early that summer, for R. Coulton Davis (Philadelphia druggist and avid collector of pattern coins) wrote to Director Snowden on June 24, 1858, indicating that a Boston newspaper had just carried a favorable story about the proposed new Indian design.[21] On June 26, 1858, Augustus B. Sage, writing on behalf of the newly formed American Numismatic Society, contacted Snowden regarding a specimen of the new Indian Head cent for the Society and another for his own collection.[22]

THE INDIAN MOTIF

In a letter dated August 21, 1858, to Mint Director James Ross Snowden, Longacre observed:

> I allude more especially to the design on the obverse.... Why should we in seeking a type for the illustration or symbol of a nation that need not hold itself lower than the Roman virtue or the science of Greece, prefer the barbaric period of a remote and distant people, from which to draw an emblem of nationality, to the aboriginal period of our own land?... Why not be American from the spring-head within our own domain?
>
> From the copper shores of Lake Superior to the silver mountains of Potosi, from the Ojibwa to the Araucanian, the feathered tiara is as characteristic of the primitiveness of our hemisphere, as the turban is of the Asiatic. Nor is there any thing in its decorative character, repulsive to the association of Liberty, with the intelligent American.[23]

On November 4, 1858, Mint Director Snowden discussed Longacre's motif in a letter to Secretary of the Treasury Howell Cobb, noting in part:

> The obverse...presents an ideal head of America—the drooping plumes of the North American Indian give it the character of North America...and that so far from being modeled on any human features in the Longacre family, or any Indians, these were based squarely on

the classical profiles on ancient sculpture.... In any event, the feathered headdress was certainly intended in at least two instances to be that of the Indian, the artists at the Mint evidently not realizing the absurd incongruity of placing this most masculine attribute of the warrior brave on the head of a woman....

Earlier, in 1854, Longacre had used a "feathered tiara" on the new designs for the gold dollar and $3 gold piece. However, it was differently styled than the headdress, typically likened to a war bonnet, used on the 1858 and later Indian Head cents.

A legend arose that Longacre's daughter Sarah posed as the model, but in actuality the image is probably a composite. Longacre himself stated the facial profile was copied from a statue, *Venus Accroupii* (Venus Crouching), apparently either in a Philadelphia museum or in the Vatican in Italy.[24] The above-quoted letter from Snowden to Cobb seemingly addresses the "Sarah question" via the sentence denying the representation of "any human features in the Longacre family."

A photograph of Sarah Longacre (born on February 20, 1828, and thus hardly a little girl when either the 1854 $3 coin or the 1858 pattern Indian Head cents were made) taken on her wedding day in 1847 is inconclusive, but shows her face to be an equal or better candidate than the somewhat unlikely profile of the aforementioned Venus (both images are presented in juxtaposition in *Longacre's Ledger*, July 1992, p. 19). The attribution of the portrait will probably never be decided to everyone's satisfaction, especially absent any surviving information from Longacre stating that his daughter Sarah was the model.

With regard to the absurdity of placing an Indian chief war bonnet on the head of a maiden, history repeated itself in 1907 when Augustus Saint-Gaudens decked Miss Liberty in a feathered headdress on the new $10 gold coin. However, ethnologically correct male Indians in headdresses were used elsewhere in the American monetary system, most notably on the $5 Silver Certificate paper currency in the Series of 1899, Bela Lyon Pratt's designs for the new $2.50 and $5 gold coins of 1908, and James Earle Fraser's Buffalo nickel of 1913.

Director Snowden wrote to Longacre on November 6, 1858, to advise that the Treasury Department had approved the new (Indian) design, the change to take effect on January 1, 1859. Longacre was to prepare the necessary dies. A slight modification was requested in the reverse die.[25]

In due course in 1859 Longacre's Indian Head design became standard on the copper-nickel cent, and 36,400,000 examples were coined for circulation. As it turned out the laurel wreath reverse was only used this year on the cent. It was not forgotten completely, however, and in 1865 it was adapted for use on the new nickel three-cent denomination.

1860: DESIGN MODIFIED

In 1860, for reasons not clear today, the reverse was redesigned to feature a wreath of oak and other leaves with a narrow shield at the top, a motif used in pattern form on certain 1859 cents. The 1859 cent seemed to present no problems in striking, and today most examples have full details.

The new oak wreath with narrow shield reverse motif may have been the work of Anthony C. Paquet, alternatively of James B. Longacre, and in any event was adapted

$3 Gold Piece (1854–1889)

Indian Head $2.50 (1908–1929)

Indian Head $5 (1908–1929)

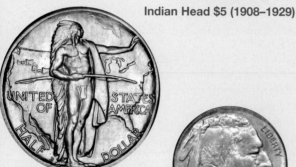

Oregon Trail Memorial
Half Dollar (1926–1939)

Buffalo Nickel (1913–1938)

Indian Head $10 (1908–1933)

$5 Silver Certificate (Series of 1899)

Some Other Native American Motifs in U.S. Currency

These designs exhibit varying degrees of historical/ethnological accuracy. For example, a woman (Miss Liberty), as depicted on the $10 gold piece, would not have worn the feathered headdress of an Indian chief.

from pattern reverses of 1858 (one with an oak wreath with an open top, and one with an oak wreath with a broad ornamented shield at its apex). The lettering ONE CENT on the 1860 issues differs from that on the 1859 cent.

The Indian Head obverse design and oak wreath and narrow shield reverse remained standard in the series through its end in 1909.

TOO MANY CENTS: AN "EVIL"

By autumn 1860 there were too many cents in circulation, not only of the Flying Eagle type minted for commerce in 1857 and 1858, but also of the new Indian Head design first minted in 1859. An article in the *Philadelphia Press*, reprinted in the October 1860 issue of *The Bankers' Magazine and Statistical Register*, advised the following:

> We are requested to state that the Spanish and Mexican fractions of the dollar will not, after today, be received at the Mint at their nominal value, exchanged for the new cents. The main object of the law authorizing these coins to be received at their nominal value of twenty-five, twelve and a half, and six and a quarter cents [Spanish 2-real, 1-real, and half-real coins], was to retire them from circulation, and thus relieve the community from worn-out and depreciated currency, which materially interfered with our excellent decimal system of coinage.
>
> The object having in a great measure had been obtained, and the amount of cents issued being quite large, Mr. Snowden, director of the Mint, recommended that a law should be passed to repeal so much of the former law, on the subject as required these exchanges to be made. This accordingly has been done.
>
> Hereafter the new cents will only be paid out in exchange for gold and silver coins of the United States, and for the copper cent of the former issues. This regulation will undoubtedly be regarded by many of our citizens as a judicious one, inasmuch as the large issue of the new nickel cents has rendered them almost as much of a nuisance as the old Spanish currency. Many persons who have obtained for the latter, at its nominal value, much larger number of the cents than they could legitimately use, have used them to pay bills of one, two or three dollars, and as this custom has been extended, it has caused considerable inconvenience.
>
> The new regulation, by destroying the cause of the over-issue of cents, will no doubt do much to diminish the evil which has resulted from it, and it is hoped that the period is not far distant when the supply of cents will not be graded on the demand for them for use in the small transactions to which silver coins are not adapted....

MORE ABOUT THE FLOOD OF CENTS

The same issue of *Bankers' Magazine* told more:

> There is much feeling manifested in this city at the persistence of the Philadelphia Mint coinage of cents, the market is so flooded with

them. The answer of the Mint is, that there is a constant demand, to meet which they must continue to coin. This demand comes from those who care nothing for the inconvenience of the community, or who do not experience any of the evils of the great surplus of cents, and are therefore inconsiderate enough to order new pieces from the Mint to meet their payments.

Banks, and a variety of other institutions and establishments which have to provide change, prefer an elegant new cent to a dirty old one, and will order from the Mint a constant supply as fast as their stock is exhausted. Of course, as they are not obliged to receive them back, they care little how many are afloat. Thus the evil goes on increasing every day.

There are 10 million cents at this moment in New York over and above the want of the community, and they serve no purpose except to rob the poor of the daily commission on their hard earnings. There is no way to get rid of them; they are sold every day at a depreciation, and immediately put into circulation to be paid out and sold over again. There is but one way to remedy the evil. Let the secretary of the Treasury order the Mint at once to stop the coinage.

If there is any demand for them, orders can be filled here at this moment, at a discount of one year's interest. Congress should then give the people the privilege of exchanging them at the Mint for silver; this would at once meet the "demand" at the Mint, and the director would take care that there were not too many coined, if the surplus were allowed to go back to its source....

The *Report of the Director of the Mint*, 1860, included this commentary:

The new cents have heretofore been issued in exchange for the fractions of the Spanish and Mexican dollar, and for the old copper cents. As the Spanish and Mexican pieces were received at their nominal value, large amounts of these coins have been brought to the melting-pot, and thus the community has been relieved from an irregular and depreciated currency. But it has required the issue of a large amount of cents, and induced a temporary redundancy of that coin in some of the Eastern cities. They are gradually, however, being distributed to all parts of our country, including a portion of the Southern states, where the copper cent was scarcely known as a circulating medium.

Since the passage of the Act of 25th of June, 1860, the issues have been limited to exchanges for the copper cents, except the supplying of the government offices with the new issue, and distant parts of the country in limited amounts. In order to accelerate the process of relieving the community from the cumbrous and inconvenient copper cents, the Mint now pays the expenses of transportation on them, and will make returns in the new issues. This arrangement will tend to relieve the country from a burdensome currency, without increasing the amount of circulation of that denomination of coins.

"In Our Youth, Our Hearts Were Touched By Fire"
(Oliver Wendell Holmes, Speaking of the Civil War)

These soldiers of the early 1850s would have grown up spending half cents and large cents (minted from 1793 onward). In 1857 their pocket change would instead include the new, smaller Flying Eagle cent, and later the Indian Head cent. Five years later, while they fought in the Civil War, all coins would become scarce, hoarded by the public. (From a painting by Henry Alexander Ogden, published by the U.S. Army Quartermaster General in 1890)

THE SITUATION IN JULY 1862

The Bankers' Magazine and Statistical Register, November 1862, reported on the dramatically changed situation in Philadelphia the preceding July:

> The great feature of [July 1862] was the heavy manufacture of cents, of which 3,600,000 were made, of the value of $36,000. There was a great rush to the Mint to procure cents. The *North American* says: "At an early hour in the morning there were not less than 150 boys and men, and 31 young ladies and girls, awaiting a supply of pennies. The boys and men carried shotbags, cigar boxes, baskets, and all sorts of contrivances in which to carry off the much-needed coin. The girls principally carried neat baskets. When the distribution came to be made, the girls were first served, to the intense chagrin of the men, who had been standing on a single foot, alternately, upon the sidewalk for two or three hours. The men and boys were not attended to until the last girl had departed."

Actually, the larger part of the story was left unsaid. The Civil War was raging, and the outcome was far from certain. Some foreign countries (Britain being the prime example) dallied with the idea of recognizing the Confederate States of America, while others sided with the Union. Meanwhile, as in other times of national emergency, the public tried to squirrel away items of lasting value. In the second week of July 1862 there was a flurry of hoarding throughout the Eastern and Midwest sections of the United States. By month's end no silver coins were seen in circulation, and copper-nickel cents were "in anxious demand, and we have heard of 2% [premium] in some instances being paid for them."[26] Gold coins had not been seen in general trade since the preceding December (1861).

As a palliative Congress passed the Act of July 17, 1862, stating that ordinary postage stamps could be used as money in paying federal debts up to $5. The intent of this law was subverted soon thereafter, and the Treasury ordered a supply of privately printed notes popularly referred to as Postage Currency, although there had been no legal provision for them. Denominations were 5¢, 10¢, 25¢, and 50¢. The first of these notes had perforated edges just like stamps. (Today these are collected as part of the Fractional Currency series.) Postage Currency notes were first distributed to Army paymasters in August 1862 and to the public in September. By early 1863 about $100,000 of these notes reached circulation every day, but the demand remained unsatisfied.

Meanwhile, in New York City in mid-July 1862, there were no silver three-cent pieces, half dimes, or other coins of intrinsic value with which to buy a glass of soda or a mug of beer or a streetcar ride, unless such coins were purchased at a premium from a speculator.

The Treasury Department stopped paying out freshly minted silver and gold coins and relegated them to bank vaults or sold them at a premium (in terms of paper money) for export. Silver coins did not return to general use until the mid-1870s and were not in generous supply until 1876; gold was back in circulation beginning on December 17, 1878 (the mandated date was January 1, 1879, but this was anticipated in practice).

For more than a decade, beginning in the summer of 1862, substituting for silver coins were many privately issued items including tickets and small notes printed in val-

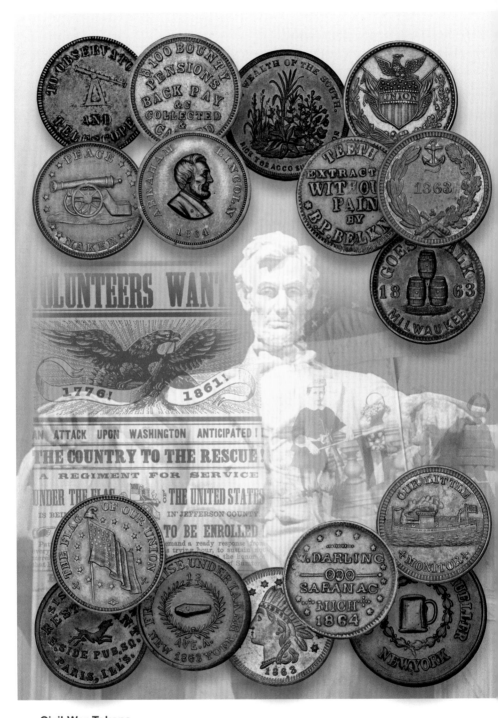

Civil War Tokens

These tokens were made in a wide range of compositions and designs. More than 10,000 different varieties have been recorded, many imitating the Indian Head cent with its headdress-clad youth. Some were political or patriotic in nature, featuring military leaders or propagating slogans. The *Guide Book of United States Coins* estimates that 50 million or more pieces were issued. (Illustations enlarged)

ues from 1¢ upward, government postage stamps placed in privately printed envelopes and brass frames (the latter known as *encased postage stamps*), and a vast flood of small one-cent-size bronze (mostly) and brass tokens, these in addition to a vast quantity of Fractional Currency bills.

Indian Head cents continued to be minted in record numbers in the summer of 1862, and from time to time quantities were released into circulation, as outlined in the newspaper report cited above. The reason why the public clamored for cents in July 1862 is that they were becoming increasingly difficult to find in circulation at the time. Many had been taken off the market, sometimes by being wrapped in paper rolls or packets of 25, 50, or 100 coins, and then stored by those who accepted them in trade. "Bus companies, theatres, and restaurants accepted these rolls everywhere. A retail store in New York received so many that the floor of the room in which they were stored collapsed."[27]

Hoarders had Flying Eagle and Indian Head cents. The public did not. By July 10, 1862, copper-nickel cents were trading at a 4% premium (in terms of paper money) in New York City, and by July 15 they cost a similar premium in Springfield, Massachusetts.[28] What a change from the glut of 1860!

In his *Fractional Money* study, 1930, p. 187, Neil Carothers commented:

> In a vain effort to satisfy the demand [for copper-nickel Indian Head cents] the Mint forced itself into a rate of production even higher than that of 1858. By the end of July the weekly issue amounted to 1,200,000 pieces. One-third of this total was reserved for Philadelphia, the remainder going to the other large cities. No applicant anywhere received more than $5 worth.
>
> The coinage jumped from 12,000,000 pieces in the [fiscal] year ending June 30, 1862, to 47,800,000 in the following year. Even this extraordinary value in cents, $478,000, was a small sum which contrasted with the $25,000,000 or more in silver coin that had disappeared. The demand for the cent pieces was never satisfied. The conditions in Philadelphia, which were duplicated in other cities, were described in the *Public Ledger* of July 18th [1862]:
>
> "The difficulty among small shopkeepers, provision dealers in the markets and in the city generally, in making change, has caused an extraordinary demand for cents, and all that can be commanded at the Mint are eagerly bought.... Though many of those who desired cents stood in line for hours, waiting an opportunity to get into the Mint, they had to go home without them, as the supply on hand was exhausted before half the applicants were accommodated."

Carothers went on to note that these cents, called *nickels* or simply *nicks* (in an era before the nickel five-cent piece, introduced in 1866, would assume that name), were in demand because the ownership of a few cents "meant that the owner could ride rather than walk. And, for months after it meant that he could buy a postage stamp without an altercation with the clerk or a cigar without receiving in change a handful of the dealer's own manufactured currency [paper tickets or notes]."

THE SCENE FROM 1863 TO 1866

By March 1863 the Treasury Department's so-called Postage Currency notes in values of 5¢ to 50¢ had become common in trade and, seemingly, should have alleviated the cent shortage. However, the public still preferred coins, silver and gold remained nowhere to be seen, and attention continued to be focused on the copper-nickel Indian Head cent. On March 9, 1863, the *Public Ledger* reported that in Philadelphia cents were "so scarce as to command a premium of 20%."[29]

By the end of the Mint's fiscal year on June 30, 1863, copper-nickel cents were sufficiently scarce that Director James Pollock reported that they were "scarcely to be had" in circulation, and stated that he could not guess "as to the amount of cents that will be required to meet the public demand."

Under the provisions of the Act of March 3, 1863, the federal government issued Fractional Currency notes in denominations from 5¢ to 50¢, but this distribution did not begin until October 10 of the same year. At this time the tattered Postage Currency notes began to be gradually retired. In autumn 1864 a new Fractional Currency denomination, the 3¢ note, reached circulation, but never became popular.[30]

Gradually, as privately issued bronze tokens were dumped into circulation by the millions and used for everyday change, Indian Head cents returned to commercial channels and circulated, but seemingly not in large numbers in any one place. As late as

Small Change After the War
By 1866, hoarding was no longer a problem. Commerce was aided by several new coins in circulation (including the two-cent piece, and three-cent and five-cent pieces in nickel).

June 30, 1864, at the end of the Mint's fiscal year, Director Pollock reported, "Large quantities are hoarded, and thus kept from circulation."

Apparently, by autumn 1864 the situation eased somewhat, for little was said later in *Mint Reports* about cent hoarding. By this time the new bronze Indian Head cent was a reality. In the same year, 1864, the bronze two-cent piece was introduced to help relieve the need for pocket change, and in 1865 the nickel three-cent piece made its debut, followed by the nickel five-cent piece in 1866. Still, silver coins remained in Treasury vaults and did not circulate, not even the lightweight trimes (silver three-cent pieces). However, by 1865 and 1866 there were enough minor coins in the channels of commerce to satisfy most needs.

BRONZE CENTS

Copper-nickel alloy was very difficult for the Mint to use. It was extremely hard, did not strike up well, and caused rapid die wear. In 1863 Mint officials noted that the public eagerly used private tokens minted of softer bronze, and pattern Indian Head cents (Judd-299, Pollock-359) were struck in a related alloy (the Mint alloy was 95% copper and 5% tin and zinc). The new bronze Indian Head cents, minted under the Act of April 22, 1864, were of lighter weight and thinner, and struck up better than the old-style coins. By the end of May 1864, the copper-nickel cent had been discontinued, and the bronze cent had become standard.

Meanwhile on April 15, 1864, Joseph Wharton, who in 1863 had purchased the nickel mine at Lancaster Gap, Pennsylvania, and who reportedly had $200,000 invested in it, published a pamphlet, *Project for Reorganizing the Small Coinage of the United States of America*, which recommended that the use of nickel be *increased*, and denominations of 1¢, 2¢, 3¢, 5¢, and 10¢ be made with an alloy of 25% nickel and 75% copper. Wharton exercised strong influence on certain members of Congress, and at his doorstep can be directly laid the widespread use of nickel in coinage during this era including the new nickel three-cent piece in 1865 and the nickel five-cent piece in 1866—all made in accordance with his 25% nickel, 75% copper suggestion.

This same Lancaster Gap nickel source, under different ownership, had supplied nickel for copper-nickel cents from 1856 onward.[31]

THE 1860s AND 1870s

After 1865, quantities struck of Indian Head cents dropped significantly as the two-, three-, and five-cent coins and Fractional Currency notes took up the slack. From then through 1878 there were only a few years in which the mintage exceeded 10 million: 1868, 1873, 1874, and 1875. For three years—1871, 1872, and 1877—production was less than 5 million annually, with 1877 registering only 852,500 coins.

By 1871 so many cents had accumulated that they had become a nuisance. Congress passed a law allowing them to be redeemed in greenbacks by the Treasury when presented in amounts of $20 or more. The Act of March 1871 provided for the melting of millions of unwanted two-cent pieces (first coined in 1864) as well as worn copper and bronze cents, with the metal to be used to strike more Indian Head cents. This piece of legislation resulted in generous mintage figures after 1872.

In 1873 the Treasury's illegal resumption of silver specie payments put a small quantity of silver coins back into commercial channels. By autumn 1876 this severely lessened the demand for minor coins, resulting in lower mintages for the cent, nickel three-cent, and nickel five-cent pieces.[32]

1879 TO 1909

Beginning in 1879, production of Indian Head cents at the Philadelphia Mint went back above the 10 million mark annually and remained there for the rest of the series through to its end in 1909. The lowest mintage of this interval was 11,765,384 (including 3,790 Proofs) for 1885, and the highest mintage and the only year to cross the 100-million mark was 1907 with a production of 108,138,618 (including 1,475 Proofs). The American economy was in a rapid-growth stage during the early 20th century, coin-operated machines were being made in unprecedented quantities, and Indian Head cents were needed in record numbers.

Until 1908, production of Indian Head cents was limited to the Philadelphia Mint. In that year 1,115,000 cents were produced at San Francisco, each coin having a tiny S mintmark below the wreath on the reverse. The first production took place on November 27, 1908.

In 1909 309,000 1909-S Indian Head cents were made, the lowest circulation-strike production in the Indian Head series.

The San Francisco Mint, 1906
When San Francisco was rocked by an earthquake in April 1906, the Mint was the only building standing for several blocks. It was up and running again by the following year, and contributed to Indian Head cent production in 1908 and 1909.

Aspects of Collecting

Being a Smart Buyer

To build your collection of Flying Eagle and Indian Head cents you will need to participate in the marketplace. These coins as well as those in other series are easy enough to buy—just by writing a check. However, the difference between a drab collection and a great one, even within the same grades, is a matter of connoisseurship.

If you go car-buying or house-buying, the seller is not likely to tell you, "This is a tired old automobile on its final laps," or "There is so much work to be done on this building that it isn't worth it." So it is with coins. Even certified coin holders give no indication as to whether the coin within is a rare beauty or as ugly as a toad. Accordingly, it is up to *you* to be a smart buyer—if you want to.

Here are some guidelines for smart buying:

Look at the coin, not at the numerical grade or color designation, except as a starting point. If it is stained, spotted, ugly, or unappealing, don't buy it. Wait for another. You'll have a later chance. A spot-free, pristine, beautiful MS-65 RD cent priced at $1,200 might be a better buy than a stained, cleaned "MS-65 RD" priced at $500.

There are a lot of traps among certified coins and even more among those that are not certified. Some pieces are very ugly. And, as grading interpretations become looser, the average quality within a grade designation is getting worse. To put it simply, the typical certified MS-65 RD cent on the market in 1987 was better in quality than the same grade in 1997, and a 2007 coin is likely to fall short of the quality of 1997. Many of yesterday's MS-64 coins are today's MS-65's and MS-66's!

Outside of certified coins, assigning a numerical grade (without respect to quality and eye appeal) to Mint State and Proof bronze Indian Head cents is often a minefield for the unwary or uneducated buyer. Unless you have some grading savvy, at least start by examining certified coins. You may not bat 1000, but you stand a better chance of batting 300 than if you buy non-certified pieces. Certification by ANACS, ICG, NGC, and PCGS has become so popular, that most dealers have sent in their higher-value coins for grading to these services. High-value coins that are *not* certified might have been rejected by these services as cleaned, retoned, or having other problems. This is not always true—some dealers don't like certified coins, and many collectors stay away from them as well—but for the beginner certification is a good first step when considering coins. In the mid-1990s ANACS was the only service to attribute Flying Eagle and Indian Head cents by Snow numbers, as cataloged by Richard Snow. Increasingly, other services are doing this as well.

Think independently. Don't let someone fool you into believing that all MS-65 RD coins are better than, for example, MS-63 BN specimens. This is not the case. There are nice coins and there are ugly coins within each grade category.

Don't be a bargain hunter. If the quality is there and the coin is *rare*, don't be afraid to pay the going rate or even more. No one ever bought the best quality for the cheapest price. This is true throughout the Flying Eagle and Indian Head cent series and is especially so among the bronze Indian Head cents of 1864 to 1909. On the other hand, among later Lincoln cents, if a coin is common in gem condition (as are, for example, Proof Lincoln cents of the past two or three decades), then finding a gem will be a snap, just about every vendor has high quality, and the effort of cherrypicking for quality will not be important. Stated another way, the discipline needed to buy a modern Proof-66

RD 2000-S Lincoln cent is one thing, and that needed to buy a Proof-66 RD Indian Head cent of 1890 is another.

Study the specific variety of the coin you intend to buy in order to learn its characteristics, its availability in various grades, and its other aspects. Fortunately for you, there is much information available on Flying Eagle and Indian Head cents—in this book and elsewhere (see the bibliography)—so you can indeed know where you are going.

Take your time. No matter how well endowed your checking account may be, allow yourself a year or two or three to put together a nice set. This will prolong the thrill of the hunt as well. No one has ever put together a *quality* collection of Flying Eagle and Indian Head cents by buying in a hurry.

A Few Words About Proofs

Toned Proof Cents
Environmental factors can lead to a variety of beautiful surface colors.

The Mint struck Proof Flying Eagle and then Indian Head cents, in quantities ranging from a couple dozen to several thousand. These were made by using dies with highly polished faces, striking the coins slowly on a medal press, and handling them with care afterward. The resultant coins had deeply mirrored fields.

Because these were sold at a premium to collectors, most were saved. We know that 2,350 Proof Indian Head cents were struck in 1878. Likely, 1,500 or so still survive. Some have been cleaned or tampered with, most pristine pieces have natural medium brown and iridescent toning, and others have mint red color in varying degrees. Some are beautiful to behold, others are not.

In contrast, circulation strikes were placed into commerce and soon became worn. The survival of Mint State coins is a matter of chance—a piece put away in a cast-iron bank in the 1880s, or left in a box of keepsakes, or perhaps picked out of circulation by a coin collector. In proportion to the original mintage figures, only a tiny fraction of 1% of the various issues have survived in Mint State.

As Proofs were made by a different method of manufacture, they can be considered "varieties" different from circulation strikes. Many specialists obtain one Proof and one Mint State coin for a given date. Generally, high-grade Proofs are apt to have more problems than are high-grade circulation strikes, simply because numismatists who owned Proofs often cleaned them.

GRADING FLYING EAGLE CENTS

The following grading guidelines are adapted from the *Official American Numismatic Association Grading Standards for United States Coins*, 6th edition.

MINT STATE (UNCIRCULATED)

Coin has absolutely no trace of wear.

MS-70 • A flawless coin exactly as it was minted, with no trace of wear or injury. Must have full mint luster and natural color.

MS-67 • Virtually flawless, but with very minor imperfections.

MS-65 • No trace of wear; nearly as perfect as MS-67 except for some small blemish. Has full mint luster but may be unevenly toned or lightly fingermarked. A few minor nicks or marks may be present.

MS-63 • A Mint State coin with attractive mint luster, but noticeable detracting contact marks or minor blemishes.

MS-60 • A strictly Uncirculated coin with no trace of wear, but with blemishes more obvious than in higher grades. May have dull mint luster; color may be uneven shades.

ABOUT UNCIRCULATED

Small traces of wear are visible on highest points.

AU-58 (Very Choice) • Has some signs of abrasion: feathers on eagle's breast; wing tips.

AU-55 (Choice) • OBVERSE: A trace of wear shows on the breast and left wing tip. REVERSE: A trace of wear shows on the bow. SURFACE: Considerable mint luster is still present.

AU-50 (Typical) • OBVERSE: Traces of wear show on the breast, left wing tip, and head. REVERSE:Traces of the wear show on the leaves and bow. SURFACE: Some of the mint luster is still present.

EXTREMELY FINE

Very light wear on only the highest points.

EF-45 (Choice) • OBVERSE: Wear shows on breast, wing tips, and head. All feathers are plain. REVERSE: High points of the leaves and bow are lightly worn. SURFACE: Traces of mint luster still show.

EF-40 (Typical) • OBVERSE: Feathers in wings and tail are plain. Wear shows on breast, wing tips, head, and thigh. REVERSE: High points of the leaves and bow are worn.

VERY FINE

Light to moderate even wear. All major features are sharp.

VF-30 (Choice) • OBVERSE: Small, flat spots of wear show on breast and thigh. Feathers in wings still show bold details. Head is worn but sharp. REVERSE: Ends of leaves and bow are worn almost smooth.

VF-20 (Typical) • OBVERSE: Breast shows considerable flatness. Some of the details are visible in feathers of the wings. Head is worn but bold. Thigh is smooth, but feathers in tail are nearly complete. REVERSE: Ends of leaves and bow are worn smooth.

FINE

Moderate to heavy even wear. Entire design is clear and bold.

F-12 • OBVERSE: Some details show at breast, head, and tail. Outlines of feathers in right wing and tail show, with no ends missing. REVERSE: Some details are visible in the wreath. Bow is very smooth.

VERY GOOD

Well worn. Design is clear but flat and lacking details.

VG-8 • OBVERSE: Outline of feathers in right wing ends show, but some are smooth. Legend and date are visible. The eye shows clearly. REVERSE:

Slight detail in wreath shows, but the top is worn smooth. Very little outline shows in the bow.

GOOD
Heavily worn. Design and legend are visible, but faint in spots.
G-4 • OBVERSE: Entire design is well worn, with very little detail remaining. Legend and date are weak but visible. REVERSE: Wreath is worn flat but completely outlined. Bow merges with wreath.

ABOUT GOOD
Outlined design. Parts of date and legend are worn smooth.
AG-3 • OBVERSE: Eagle is outlined, with all details worn away. Legend and date are readable but very weak and merging into rim. REVERSE: Entire design is partially worn away. Bow is merged with the wreath.

GRADING INDIAN HEAD CENTS

MINT STATE
Absolutely no trace of wear.
MS-70 • A flawless coin exactly as it was minted, with no trace of wear or injury. Must have full mint luster and natural color.
MS-67 • Virtually flawless, but with very minor imperfections.
MS-65 • No trace of wear; nearly as perfect as MS-67 except for some small blemish. Has full mint luster but may be unevenly toned or lightly finger-marked. A few minor nicks or marks may be present.
MS-63 • A Mint State coin with attractive mint luster, but noticeable detracting contact marks or minor blemishes.
MS-60 • A strictly Uncirculated coin with no trace of wear, but with blemishes more obvious than in higher grades. May have dull mint luster; color may be uneven shades of brown.

ABOUT UNCIRCULATED
Small traces of wear are visible on highest points.
AU-58 (Very Choice) • Has some signs of abrasion: hair above ear; curl to right of ribbon; bow knot.
AU-55 (Choice) • OBVERSE: Only a trace of wear shows on the hair above the ear. REVERSE: A trace of wear shows on the bow knot. SURFACE: Considerable mint luster is still present.

AU-50 (Typical) • OBVERSE: Traces of wear show on the hair above ear, and curl to right of ribbon. REVERSE: Traces of wear show on the leaves and bow knot. SURFACE: Significant mint luster is still present.

EXTREMELY FINE

Very light wear on only the highest points.

EF-45 (Choice) • OBVERSE: Wear shows on hair above ear and curl to right of ribbon, and on ribbon end. The diamond design and letters in LIBERTY are very plain. REVERSE: High points of the leaves and bow are lightly worn. SURFACE: Traces of mint luster still show.

EF-40 (Typical) • OBVERSE: Feathers are well defined and LIBERTY is bold. Wear shows on hair above ear, curl to right of ribbon, and ribbon end. Most of the diamond design shows plainly. REVERSE: High points of the leaves and bow are worn.

VERY FINE

Light to moderate even wear. All major features are sharp.

VF-30 (Choice) • OBVERSE: Small, flat spots of wear on tips of feathers, ribbon, and hair ends. Hair still shows half of details. LIBERTY is slightly worn and letters are generally sharp. REVERSE: Leaves and bow are worn but fully detailed.

VF-20 (Typical) • OBVERSE: Headdress shows considerable flatness. Nearly half of the details still show in hair and on ribbon. Head is slightly worn but bold. REVERSE: Leaves and bow are almost fully detailed.

FINE

Moderate to heavy even wear. Entire design is clear and bold.

F-12 • OBVERSE: Some details show in the hair and feathers. Ribbon is worn smooth. LIBERTY normally shows with no letters missing. REVERSE: Some details are visible in the wreath and bow. Tops of leaves are worn smooth.

VERY GOOD

Well worn. Design is clear but flat and lacking details.

VG-8 • OBVERSE: Outline of feathers show but some are smooth. Legend and date are visible. Some letters in LIBERTY show; any combination of two full letters and parts of others is sufficient. REVERSE: Slight detail in wreath shows, but the top is worn smooth. Very little outline shows in the bow. Rim is complete.

GOOD

Heavily worn. Design and legend are visible, but faint in spots.

G-4 • OBVERSE: Entire design is well worn with very little detail remaining. Legend and date are weak but visible. REVERSE: Wreath is worn flat but completely outlined. Bow merges with wreath. Rim is incomplete in spots.

ABOUT GOOD

Outlined design. Parts of date and legend are worn smooth.

AG-3 • OBVERSE: Head is outlined, with nearly all details worn away. Legend and date are readable but very weak and merging into rim. REVERSE: Entire design is partially worn away. Bow is merged with the wreath.

SEEKING HIGH-QUALITY FLYING EAGLE AND INDIAN HEAD CENTS

With a firm understanding of grading we go on to some other aspects of Flying Eagle and Indian Head cents, mainly those of the surface appearance. These and other considerations are, of course, all interrelated so far as market value and desirability are concerned.

For the best use of your money, determine to be a connoisseur. Along the way it is important to know what *not* to buy as well as what you should acquire. Thomas Edison is said to have made 500 non-working light bulbs before *the* light bulb was invented in 1879. If you consider 20 coins before buying *the* coin, you have accomplished much.

CLEANING

Immersing a brown-toned Indian Head cent in silver dip or another cleaner will make it "brilliant," perhaps a bright orange somewhat similar to what it looked like when first minted, but to the expert's eye, ever so slightly paler and not quite the "right" hue. Cleaning a bronze coin strips the surface of its toning and makes chemically active copper metal even more susceptible to atmospheric effects. Most dipped pieces soon become blotchy or unevenly colored. Most mottled and stained Proof bronze cents in certified holders marked "BN" or "RB" have probably been cleaned. Some blotchy "RD" coins may represent recently dipped pieces that have been certified, but which changed color within the holders.

As a connoisseur you must avoid blotchy coins. Most advanced specialists would agree that a run of nicely matched, brown-toned AU-55 cents is much more desirable than a far costlier collection of blotchy MS-63 RB pieces. *Quality* is the key word that you as a connoisseur should always keep in mind. *Quality* first, *price* second.

The "secret" to success in buying is simply to avoid coins that are stained and ugly, even if the price is a bargain. Let someone else buy them. The popular coin publications are filled with all sorts of claims and offers, and all too often that bargain "gem brilliant Uncirculated" or "selected brilliant Uncirculated" proves to be a scrubbed-up About Uncirculated coin. Or, that certified Proof-64 RB cent may indeed be Proof-64, but so spotted that it is ugly as sin, and will be something you'll always regret buying, no matter how much of a "bargain" it is.

Bill Fivaz has commented: "Don't buy a problem. It will always be a problem. It doesn't get any better, and it could get worse!"[33]

Similarly, Richard Snow has remarked, "There is no price *too low* for a problem coin."[34]

"GOOD" CLEANING

And yet, some cleaning and techniques can improve a coin's surface. A bright unnatural orange coin that has been dipped will retone a nice brown if it is exposed to the atmosphere, such as on a windowsill under a little wire basket to prevent it from slipping away. Or, a mixture of sulfur powder and mineral oil applied with a cotton swab may do the trick. This is not a suggestion for you, but merely an indication of what can be done to bring back the latent beauty of a cent that has been made ugly. Dr. Sheldon in *Early American Cents* gives some good advice.

A *copper-nickel* cent that is stained or blotched, if it is in a higher grade, may sometimes be dipped with good effect. However, repeated dipping will yield only a dull, unattractive surface, a coin with no "life."

Dipping a *bronze* Indian Head cent usually lessens its value from the outset.

Brushing a circulated bronze coin with a camel's hair brush may remove dust and impart a glossy surface. Again, consult Dr. Sheldon on this one.

Acetone (a volatile solvent available at drug and hardware stores, and which must be carefully used) or plain old soap and water can be used effectively to remove dirt and verdigris from the surface of an Indian Head cent.

In all in instances, do your experimenting with a common, cheap bronze Lincoln cent, not a numismatically valuable older coin.

A BIT OF PHILOSOPHY

If you are knowledgeable about the problems and pitfalls, you will buy coins more effectively, and the pleasures of making a good buy will be more exciting, more real. If you buy that MS-65 RD Indian Head cent and know full well what the grading game is about, then you are home free. If you have looked at 16 coins and have passed them by, and finally have found Coin No. 17, the sparkling gem you've been hoping for, you will be happy and satisfied. You'll really appreciate what you have, just as Edison realized the importance of Light Bulb No. 501.

On the other hand, if you buy a coin described as MS-65 RD, but are not sure whether the price is right or what the coin should look like or whether quality is important, but are relying simply upon someone else's sales pitch or the inducement of a low price, the day of reckoning awaits you.

There are pleasures in collecting Flying Eagle and Indian Head cents, and these pleasures are *delicious* once you have some knowledge. There is an Unclouded Sky in numismatics if you are a connoisseur. Become a connoisseur, a smart buyer, and you'll have a really great time.

FOUR STEPS TO SUCCESS

An important aspect for you to know, but not at all treated in the wide marketplace, is that for any Proof Flying Eagle or Indian Head cent to be other than gem grade, say Proof-65 or better, it has been subject to some handling. If it has *hairlines*, this is because the coin has been *cleaned*. However, the grading services are inconsistent as to how they handle this. Generally, an Indian Head cent with hairlines, for example, will be graded less than Proof-65, and assigned some grade such as Proof-62 or Proof-63. If the cleaning is severe, it might be called Proof-60. A correct listing would be as follows: "Proof-62 due to hairlines from cleaning." Some services will return a coin ungraded if it has been *severely* cleaned; others may put a "net grade" on it. There is little consistency in this regard. The problem is not as acute with circulation strikes, as the mint luster will often mask hairlines.

Any Flying Eagle or Indian Head cent, if as brilliant as when first minted, with a bright edge, is a coin that has been dipped (immersed in a liquid silver cleaner or chemical metal brightener). Any such coin, if held by the most careful of numismatists and their successors, that has come down to the present day will *always* show some light toning. This is reflected by examining coins held in old-time collections, such as the T. Harrison Garrett and James M. Clapp collections assembled in the 19th century.

Then there is the matter of sharpness of strike. Some cents are flat in areas, while others have the needle sharpness denoted as *Full Details* (FD), with every feature defined. Flying Eagle cents often have some lightness on the eagle's head and tail feathers, less often on the reverse wreath. Indian Head cents often have indistinct detail at the tips of the headdress feathers, this being particularly true of the copper-nickel issues from 1859 to 1864. Certified holders say *nothing* about strike—weak, average, or with Full Details. It is up to *you* to determine this! Tracking down these features can be a pleasant endeavor.

You can see that grading-service nomenclature such as MS-63 and Proof-67 doesn't tell you much if you really want to be a connoisseur. Instead, you need to apply your own expertise and thinking.

Some time ago, for Whitman Publishing, I devised the following four-step process for successful collecting. It has caught on with a number of readers who have applied it to their own fields of interest. Adapted for the present text, here it is:

Step 1: Observe the Numerical Grade

You are holding a coin in your hand. Should you buy it? Your first step is to look at the assigned grade of the coin, or, if you are familiar with grading, to assign your own number. Experienced collectors and dealers will often share their opinions with you. Without being an annoyance, see if you can "ask around" for help.

If you are just entering numismatics, you would do well to only consider coins that have been certified by the four leading grading services—ANACS, ICG, NGC, and PCGS. All but ICG publish population reports delineating the coins that have passed through their hands. Retail price information for many commercially graded coins can be found in many places, in particular *The Certified Coin Dealer Newsletter*. However, the *Newsletter* states that prices listed there are only for average-quality coins.

The grade listed on a certified coin holder, or noted by a dealer on a cardboard or other holder, is simply the *starting point* in the buying process. This is one of the most important concepts for success.

When you visit a coin shop or a convention, or contemplate a catalog or Internet offering, have an approximate grade in mind for each coin you are seeking. If you are looking for a rare 1877 Indian Head cent, and have $1,000 to spend, there is not much sense asking to see MS-65 or other high-grade coins. Nor is there any reason to waste your time looking at well-worn pieces in G-4 grade. These are the market prices from the listings given later in this book:

> 1877 cent: G-4: $625 • VG-8: $800 • F-12: $1,200 • EF-40: $2,200 •
> AU-50: $2,600 • MS-60: $3,400 • MS-63: $4,000

At a coin show, or when sending a "want list" to a dealer, ask to see coins in the range of VG-8 to F-12 as these are more or less in the price range you want to pay.

No matter what grades you ask for, reject any coins that seem to be overgraded. This comment is made with the realization that you will need some experience, for lacking this, you will not know accurate grading from inaccurate. The best way to gain experience is to visit a coin show or a coin shop and look through as many Flying Eagle and Indian Head cents as you can. This might range from a few Flying Eagle cents to dozens or even hundreds of Indian Head cents. Stocks of Proofs are apt to be smaller. Today the Internet offers some at-home opportunities. While the grade may be hard to figure out from a low-resolution Internet image, and coins can be turned in the light and photographed to make them look more attractive than they really are, other aspects such as sharpness can be discerned.

Read the *Official ANA Grading Standards for United States Coins*. Spend time looking at cents, preferably in person, perhaps with this book in your hand. If you do this at a show or in a shop, it is good form to advise the dealer what you are doing—seeking education—and to make a courtesy purchase of a coin or a book or two. In less time than you realize, you will learn the fundamentals of grading.

Step 2: Determine First-Glance Eye Appeal

Now, the process becomes easier! At this point take a quick glance at the coin. Is it "pretty"? Is the toning (if present) attractive, or is it dark or blotchy? Is the coin stained? If it is brilliant, is it attractively lustrous, or is it dull and lifeless? Are there black spots here and there on the surface? Here the Internet can offer many opportunities for education. When buying from a dealer or on an Internet listing, insist on a return privilege if *for any reason* you do not like the coin. If the vendor does not want to offer this privilege, find another seller.

If the coin is not attractive, then reject it and go on to look at another. Even if the price seems to be a super-bargain, cast the coin aside. Stop right here, and go back to Step 1 with another coin. An ugly coin graded as MS-65 RD or Proof-63 RB is still ugly, and would not be bought by a connoisseur for *half* of the current market price! Do not be tempted by overgraded and/or ugly coins offered at "below wholesale" prices. Keep your wallet in your pocket. The good news is that attractive Flying Eagle and Indian Head cents do exist, and in fair numbers. However, they need some scouting to find.

If the coin is attractive to your eye, then in some distant future year when time comes to sell it, the piece will be attractive to the eyes of other buyers—an important consideration. Now, with an attractive coin in hand, you have a candidate *for your further consideration.*

Step 3: Evaluate Sharpness and Related Features

At this point you have a coin that you believe to be more or less in the numerical grade assigned on the ANACS, ICG, NGC, or PCGS holder, or in a dealer's holder of another type, or, if you are in the fast lane, determined by your own experience. You also have for consideration one that has passed your test for excellent eye appeal.

The next step is to take out a magnifying glass and evaluate the coin's sharpness. Here, one rule does not fit all, but general guidelines apply. For a Flying Eagle cent, check the head and tail of the eagle. If those features are needle-sharp (with Full Details), then look at the rest of the coin. For an Indian Head cent, the tips of the head-dress feathers are the first place to look, after which you need to check the rest of the coin. Full Details coins are much more plentiful in the Flying Eagle and Indian Head cent series than, for example, among Indian Head / Buffalo nickels, Standing Liberty quarters, or Liberty Walking half dollars.

To determine sharpness, you must examine the coin! There is *no* alternative unless you enlist a trustworthy dealer or friend to do this for you, and share your guidelines.

Also check for surface quality. Is the luster satiny or frosty, with full sheen—or is the coin struck from overused dies showing metal flow and granularity? Again, certified holders reveal nothing about this. Is the planchet of good quality, or is it rough? Generally, Proofs are more sharply struck and present fewer difficulties than do circulation strikes.

If the coin you are considering buying has passed the preceding tests, it is ready *for further consideration.* Chances are good that you are holding a very nice coin in your hand!

Step No. 4: Establish a Fair Market Price

If you've done everything right, you have a Flying Eagle or Indian Head cent that is correctly graded, of superb eye appeal, and sharply struck (a realistic goal for all basic dates in the series). Now, to the price you should pay.

For starters, use one or several handy market guides for a ballpark estimate. Unlike many other specialties, nearly all issues in the Flying Eagle and Indian Head cent series are actively traded, and there is no lack of information. This book includes market values for every coin, in several grades.

Now comes the fun part: If the coin is common enough in a given grade, with sharp strike, with fine planchet quality, and with good eye appeal, then the market price is very relevant, as you can shop around. If a coin is common in the grade you want, and with all other desired features, and you have ascertained that the market price level is about $700, then there is no sense paying $800 or $950. Wait until you find one at or near $700. On the other hand, chances are good that you will not find a problem-free coin for, say, $500 or $600. If something is offered to you for *below wholesale*, this simply means that any dealer wanting to buy a choice coin will not buy *this* one—and, accordingly, it is available for less!

You are *very lucky* in that for Flying Eagle and Indian Head cents, hardly anyone looks at sharpness and overall quality. Ninety or more out of every hundred buyers consider only the certified grade. This is amazing, but true. You are also lucky that each and every issue does exist with Full Details. Bide your time until you find them. When you do, the market premium will be modest or even non-existent over a typical coin of lower quality.

NOTES

1. 125th Congress, Document No. 7, House of Representatives, 1st Session, titled *Substitute for Copper. Memorial Lewis Feuchtwanger*, September 13, 1837.

2. Director Snowden in *A Description of Ancient and Modern Coins...*, 1860, p. 120, specifically called this a *cereal wreath*. In the 19th century it was occasionally called a *tobacco wreath*.

3. Although the top ends of the wreath do not particularly resemble corn ears, this is what they were intended to be. Thomas K. DeLorey, in a letter to Q. David Bowers, June 3, 1996, commented: "The original wax model for the agricultural wreath, now in my possession, shows the detail of the two corn ears at the tops of the wreath as long, feathery fronds, signifying the tassel normally found on a corn ear. However, none of this detail survived the transfer to the various incarnations of this wreath, and in each case Longacre was forced to replace it with a series of dots resembling kernels of corn themselves."

4. Original Saint-Gaudens letter owned by Les Perline.

5. This and other references from most of the year 1836 refer to *dies* rather than models, perhaps verifying that the pantograph method of model-to-hub reduction was not yet in use. A Contamin portrait or transfer lathe was installed in 1837, after which the process became mechanized.

6. Gold shipments received as indemnification from France. In addition, many gold coins of heavy weight ("old tenor" coins) minted prior to the Act of June 28, 1834, came into the Mint and were converted to coins of the new standard, which was instituted on August 2, 1834.

7. Modern numismatic scholars, Tom DeLorey and John Dannreuther among them, have endeavored to undo some of Breen's gratuitous assumptions.

8. Walter Breen, *The United States Minor Coinages 1793-1916*, p. 14; modified by his *Encyclopedia of Proof Coins*, p. 245. Also R.W. Julian, "The Flying Eagle Cent," *COINage*, October 1987.

9. June 4, 1853, is the date personally stated by Snowden in his *Medallic Memorials of Washington*, p. 194: "...entered upon the duties of the office on the 4th day of June, 1853." Numerous later accounts state June 3, 1853. Although he began serving in 1853, he was not officially confirmed until February 4, 1854.

10. James Ross Snowden, *The Medallic Memorials of Washington*, page v (part of an account of how the Washington Cabinet was formed).

11. Today it is more popular to state the diameter as 19.1 mm, obscuring the "useful" diameter originally intended.

12. Quoted by Kevin Flynn in "Two Obverse Types Used on 1857 Flying Eagle Cents." *Numismatic News*, April 2, 1996, here slightly edited. Certain other letters were quoted by Larry R. Steve and Kevin Flynn in *Flying Eagle and Indian Head Die Varieties*.

13. *Specie* here refers to gold coins. Passengers from California typically brought their profits (if they had them) in the form of privately minted as well as San Francisco Mint gold coins and arrived in the East aboard steamers, connecting at Aspinwall, the Atlantic terminus of the Panama Railroad (opened in 1855). Copper-nickel cents were never considered to be specie; this term was reserved for coins struck in silver or gold, although the newspaper reporter used the word in the cent connection.

14. $5 worth of 1/16th dollars had to weigh more than $4.30 face value worth of current silver coins (half dimes to half dollars); $5 worth of 1/8th dollars had to weigh more than $4.50 worth of silver coins; $5 worth of 1/4th dollars had to weigh more than $4.80 in silver coins.

15. Millions were taken north to Canada, and in the early and mid-1860s large cents circulated actively there at a time when they were no longer plentiful in everyday transactions in the United States, having been mostly replaced by copper-nickel cents.

16. *Flying Eagle & Indian Cents*, p. 49.

17. Snowden, *A Description of Ancient and Modern Coins...*, 1860, p. 120. "Eagle volant" simply means "flying eagle."

18. Citation supplied by R.W. Julian, letter to Q. David Bowers, April 24, 1996; also "The Adoption of [the] Indian Head Cent," Walter Thompson, *Numismatic Scrapbook Magazine*, July 1961.

19. Snowden, *A Description of Ancient and Modern Coins...*, 1860, p. 120.

20. Steve-Flynn, *Flying Eagle and Indian Head Die Varieties*, p. 213.

21. Citation from R.W. Julian, letter to Bowers, April 16, 1996. Additional information from Walter Breen, letter, February 12, 1992. Also, letter from R.W. Julian, March 20, 1992. Robert Coulton Davis was one of the earliest specialists in pattern coins and wrote the first serious study on them, which appeared serially in *The Coin Collector's Journal*, 1885–1887.

22. Citation provided by R.W. Julian, letter to Bowers, April 24, 1996.

23. Information from Dr. George R. Conger, "The Controversial Feathered Headdress," *Longacre's Ledger*, April 1992; and Joy Goforth, "Who Came First? Goddess, Sarah, or Indian?" *Coin World*, January 4, 1984 (reprinted from Goforth's article in the November 1983 issue of *Mint Press*, there titled "Goddess of Liberty").

24. Breen, *Encyclopedia*, p. 217, locates the statue "in a Philadelphia museum." Cornelius Vermeule, *Numismatic Art in America*, is the source for the Vatican location. Sarah Longacre biographical and portrait information is adapted from "An Argument Favoring Sarah as Longacre's Model," *Longacre's Ledger*, July 1992, which in turn was based upon several cited sources.

25. Citation per R.W. Julian, letter to Bowers, April 24, 1996. The slight modification may have referred to the laurel leaves which were increased in number to six per bunch or cluster, from the five used on patterns. This letter does not preclude Longacre's assigning certain work to his assistant, Anthony C. Paquet, as instructions from the Mint director were typically given to the chief engraver, not to assistants.

26. Neil Carothers, *Fractional Money*, p. 187, quoting the July 4, 1862, *Public Ledger*.

27. Carothers, *Fractional Money*, p. 187.

28. Carothers, *Fractional Money*, p. 187.

29. Carothers, *Fractional Money*, p. 189.

30. In 1869 another denomination, 15¢, was added to the Fractional Currency lineup, but it, too, was never widely used. Fractional Currency notes of all kinds tended to become tattered and soiled easily and hard to stack and count. The public called these notes *stamps*.

31. Carothers, *Fractional Money*, p. 197.

32. The Treasury illegally began silver specie payments, dimes to half dollars, in the spring of 1873; Congress belatedly authorized the action in 1875 (R.W. Julian, letter to Bowers, April 24, 1996).

33. Letter to Bowers, March 29, 1996.

34. Letter to Bowers, April 10, 1996.

How To Use This Book

"Snapshot" essays introduce each year, placing its coins in historical context. Then each cent is studied, by mints and varieties within each year. Each cent is illustrated at 1.5x actual size. For some coins, greater enlargements focus on important details or aberrations. *Circulation Mintage* is for those coins struck for use in commerce; *Proof Mintage* is for those struck for presentation or for collectors. Mintage numbers are generally gathered from the *Annual Report of the Director of the Mint*, but some are given as estimates (especially in the cases of varieties and early coins).

The Whitman Coin Guide (WCG™) offers data for the collector, in a convenient format:

Market Values • Circulation Strikes and Proof Strikes

G-4	VG-8	F-12	VF-20	EF-40	AU-50	MS-60	MS-63
MS-64	MS-65	MS-66	PR-60	PR-63	PR-64	PR-65	PR-66

Availability (Certified Populations)

G - VF	EF-40	EF-45	AU-50	AU-53	AU-55	AU-58	MS-60	MS-61	MS-62	MS-63	MS-64	MS-65	MS-66	MS-67	MS-68	MS-69	MS-70
<PF-60	PF-60	PF-61	PF-62	PF-63	PF-64	PF-65	PF-66	PF-67	PF-68	PF-69	PF-70						

Field populations: Circulation strike (<MS-60), 000,000; circulation strike (MS-60+), 000,000; Proof, 000,000.

Market Values—Circulation Strikes: Market values are given for circulation-strike cents, both circulated (G-4 to AU-50) and Mint State (MS-60 to MS-66). (For details of the 70-point grading system, see the *Official American Numismatic Association Grading Standards for United States Coins*.) Among Mint State bronze coins, *BN* indicates Brown color, *RB* indicates Red Brown, and *RD* indicates Red.

Market Values—Proof Strikes: Market values are also given for Proof cents (when appropriate), from PF-60 to PF-66 (those levels most readily available). As with Mint State coins, *BN*, *RB*, and *RD* indicate Brown, Red-Brown, and Red color.

Certified Populations: The WCG™ presents the number of times the major third-party grading services (ANACS, NGC, and PCGS) have graded cents of a particular date/mint, in circulation-strike grades ranging from EF-40 to MS-70, and Proofs ranging from PF-60 to PF-70. (Summary totals are given for circulation-strike coins graded Good to VF, and for Proofs graded less than PF-60.) These numbers reflect data available as of early 2006.

Note: As time passes, many certified population numbers will increase, as new coins are submitted for grading and previously graded coins are resubmitted. Population reports should not be seen as a perfect reflection of a coin's rarity. High-value coins are likely to have a high percentage of existing pieces submitted for grading than are lower-value coins. Furthermore, a coin with an estimated mintage of, for example, 1,500 pieces might have a certified population greater than 1,500, due to the same coins being submitted and re-submitted several times (by owners hoping to increase their assigned grades).

Field Populations: For each coin, the author has given an estimate for the quantity surviving today in circulated grades (<MS-60), Mint State, and (when appropriate), Proof.

The author describes each coin in detail, with observations on its production, survivability, and any related varieties. He offers guidance on acquiring each coin for circulated, Mint State, and (when available) Proof collections, and describes any challenges pertinent to each coin. The *Optimal Collecting Grade* is the author's opinion of a grade that offers a combination of high quality of preservation *and* reasonable market price—in other words, "a lot of coin for the money."

A Snapshot of the Year 1856

The spring of 1856 saw a very public demonstration of the growing friction between pro- and anti-slavery interests in the United States. The stage was the chambers of the U.S. Senate—but the confrontation was far from a gentlemanly disagreement. South Carolina Congressman Preston Brooks, offended by a robust verbal attack on his pro-slavery uncle, Senator Andrew P. Butler, escalated the war of words into one of physical violence. Brooks attacked his uncle's critic, Massachusetts senator Charles Sumner, beating him so violently with his cane that he nearly killed him. Georgia senators who witnessed the attack laughed, and later other pro-slavery Southerners presented Brooks with congratulatory canes—not-so-subtle encouragement that other abolitionists should be beaten as well. Sumner, meanwhile, required several years to recover from the attack and resume his duties, never again at full capacity.

At the national level, James Buchanan defeated his Republican opponent, the famous explorer John C. Frémont. The Pennsylvania Democrat would be the country's first and only bachelor in the White House.

Numismatically, the year 1856 saw the first "Type 3" gold dollars struck, at the Philadelphia Mint. These were distinguished from their immediate predecessors by a larger Indian princess portrait on the obverse. The old smaller portrait was struck on gold dollars at the San Francisco Mint, which also struck its first dimes, of the Liberty Seated type with stars on the obverse.

1856 Liberty Seated Dime

President James Buchanan
The Pennsylvania Democrat finally won the White House after three unsuccessful bids.

1856 Type 3 Gold Dollar

1856 FLYING EAGLE CENT

CIRCULATION MINTAGE:
EST. 800

PROOF MINTAGE:
EST. 1,500

Enlarged 1.5x—Actual Size: 19mm

Market Values • Circulation Strikes and Proof Strikes

G-4	VG-8	F-12	VF-20	EF-40	AU-50	MS-60	MS-63
$6,200	$6,800	$7,500	$8,750	$10,000	$12,000	$14,000	$18,500
MS-64	MS-65	MS-66	PF-60	PF-63	PF-64	PF-65	PF-66
$45,000	$100,000	$175,000	$12,500	$20,000	$23,500	$30,000	$65,000

Certified Populations

G - VF	EF-40	EF-45	AU-50	AU-53	AU-55	AU-58	MS-60	MS-61	MS-62	MS-63	MS-64	MS-65	MS-66	MS-67	MS-68	MS-69	MS-70
80	43	31	32	6	25	28	13	20	47	94	225	14	2	0	0	0	0
<PF-60	PF-60	PF-61	PF-62	PF-63	PF-64	PF-65	PF-66	PF-67	PF-68	PF-69	PF-70						
153	27	43	126	704	1,326	293	24	11	0	0	0						

Field populations: Circulation strike (<MS-60), 500; circulation strike (MS-60+), 300; Proof, 600.

1856 Cent Production: The 1856 Flying Eagle cent was first produced in late 1856 and early 1857 as a pattern coin, to persuade Congress to drastically change the cent coinage from the large copper pieces then in circulation to a small copper-nickel coin. As this was the first use of this metal for the United States' coinage, trials were needed to both test the striking qualities of the alloy and demonstrate the utility of the new coin to the congressmen who were then writing what would become the Mint Act of February 21, 1857.

The original production was minted in both Proof and circulation strikes, with the vast majority being circulation strikes. U.S. Mint correspondence shows that at least 634 pieces were officially distributed to President Franklin Pierce, Treasury Secretary James Guthrie, and members of Congress. Initially, Pierce was presented with four examples and Guthrie was given four, with two more placed in the Mint Cabinet. It is unknown if these were a special striking in Proof format.

It is to be assumed that a simulated press run at normal speed was conducted to test the new alloy, size, and design. In late 1856 a relatively large run of circulation-strike coins was produced. Early the next year Secretary Guthrie received 200 of this test run and 100 more were sent to the chairman of the Ways and Means Committee, Representative Lewis Davis Campbell. Over the next few weeks, members of the Senate received 62 pieces and at least 264 were sent to the House of Representatives. Undoubtedly, Director James Ross Snowden held extra pieces at the Mint for personal distribution to employees. As far as anyone at the Mint was concerned, this initial production of the 1856 Flying Eagle cent was purely a pattern striking, meant for official purposes. However, the changeover to the copper-nickel small cent would create many new coin collectors, many attempting to assemble complete date sets of the now discontinued large cents.

When the new 1857-dated copper-nickel cents flooded into circulation on May 25, 1857, rumors about the rare 1856-dated copper-nickel cents prompted people to look through their change for the coin. The prices of extant examples skyrocketed. Soon it was trading for 200 times its face value—in an era when $2 was a workingman's daily wages. The first coin-collecting boom in this country had begun.

This new interest in collecting was not lost on the officials at the Mint. Director Snowden was writing a manual on Washington tokens and medals, soon to become a popular collecting subject. He was interested in acquiring any pieces not presently in the Mint's holdings. To augment this collection, he struck additional 1856 copper-nickel cents and began to sell them to collectors in 1859. Almost all of these additional pieces were struck in Proof, a format desired by collectors at the time.

It is unknown what price the Mint charged for these newly struck pieces, but auction records show a drop in prices for 1856 copper-nickel cents, down to 25 cents. Perhaps since the rarity of the 1856 copper-nickel cent was not firmly established, buyers were unwilling to stretch on purchasing the coins.

It is possible that the additional 1856 copper-nickel cents were first made in a single large batch in 1859, but we have no way of knowing when they were last struck. We can surmise that not all were immediately distributed, as the Mint's surplus of 1856 cents kept the price below $2 well into the 1870s. No records were kept regarding the mintage of these pieces.

Survivability: The original 1856 Flying Eagle cents were distributed to members of Congress. Mint employees also kept some of this issue. The James B. Longacre estate had 11 pieces. When the estate was auctioned in 1870, these coins brought $1 each. As these were popular trading items for coin dealers, they were kept mostly in decent shape over the years. Non-collector owners, such as congressmen, probably spent the circulated examples that are encountered today. Today the average grade of the original striking period is About Uncirculated, with high grades of Mint State being very scarce. Coins grading below Very Fine are also very difficult to find, since few circulated for very long periods.

The restrikes from 1858 to 1860 likewise went into collections where they were cared for by their owners. However, quite a number of worn examples are found today. These pieces probably entered circulation during the Civil War, when the Mint was desperate to supply the nation with cents. I imagine the unsold examples could have inadvertently been mixed with a regular shipment of cents. Very worn examples are occasionally seen and must have stayed in circulation well into the 1870s.

Collecting Challenges: All 1856 dies seem to have been prepared carefully with a Proof finish. Examples of what we call Mint State today usually have semi-prooflike fields, but evidence of normal striking conditions, such as weak strikes and strike doubling. The challenge for today's collectors is in determining which coins are Proof and which are Mint State. By comparing the striking quality of known die pairs in the order of their use it is known that the majority, if not all, of the coins distributed to Congress were from what is called the Snow-3 die pair.

The biggest challenge facing collectors is being able to afford an 1856 Flying Eagle cent. Presently, even coins worn down to Good will cost $6,000 or so. Many collectors desire the Mint State version more than the Proof because they were minted during the original striking period. Prices over the years have escalated for Mint Sate pieces due to this extra demand. Collectors must decide if a PF-65 would be a better buy than an MS-63.

Prospective purchasers should study the series before purchasing any 1856 Flying Eagle cent offered. My *Flying Eagle and Indian Cent Attribution Guide, Vol. 1 (1856–1858)* details the various striking periods and their formats in great detail. In general, the die pairs known as Snow-3 are mostly Mint State coins from the original striking period and are easily distinguished by the repunching on the 5 in the date. The majority of the Proofs are from the die pair known as Snow-9. These have a centering dot on the reverse under the upper-left serif of the N in CENT. There are other die pairs, but these are rare, and of interest only to the specialist.

Over the years, grading services have had difficulty with correct attributions on the format of 1856 Flying Eagle cents. Not until the release of the Snow attribution guide in 2000 were the details of the striking formats clearly presented. Since then, ANACS has attributed each format accordingly. In the 13 years prior to the release of the book PCGS and NGC graded many Mint State pieces as Proof and many Proofs as Mint State. This problem confused collectors and created problems for these grading companies, rendering population reports useless. Presently, they have both decided to grade all 1856 Flying Eagle cents with a PR designation. Today this is a hotly debated topic among collectors.

Snow-3 (Repunched 5)

Snow-9 (Reverse Center Dot)

Collecting Circulated Pieces: The Optimal Collecting Grade is EF-40. Clearly, this is the most expensive coin in the collection of Flying Eagle and Indian Head cents. Many collectors ponder the need to include this coin, as it technically is a pattern and was not officially released for circulation. However, the great historical importance of this coin has caught the fancy of enough collectors to warrant a significant premium. There will be a slight premium for the Snow-3 die pair over the Snow-9, but not as much as is seen for high-grade specimens. After a brief time in circulation it is not possible to determine whether a coin started out as a Proof or a circulation strike, so collectors are less inclined to pay great premiums for the Snow-3 in these grades.

The best criterion for choosing a circulated 1856 Flying Eagle cent is the eye appeal of the coin. You should select one with few problems and no evidence of cleaning.

Collecting Mint State Pieces: The Optimal Collecting Grade is MS-63. These are usually from the Snow-3 die pair. Because they have been shown to be from the original striking period (distributed to congressmen), they are under very high demand. They were made in smaller numbers than the Proof issues.

It is important to find an example with a good strike. Many of these Mint State coins show strike weakness on the eagle's head and tail. The surfaces are usually satiny with the fields slightly prooflike. Weakness on the eagle's breast feathers is normally evident and should not be a concern.

Values for the Snow-3 die pair have risen dramatically over the past decade. A record price of $172,500 was set for a PCGS MS-66 Snow-3 at the 2004 Florida

United Numismatists show sale by Heritage Rare Coin Galleries. This is the finest Snow-3 graded Mint State by PCGS. To show the dramatic price rise, consider that this same coin sold a year earlier, at the 2003 FUN show sale, for $103,500. In 1997 my firm, Eagle Eye Rare Coins, had sold this coin for $45,000.

Collecting Proof Issues: The best value for the money is probably a PF-63 or PF-64, which are presently in the $20,000 to $24,000 range. Quality for the grade is a key issue when selecting a coin to add to your collection. An attractive high end for the grade PF-63 is a much better coin to purchase than a low-end PF-64. The majority of Proofs are from the Snow-9 die pair described above. These will have very sharp details on the design elements, and squared rims. The surfaces will not be deeply mirrored like other Proofs from this period, but on unimpaired examples there should be some reflectivity. The mintage of the Proofs is estimated to be no fewer than 1,500 pieces. This is a very large quantity of Proofs to be struck during this era, especially since they are all struck from one die pair. The Proof mintage of any other coin up to this time was no more than 500 pieces. This high level of production took its toll on the quality of the Flying Eagle cent Proofs. Later-die-state coins show die cracks and evidence of repeated polishing of the dies. This quality issue has added confusion to the Proof status of these coins.

Varieties: Presently 10 die pairings have been described and listed with Snow numbers. These are enumerated in *The Flying Eagle and Indian Cent Attribution Guide, Volume 1 (1856–1858)*. Adventurous collectors have targeted the Snow-1, "Tilted ONE CENT" and Snow-4 "Low Leaves Reverse" as interesting (and rare) varieties. Some collectors have attempted to acquire complete die-pair sets. Although no one has yet accomplished this feat, one collector (Dr. Thomas Fore) has come close.

A SNAPSHOT OF THE YEAR 1857

The United States had enjoyed prosperity and an economic boom from the mid-1840s into the 1850s, following the Panic of 1837 and the so-called Hard Times that lasted until about 1844. Twenty years after the earlier collapse, however, a variety of factors combined to create the Panic of 1857. In New York City, in August, one of the nation's largest finance houses, the Ohio Life Insurance and Trust Company, collapsed with massive liabilities. The financial crisis stopped the functions of many banks in Baltimore, Washington, Philadelphia, and New York (the latter having only *one* operational bank on October 13!). Stock values fell, thousands of people lost their jobs, nearly 5,000 companies failed nationwide, and banks stopped paying out gold and silver for paper money. Commentators of the day attributed the panic to unfavorable foreign trade, bad banking practices, land speculation, and journalists and rumormongers discrediting railroad securities and the credit of city and country banks.

Fugitive Slaves
The Supreme Court's 1857 decision marked a setback for their freedom.

On the judicial front the United States Supreme Court denied freedom to fugitive slave Dred Scott, who petitioned for his liberty in the free territory of Minnesota. The Court's landmark decision was that blacks could not bring suit in federal court, and that Congress did not have the authority to prohibit slavery in the territories.

The year 1857 was very important from a numismatic standpoint. The Coinage Act of February 21, 1857 abolished two warhorses of the American economy: the half cent (struck intermittently since 1793) and the copper large cent (struck continuously since 1793 with the exception of 1815). The large cent was replaced with the smaller, more economical Flying Eagle cent, in a new composition of 88% copper and 12% nickel. In late May the U.S. Mint erected a temporary structure in its yard, with two windows, one for exchanging the public's old large cents and half cents for the new Flying Eagle coins, and the other for exchanging worn Spanish colonial silver coins, which were still in circulation (and whose legal tender status was abolished by the Act of February 21).

◆

1857 Cent Production: Soon after the Mint Act of February 21, 1857 was enacted, production began on the regular-issue 1857 Flying Eagle cent. By May 25, the official release date, the excitement of the populace overwhelmed the U.S. Mint. Two special outdoor booths were set up in the Mint yard to accommodate the massive demand. In addition to the novelty of the new coin, the rush to get the new cent was augmented by the mandate that they be exchanged for the old copper cents and half cents, which were to be slowly removed from circulation. The cents were mostly paid out in bags of 500 pieces.

Up until 1860, certain foreign silver coinage, mostly Spanish coins minted in Mexico, was legal currency in this country. The new Mint Act called for the removal of these coins in exchange for the new cents or federal silver coinage. Most people chose to exchange for silver, even at a discount.

1857 FLYING EAGLE CENT

Enlarged 1.5x—Actual Size: 19mm

CIRCULATION MINTAGE:
17,450,000

PROOF MINTAGE:
TRADITIONALLY ESTIMATED AT 485;
POSSIBLY AS LOW AS 50

Market Values • Circulation Strikes and Proof Strikes

G-4	VG-8	F-12	VF-20	EF-40	AU-50	MS-60	MS-63
$22	$24	$34	$50	$140	$180	$320	$650
MS-64	MS-65	MS-66	PF-60	PF-63	PF-64	PF-65	PF-66
$1,500	$3,500	$15,000	$6,000	$8,200	$17,500	$40,000	$65,000

Certified Populations

G - VF	EF-40	EF-45	AU-50	AU-53	AU-55	AU-58	MS-60	MS-61	MS-62	MS-63	MS-64	MS-65	MS-66	MS-67	MS-68	MS-69	MS-70
634	504	361	383	74	365	349	158	236	668	4,542	8,266	2,051	123	0	0	0	0
<PF-60	PF-60	PF-61	PF-62	PF-63	PF-64	PF-65	PF-66	PF-67	PF-68	PF-69	PF-70						
0	3	1	4	34	226	53	3	0	0	0	0						

Field populations: Circulation strike (<MS-60), 75,000; circulation strike (MS-60+), 8,000; Proof, 50-75.

The shape of the lettering on these new dies was slightly altered, most noticeably on the O in OF, which is oval shaped. Some of the undated dies from 1856, which had a somewhat squared O in OF, were dated 1857 and used for this production. This creates two minor types of 1857 Flying Eagle cents: Type of 1856 and Type of 1857. The Type of 1857 is far more common and is usually not considered a variety.

Survivability: This issue was initially heavily saved because of its novelty. One of the effects of the redemption for old coppers is that many people may have obtained large quantities at one time. It was difficult to spend cents for anything but small purchases, so enterprising individuals would bundle the coins up into 25¢, 50¢, and $1 bags. Lack of wear from personal contact may have contributed to their survivability. Within six years they were withdrawn from circulation, along with all the other hard currency, during the Civil War. After 1863 they came back into circulation and stayed there in quantity until the redemption program of the 1870s. After 1880, they began to be curiosities in circulation.

1857, Type of 1856

1857, Type of 1857

The coins remaining today are in either very low grade (below Fine) or Mint State. Problem-free Extremely Fine and About Uncirculated coins are very difficult to locate.

Collecting Challenges: These coins are available readily enough that collectors should be patient to find attractive examples with good strikes and few problems. The Type of 1856 design is of fairly minor importance and was not well known until the 1980s. As such it is not included in any of the popular albums made for circulated coins, or in Whitman's *Guide Book of United States Coins* (the "Red Book"). Even so, some specialists desire to acquire an example.

Collecting Circulated Pieces: The Optimal Collecting Grade is EF-40. Examples in Good to Fine are very plentiful. The higher-grade examples are fairly expensive, but the price is based on demand for a popular coin, so they tend to be easily resold at a price close to retail. On the other hand, low-grade examples are plentiful enough that their resale value is much lower than their retail price.

Collecting Mint State Pieces: The Optimal Collecting Grade is MS-64. Examples in this grade are very popular and in high demand. They are also widely available, so it is important to search out quality pieces. Because of price resistance, examples in MS-63 and lower are in demand if they are attractive. MS-64 examples offer the best value for the money spent. Prices for MS-65 are much higher than for MS-64 because of the demand for "gem" sets against a small supply of available pieces. Beware of lower-quality MS-65 coins that may in fact be no better than the nicer MS-64 examples available. A patient collector will be rewarded with a beautiful example of this popular design.

Collecting Proof Issues: Proof examples are very well struck and have very deep mirror fields. These are some of the most beautiful Flying Eagle cents made. All Proof 1857 cents come from the Type of 1857 dies. A few prooflike examples of the Type of 1856 design are known, and can be confused as Proofs. Some have even been mistakenly certified as Proofs.

The Proofs are much rarer than the published mintage suggests. The Red Book lists an estimated mintage of 485 pieces; however, nowhere near those numbers are known today. Perhaps no more than 50 were struck. Unimpaired specimens in PF-63 or higher are easily five-figure coins. Needless to say, this is one of the toughest dates in the series.

Varieties: This is one of the more popular dates with variety collectors. Two design types, Type of 1856 and Type of 1857, are available to collectors should they desire to acquire them.

The top varieties for this date are the multi-denominational clashed dies: Snow-7, Snow-8, and Snow-9. These have imprints on the die, called *clash marks*, which are caused not by the opposing die, but by a totally different denomination! Snow-7 has obverse clash marks from the obverse of a $20 gold piece! Snow-8 shows reverse clash marks from the reverse of a Liberty Seated quarter dollar. Snow-9 shows clash marks from the obverse of a Liberty Seated half dollar. These three varieties are widely collected as a set.

There are no fewer than 11 known doubled dies, some of which, like the Snow-3, Snow-4, and Snow-15, are quite dramatic. There are a few repunched dates known as well, including one on the Type of 1856 design. One interesting variety, S-16, shows the base of all four digits punched into the eagle's neck feathers, twice!

1857 Multi-Denominational Clashed Dies: Snow-7, -8, -9

These three varieties, clashed dies from denominations totally unrelated to the cent, are some of the most interesting among all United States coinage! In general, clashed dies are not rare, nor are they very interesting or collectable to most collectors. However, these clash marks are produced from dies other than the Flying Eagle cent and as such have great appeal with collectors.

Clashed dies are produced when dies impact each other. A reversed impression of each die is left on the opposing die. All coins later struck from these dies will show the marks as a slightly raised shelf. This may happen during the setup of the dies in the press. If the dies are initially set too close, the dies will clash during the startup of the press. This is commonly seen in the Indian Head Cent series. On the obverse the clashes are usually in the form of a jagged gear-shaped shelf by the forehead of Lady Liberty. This is from the impression of the inside of the wreath from the reverse die. The reverse will likewise show the clash impression from the forehead and nose inside the wreath, by the O in ONE. Collectors take these typical clash marks as normal artifacts of coin production and place little added interest in them. The clash marks described here, however, are much different.

The study of these coins has been ongoing by many specialists since they were first identified. In 1977 an 1857 quarter dollar with strange clash marks on its reverse was sent to Tom DeLorey, editor of *Coin World's Collector's Clearinghouse*, for identification by Jesse Perrotta. The coin was correctly identified as having clash marks from the reverse die of a Flying Eagle cent. At the same time, purely by chance, Bill Fivaz sent DeLorey another 1857 clashed die coin. This time it was a Flying Eagle cent with a clash on its obverse from a half dollar (Snow-9). DeLorey's findings were subsequently published in *Coin World* under the title "Was Mischief Afoot in 1857 Die Clashes?" The strange clash marks were ascribed to the possibility that someone at the Mint was making mismatched coins with various denominations. Today we call these types of coins *mules*. They have been surreptitiously produced in the past, most recently in 2000 with the Sacagawea dollar / Washington quarter coins.

Nearly a decade later, Bill Fivaz, who owned a clashed quarter and the Snow-9 half dollar clash, was told of a Flying Eagle cent with clash marks on its reverse from the reverse of a half dollar! After buying that coin and studying it, he discovered that it was not clashed with a half dollar, but with a quarter! It was the missing link to the quarter clashed with the cent in his collection. Today this variety is classified as Snow-8.

The last one of the known 1857 clashed dies to be discovered was the Snow-7 $20 clashed obverse. Bill Fivaz also brought this one to light, but he did not claim to be the discoverer. David McCann later was identified as the initial finder.

One theory, of a surreptious "Midnight Minter," has undergone some rethinking as these coins and their manufacture have been studied further. An alternate theory has emerged, due mainly to research by Chris Pilliod, whose article "What Error Coins Can Teach Us About Die Settings" appeared in the April 1996 issue of *The Numismatist*. This article used striking errors to determine if a given die was used in the upper position in the coining press (called a hammer die) or if it was in the bottom position (called an anvil die). Pilliod showed that the Flying Eagle series had its die setting opposite from the 1857 quarter dollar, half dollar, and double eagle dies.

Series	Hammer die	Anvil die
Flying Eagle Cent	Reverse	Obverse
Liberty Seated Quarter	Obverse	Reverse
Liberty Seated Half	Obverse	Reverse
Liberty Head Double Eagle	Obverse	Reverse

The significance of this is apparent when it is noticed that the various clashed die varieties show combinations that are predicted by Pilliod's research. All show either obverse/obverse or reverse/reverse combinations. Also consistent with this is the observation that the designs are aligned right side up, rather than rotated 180 degrees as is seen on normal clashed dies. In light of Pilliod's study and the fact that no actual coins exist from these die combinations, Q. David Bowers concluded in his *Buyer's and Enthusiast's Guide to Flying Eagle and Indian Cents* that these clashed dies were not the product of surreptitious behavior at the Mint at all. It was suggested that these were caused by accident during the changing of the dies during normal coinage production. In the course of changing the dies from one denomination to another, the collar would have to be removed as well as the two dies. This would allow the press to actually cycle with two denomination dies. It may have been a common practice to cycle the press once to seat the dies in the press.

The following is the probable scenario of their production, by Bowers.

Producing the Snow-7 Double Eagle Clashed Die

It is 1857, and a coining press has been used recently to strike $20 gold pieces. A $20 obverse die is in the hammer position and a $20 reverse die is in the anvil position. It is desired to strike Flying Eagle one-cent pieces using this press, to fill the great demand for this new coin. The public is starved for them, and there are shortages for a long time after the first release of the new Flying Eagle cents on May 25, 1857.

1857 Snow-7
Enlarged 1.5x—Actual Size: 19mm

The $20 reverse die in the anvil position is removed and replaced with a one-cent Flying Eagle obverse die. With the newly fitted one-cent obverse die in place in the anvil, opposite the $20 obverse still in place in the hammer position, the press is run through a cycle, and the $20 obverse die in the hammer position strikes the one-cent obverse die in the anvil position. Clash marks occur on both obverse dies.

The clashed $20 obverse die is removed from the press and put in

1857 Snow-7 Composite
Enlarged 1.5x—Actual Size: 34mm

storage, and a new reverse die for a one-cent piece is put in the hammer die position. Cents are struck, each of which shows the clash mark of a $20 die on its obverse.

Whether $20 pieces were ever struck from the now-damaged obverse $20 die is not known; none have been identified thus far by numismatists.

1857 Snow-9
Enlarged 1.5x—Actual Size: 19 mm

1857 Snow-9 Composite
Enlarged 2x—Actual Size: 30.6mm

Producing the Snow-9 Half Dollar Clashed Die

It is 1857, and a coining press has been used recently to strike Liberty Seated fifty-cent pieces. A fifty-cent obverse die is in the hammer position and a fifty-cent reverse die is in the anvil position. It is desired to strike Flying Eagle one-cent pieces using this press, again to fill the demand for this new denomination.

The fifty-cent reverse die in the anvil position is removed and replaced with a one-cent Flying Eagle obverse die. With the newly-fitted one-cent obverse die in place in the anvil, opposite the fifty-cent obverse still in place in the hammer position, the press is run through a cycle, and the fifty-cent obverse die in the hammer position strikes the one-cent obverse die in the anvil position. Clash marks occur on both obverse dies.

The clashed fifty-cent obverse die is removed from the press, put in storage, and a new reverse die for a one-cent piece is put in the hammer die position. Cents are struck, each of which shows the clash mark of a fifty-cent die on its obverse.

Whether 1857 half dollars were ever struck from the now-damaged obverse fifty-cent die is not known; none have been identified thus far by numismatists.

Producing the Snow-8 Quarter Dollar Clashed Die

It is later in 1857, and a coining press has been used recently to strike 1857 Flying Eagle cents. Now, either the demand for cents has eased, or the demand for quarter dollars has taken precedence. A one-cent reverse die is in the hammer position and a one-cent Flying Eagle

1857 Quarter
Enlarged 1.5x—Actual Size: 24.3mm

1857 Snow-8 Composite
Enlarged 2x—Actual Size: 24.3mm

1857 Cent
Enlarged 1.5x—Actual Size: 19mm

obverse die is in the anvil position. It is desired to strike Liberty Seated quarter dollars using this press.

The one-cent Flying Eagle obverse die in the anvil position is removed and replaced with a quarter dollar reverse die. With the newly-fitted quarter dollar reverse die in place in the anvil, opposite the one-cent reverse still in place in the hammer position, the press is run through a cycle, and the one-cent reverse die in the hammer position strikes the quarter dollar reverse die in the anvil position. Clash marks occur on both reverse dies.

The clashed one-cent reverse die is removed from the press, and put in storage (thus there is the possibility, however remote, that this die could have been used in 1858 in addition to in 1857), and a new obverse die for a quarter dollar is put in the hammer die position. Liberty Seated quarter dollars are struck, each of which shows the clash mark of a one-cent die on its reverse. Later, the clashed one-cent wreath reverse die is combined with a Flying Eagle obverse, and Flying Eagle cents are struck showing quarter dollar clash marks on the reverse; made in the ordinary manner.

Other multi-denominational clashed dies have been found—an 1864 two-cent piece with a reverse clash from the obverse of an Indian Head cent; an 1868 three-cent piece with obverse clash marks from the reverse of an Indian Head cent; and an 1870 Shield nickel with its obverse clashed with the obverse of an Indian Head cent—so this type of variety is not specific to 1857.

A Snapshot of the Year 1858

In 1858 the United States continued unknowingly on its path toward unmatched internal conflict, despite the best intentions of those who sought accord. Abraham Lincoln, accepting the Republican nomination for senator in Illinois, stated that, "A house divided against itself cannot stand." Slavery continued as the topic of the day in Congress and in numerous local and state debates, with such abolitionists as Harriet Beecher Stowe (author of *Uncle Tom's Cabin*), Sojourner Truth, and Harriet Tubman lecturing throughout the country.

Life in America was made more convenient with the patent of the glass Mason jar, which allowed farm families and others to preserve food without refrigeration or drying. George Pullman introduced the first practical upscale sleeping car for the Chicago & Alton Railroad. Henry Gray's *Anatomy of the Human Body* saw its first edition and was soon established as a cornerstone of modern medical research. The *Atlantic Monthly* began publication. And in late October, R.H. Macy Company opened shop in New York City, a fledgling start to the famous retail empire.

On May 11 Minnesota joined the Union as the 32nd state.

1858 was the year the Overland Mail Company tested the limits of transportation technology with a stagecoach drawn by six horses, capable of traversing more than 100 miles in a day. Among the firm's investors was William G. Fargo, who planned to build

Abraham Lincoln
Although Lincoln lost to Stephen A. Douglas in the 1858 Senate election, their debates solidified his own national reputation.

a national mail service. In early October the Overland Mail coach rattled into San Francisco after leaving St. Louis a mere 20 days earlier. Its passengers included a *New York Herald* journalist, who noted that the coach ran day and night, non-stop except to change horses, through 2,600 miles of desert, plain, mountain, and hostile Comanche Indian territory.

The year 1858 saw beginnings and a significant ending in American numismatics. The end was for the Flying Eagle cent, which would be replaced the following year by the Indian Head design. The U.S. Mint offered Proof sets for sale to the general public for the first time, and collectors could also purchase sets of 12 different copper-nickel cent pattern varieties. Coin collecting continued to increase in popularity, spurred on by the previous year's switchover from the old large cent and the introduction of the small Flying Eagle cent. J.H. Hickcox published the first information guide for practical use by collectors, *An Historical Account of American Coinage*. Edward Cogan began his business as one of the country's first professional numismatists (although bullion dealers and banks were still most collectors' prime sources for rare coins). And the American Numismatic and Archaeological Society, later (as today) known as the American Numismatic Society, was formed.

1858, Large Letters Flying Eagle Cent

CIRCULATION MINTAGE:
EST. 12,300,000 LARGE LETTERS CENTS
(OF 24,600,000 TOTAL)

PROOF MINTAGE:
EST. 100

Enlarged 1.5x—Actual Size: 19mm

Market Values • Circulation Strikes and Proof Strikes

G-4	VG-8	F-12	VF-20	EF-40	AU-50	MS-60	MS-63
$22	$24	$34	$50	$140	$180	$300	$600
MS-64	MS-65	MS-66	PF-60	PF-63	PF-64	PF-65	PF-66
$1,500	$3,750	$17,500	$5,000	$8,000	$15,000	$25,000	$40,000

Certified Populations

G - VF	EF-40	EF-45	AU-50	AU-53	AU-55	AU-58	MS-60	MS-61	MS-62	MS-63	MS-64	MS-65	MS-66	MS-67	MS-68	MS-69	MS-70
35	7	17	6	6	19	30	2	18	62	800	2,450	1,160	151	10	0	0	0
<PF-60	PF-60	PF-61	PF-62	PF-63	PF-64	PF-65	PF-66	PF-67	PF-68	PF-69	PF-70						
0	1	3	11	75	165	132	31	30	0	0	0						

Field populations: Circulation strike (<MS-60), 50,000; circulation strike (MS-60+), 5,000; Proof, 100.

1858, Large Letters Cent Production: The high output needed to replace 64 years of large copper cent coinage continued unabated in 1858. The Mint was having problems striking up the coins in the hard copper-nickel alloy. The dies tended to deteriorate more quickly than normal. New, shallower-relief dies were made for both the obverse (Small Letters) and the reverse (Low Leaves) to help extend the die life.

Survivability: Although scarcer today than the 1857 cents, these were distributed much more widely and are found more often in lower grades. At the time of the Civil War coinage shortage (from the summer of 1862 to early 1863), these were largely removed from circulation, only to reappear after the war. Any high-grade examples were probably held back from circulation at this time. By the time of the coinage redemption of the 1870s most were called in and melted. The remaining pieces are either very worn or in very high grade. Problem-free EF and AU coins are very scarce.

Collecting Challenges: These are a bit scarcer than the 1857 issue, mainly because collectors have divided the issue between the two obverse design types. The Optimal Collecting Grade for this date is MS-64. Coins in this grade are plentiful enough that quality pieces should be sought out.

Few collectors are aware of the reverse design changes made this year to help improve the die life. The type carried over from 1857 is a high-relief design, called *High Leaves* because the inner leaves are closer to the base of the C and T in CENT. The new lower-relief design, used this year only, is called *Low Leaves*. (See illustrations on page 66.) Both can be found paired with the Large Letters obverse. Coin albums, which have changed little since the 1960s, do not carry holes for these reverse types. These types are briefly mentioned in the Red Book. Collector interest in reverse designs may shift the current lack of demand. If awareness increases, then specialists will need two examples of the 1858 Large Letters cent instead of just one.

Collecting Circulated Pieces: The Optimal Collecting Grade is EF-40. Examples in low grades are plentiful and do not offer the best value because of a low resale percentage. These may be difficult to find problem free, so a bit of patience is advised. Adventurous collectors may try and acquire both reverse types as well.

Collecting Mint State Pieces: The Optimal Collecting Grade is MS-64. These are generally more readily available than lower grades as the cheaper pieces are bought up quickly. MS-65 gems are very tough to locate. Some examples come with prooflike fields and are worth a premium.

Collecting Proof Issues: The estimated mintage of 80 reported in the Red Book is a low estimate based on year sets sold that year. The actual mintage is probably 100 or more, as a few extra pieces, probably numbering only 20, were struck for some pattern sets made this year.

The Proofs of this year are usually exceptional with deep mirror fields and outstanding strikes. The 1858 Large Letters Proofs are paired only with the High Leaves reverse.

Varieties: The major variety of this year is the 1858/7, which is so popular it is given a separate listing in this guide. There is another lesser-known 1858/7 overdate (Snow-7), which is also a doubled die. There are six other obverse doubled dies known, most of which are available for a moderate premium, if found.

Some of the Low Leaf reverse dies are found with minor doubling as well. Two repunched dates are known, one of which (Snow-4) is very wide, and is also a doubled die!

Collectors might not be aware that prior to 1909 all dates were added to coinage dies separately from the rest of the design elements. This is why doubled dies affect the design and letters but not the date, while repunched dates affect only the date.

High Leaves Reverse (Type of 1857)
Enlarged 2x—Actual Size: 19mm

Low Leaves Reverse (Type of 1858)
Enlarged 2x—Actual Size: 19mm

1858, Small Letters Flying Eagle Cent

Circulation Mintage:
Est. 12,300,000 Small Letters cents
(of 24,600,000 total)

Proof Mintage:
Est. 200

Enlarged 1.5x—Actual Size: 19mm

Market Values • Circulation Strikes and Proof Strikes

G-4	VG-8	F-12	VF-20	EF-40	AU-50	MS-60	MS-63
$22	$24	$34	$50	$140	$180	$320	$650
MS-64	MS-65	MS-66	PF-60	PF-63	PF-64	PF-65	PF-66
$1,500	$4,000	$20,000	$5,000	$8,200	$15,000	$30,000	$45,000

Certified Populations

G - VF	EF-40	EF-45	AU-50	AU-53	AU-55	AU-58	MS-60	MS-61	MS-62	MS-63	MS-64	MS-65	MS-66	MS-67	MS-68	MS-69	MS-70
29	16	13	15	5	16	32	4	31	74	1,330	2,080	610	121	0	0	0	0
<PF-60	PF-60		PF-61		PF-62		PF-63		PF-64		PF-65		PF-66	PF-67	PF-68	PF-69	PF-70
0	0		1		2		10		90		60		60	0	0	0	0

Field populations: Circulation strike (<MS-60), 50,000; circulation strike (MS-60+), 4,000; Proof, 80.

1858, Small Letters Cent Production: The Small Letters design was an attempt to lower the relief of the Flying Eagle design. It is believed that Assistant Engraver Anthony C. Paquet supplied the letter punches for this variety. The obvious difference is the smaller letters, which are similar to a font used on some medals ascribed to Paquet's hand. Whitman's Red Book describes the difference as having the AM (in AMERICA) separated, which is a very easy way to describe the differences. The eagle was also modified slightly, although most collectors key in on the lettering style. As this was also the last year of the Flying Eagle motif, the Small Letters can be considered a one-year design change.

Large Letters

Small Letters

There is no record as to when the letter style was changed, but it was used extensively on pattern issues of this year, so perhaps it was initially a pattern design made early in the year that was found acceptable to be put into regular production the same year. If so, the Small Letters dies may have been used side by side with any Large Letters dies made at the beginning of the year.

It is interesting to note that the Mint increased the die spacing to maximize the longer die life promised by the shallower design. As a result, many more Small Letters coins are found weakly struck. It is not unusual to find these coins with an anomaly called *strike doubling*, which is caused by a shifting of the dies at the time the coins are struck. The result is a slight doubling around some of the design elements, including the date and letters. Many collectors confuse this doubling with the highly prized doubled dies. In the Flying Eagle series, true doubled dies will be seen only in the eagle and letters, not the date, which is added to the die in a separate process. A Flying Eagle cent with doubling on the letters and date is most likely a strike-doubled coin, and not worth an added premium.

Survivability: There is no information regarding the release of these coins. It is believed that they were first issued side by side with the Large Letters cents until those dies were used up. Today, we find no overwhelming scarcity of the Small Letters design over the Large Letters design. As such, the estimated mintage for both the Small Letters and Large Letters designs is given as half the total mintage.

As with all the copper-nickel cents, these were popular and circulated widely. By 1860, their presence in circulation was overwhelming. It was not uncommon to bundle the cents in 25- and 50-coin bags. During the coinage crisis of the Civil War, these coins were totally removed from circulation. In 1863, they quickly returned to circulation where they stayed until the redemption period of the 1870s. Most of the issue was melted at this time. The coins that survived are either median Mint State grades that never returned to circulation after the war or very well-worn coins that stayed in circulation until the 1880s.

Collecting Challenges: These are widely available in low grades and in moderate Mint State grades (such as MS-63). It is difficult to find fully struck examples, but it is better to be patient and wait for the right coin to present itself than to quickly fill a hole in your album with a weakly struck example.

There were two reverse styles used this year: High Leaves and Low Leaves (see also 1858, Large Letters). Both are found paired with the Small Letters obverse, with the High Leaves reverse a bit harder to find. If collectors start adding all four die combinations (including the two Large Letters combinations) to their sets, the added demand should push the value of all 1858 Flying Eagles slightly higher.

High Leaves Reverse (Type of 1857)
Enlarged 2x—Actual Size: 19mm

Collecting Circulated Pieces: The Optimal Collecting Grade is EF-40. As low-grade examples are quite plentiful, it would be advisable to purchase higher-grade examples with original uncleaned surfaces. Selecting a well-struck example is also desirable for an attractive collection. The overwhelming demand for this issue is in the About Uncirculated grade, and as such, their prices have advance steadily over the years.

Low Leaves Reverse (Type of 1858)
Enlarged 2x—Actual Size: 19mm

Collecting Mint State Pieces: The Optimal Collecting Grade is MS-64. This is the toughest Flying Eagle cent (of the regular issues) to locate in top condition. The prices in Mint State are not much higher than those of the 1858 Large Letters or even the 1857. Some prooflike pieces exist, which are quite attractive and command an added premium.

Collecting Proof Issues: Proof Flying Eagle cents are some of the most attractive coins in numismatics! They all are rare, so when examples become available, they are very expensive or sell very quickly. Most if not all of the Proof issues were struck to be included in a 12-piece pattern set the Mint sold to collectors between 1858 and 1860 (see below).

There are prooflike Mint State examples that may be confused for actual Proof coins. True Proofs should have deeply mirrored fields and superb strikes. The 1858 Small Letters Proof is found with both the High Leaves (rare) and Low Leaves reverse. Few collectors attempt to acquire both types, mainly due to the cost.

Varieties: A few scarce repunched dates are known for this year. Only one obverse doubled die is known. All other reported obverse doubled dies have proven to be strike-doubled coins, which garner no additional premium. Some of the Low Leaves dies show reworking on the denomination—these are doubled dies, but are really too minor to attract much attention.

Patterns: The Mint was busy this year trying to increase the die life and striking quality of the cents. In addition to the Small Letters obverse, which was put into production, two other obverse designs were tested: a Small Eagle and an Indian Head design. These were struck together with four reverse wreaths, including the regular wreath then in production, the Plain Oak Wreath, the Oak Wreath With an Ornamented Shield, and the Laurel Wreath.

The Mint produced 12-piece sets of all these die combinations (11 pieces with the regular-issue Small Letters Flying Eagle cent). This became a staple of the Mint's sales (along with the 1856 Flying Eagle cent) and about 150 to 200 sets were produced and sold over the next few years. Some combinations, such as the 1858 Indian Head / Laurel Wreath die combination, were struck in larger quantities to satisfy demand. Today, many advanced collectors are interested in assembling this set. Some examples of these pattern coins are found in circulated grades.

1858, 8 Over 7 Flying Eagle Cent

Enlarged 1.5x—Actual Size: 19mm

CIRCULATION MINTAGE:
UNKNOWN (EST. 100,000)

PROOF MINTAGE:
NOT MADE IN PROOF FORMAT

Market Values • Circulation Strikes (Early-Die-State Specimens)

G-4	VG-8	F-12	VF-20	EF-40	AU-50	MS-60	MS-63
$100	$125	$250	$500	$1,000	$2,000	$4,000	$10,000
MS-64	**MS-65**	**MS-66**	**PF-60**	**PF-63**	**PF-64**	**PF-65**	**PF-66**
$20,000	$50,000						

Certified Populations

G - VF	EF-40	EF-45	AU-50	AU-53	AU-55	AU-58	MS-60	MS-61	MS-62	MS-63	MS-64	MS-65	MS-66	MS-67	MS-68	MS-69	MS-70
93	65	23	27	5	23	14	7	10	25	170	336	54	0	0	0	0	0
<PF-60	**PF-60**	**PF-61**	**PF-62**	**PF-63**	**PF-64**	**PF-65**	**PF-66**	**PF-67**	**PF-68**	**PF-69**	**PF-70**						

Field populations: Circulation strike (<MS-60), 2,000; circulation strike (MS-60+), 100-300.

1858, 8 Over 7 Cent Production: This very popular variety was created when a left-over 1857 obverse die was repunched with an 1858 date. Apparently some perfectly usable dies were available at the end of the year and, rather than be discarded, their dates were repunched with the 1858 date. Sometime in the middle of the striking run, the obverse die was taken out and resurfaced, removing evidence of the overdate. These later-die-state pieces are passed over by knowledgeable collectors and may sell only at a slight premium.

The die has some interesting attributes that can make identification easier. There is a remnant of a numeral 1 punched in the field directly between the date and the eagle. This looks like a small triangular dot. This die also has what is called a *broken wing tip* on the eagle's right wing. This broken wing tip is found on a number of other 1857 dies as well, so this is a design deviation, called a hub variety, and is not unique to the 1858/7 die.

Survivability: These were released into circulation as normal 1858 Large Letters cents and circulated with all the other cents. There was no collector knowledge of the variety at the time and all that have survived today have done so mainly by chance. Perhaps only 2,000 pieces exist in all grades. Of these, perhaps only 300 or so would qualify as early-die-state pieces with the overdate showing clearly.

Collecting Challenges: If paying full price, it is important that you select early-die-state coins with the 7 clearly showing. Certification does not guarantee an early-die-state coin. Because of its rarity in high grades, collectors must sacrifice quality, or face missing out on acquiring an example.

Nearly all examples are struck with the dies skewed, or out of parallel alignment. This causes the area by the eagle's tail and the opposing area of the wreath (upper left reverse) to be very weakly struck.

Collecting Circulated Pieces: The Optimal Collecting Grade is VF-20. Low-grade examples may still be found unattributed as overdates. If paying full price, a collector should select an example with significant detail remaining. Late-die-state pieces without the 7 showing should be avoided unless the premium is very small.

Collecting Mint State Pieces: The Optimal Collecting Grade is an early-die-state example in MS-63. Fewer than 100 Mint State pieces are known to exist. Of these, perhaps 35 or so would qualify as early-die-state pieces. The die state is sometimes denoted in listings as EDS (for Early Die State) or LDS (for Late Die State). If this information is lacking, it would be wise to check with the seller to determine which it is. While examples may usually be available, they are typically priced very high. It is important to select an early-die-state piece over the aesthetics of any piece presented. The weakness on the tail and wreath should be overlooked, since this is an unavoidable problem.

Varieties: These are listed in most major guides, including Whitman's Red Book. The variety is called the 1858 LL Snow-1, or simply 1858 S-1. There is a more rare, but lesser known, overdate, which is called Snow-7.

1858 LL Snow-1 (1858/7)   1858 LL Snow-7 (1858/7)

1858 LL Snow-1 Obverse   1858 LL Snow-1 Reverse

1858 LL Snow-1, Mid–Die
State (Detail)

1858 LL Snow-1, Mid–Die
State (Detail)

A Snapshot of the Year 1859

In February 1859 Oregon joined the Union as the 33rd state. Through the year the national tension over slavery continued to strain. The federal Supreme Court ruled to uphold the Fugitive Slave Act of 1850, reversing a Wisconsin court decision that held it unconstitutional. In October fiery Connecticut abolitionist John Brown and a group of more than a dozen white and five black supporters stormed the federal arsenal at Harper's Ferry, Virginia, hoping to engender a widespread slave revolt. Within days Brown and his raiders were captured by marine troops under the command of Colonel Robert E. Lee. Brown was tried, convicted of treason and other charges, and hanged on December 2. Ralph Waldo Emerson called the martyred abolitionist a "new saint" who would "make the gallows glorious like the Cross." Henry Wadsworth Longfellow warned of the "whirlwind which will soon come" as a result.

Americans continued to test the limits of transportation in 1859. In July, aeronaut John Wise and three companions became the first to transport mail by balloon. Their airship *Atlantic* floated 812 miles from St. Louis, Missouri to Henderson, New York, in just under 20 hours.

In the South, rancor against the North continued to grow, with one Richmond, Virginia newspaper advertisement offering $25,000 for the heads of selected Northerners. Another newspaper suggested that Southerners who kept company with Yankees should be watched carefully.

Countless Americans profited from the nation's natural resources, including prospector George Hearst, who would parlay his $450 investment in Nevada's Comstock Lode of silver into an empire that included publishing efforts expanded by his son William Randolph. Thousands sought their fortunes in the gold rush around Denver (in Kansas Territory), and in Pennsylvania—with its coalfield 12 times larger than any in Europe—an "oil rush" was on after Edwin Drake struck black gold in Titusville.

On the numismatic scene, silver dollars were pumped out of three mints in a steady flow: Philadelphia, New Orleans, and San Francisco. The Indian Head cent debuted as a replacement for

John Brown's Raid
Many people believed the abolitionist was insane. During his trial Brown insisted that his mission to free the slaves came from God.

the Flying Eagle; this was the only year its design would feature a laurel wreath. The Philadelphia Mint's half dimes this year featured stars that were hollow in the center, and slimmer arms on Miss Liberty. The Mint struck a wide array of pattern coins, including trial half dimes, dimes, and half dollars.

1859 INDIAN HEAD CENT

CIRCULATION MINTAGE:
36,400,000

PROOF MINTAGE:
EST. 800

Enlarged 1.5x—Actual Size: 19mm

Market Values • Circulation Strikes and Proof Strikes

G-4	VG-8	F-12	VF-20	EF-40	AU-50	MS-60	MS-63
$15	$20	$25	$60	$110	$200	$240	$500
MS-64	MS-65	MS-66	PF-60	PF-63	PF-64	PF-65	PF-66
$1,100	$3,000	$9,000	$900	$1,600	$3,000	$5,500	$7,500

Certified Populations

G - VF	EF-40	EF-45	AU-50	AU-53	AU-55	AU-58	MS-60	MS-61	MS-62	MS-63	MS-64	MS-65	MS-66	MS-67	MS-68	MS-69	MS-70
144	282	258	251	60	199	266	98	150	340	2,784	4,683	1,401	114	10	0	0	0
<PF-60	PF-60	PF-61	PF-62	PF-63	PF-64	PF-65	PF-66	PF-67	PF-68	PF-69	PF-70						
3	3	1	14	250	905	383	246	22	0	0	0						

Field populations: Circulation strike (<MS-60), 80,000; circulation strike (MS-60+), 7,500; Proof, 600.

1859 Cent Production: Production of the copper-nickel cent had always been a problem for the Mint. In attempting to extend the life of the dies, various design changes were tested in 1858. Both the obverse and reverse were altered to a lower relief, but this was still not satisfactory. The problem was that the head and tail of the eagle were directly opposite the wreath details on the reverse. In an effort to fix this problem, the Mint tried a smaller eagle on patterns, but this was also deemed unsatisfactory. The Indian Head design was also tested in 1858 and was found to be superior to the Flying Eagle. The head was centrally located on the coin and did not interfere with metal flow into the reverse die.

The design is not an American Indian, but "Liberty" in an Indian headdress. The reverse design selected is a plain olive wreath circling the denomination. However, the wreath has long been called *laurel* in the literature, following a tradition started by Mint Director J.R. Snowden in 1860.

The production of cents this year set a record for all United States coins up until that time. It was surpassed in the Indian Head cent series up to 1880 only by the 1863 issue.

Survivability: Given the high mintage, these have survived in reasonable quantities. The issue circulated for only three years before being pulled out of circulation during the Civil War coinage crisis. In 1863 they reappeared and circulated in quantity for 10 more years before the wholesale withdrawal and melting of most copper-nickel cents in the 1870s. By the 1890s they were rare in circulation. Merchants who thought them a nuisance due to their greater thickness over the bronze cents had constantly removed them and returned them to the banks.

Examples are plentiful in grades Very Fine and below. Mint State examples are also widely available, but are premium priced due to type set collector demand.

Collecting Challenges: This date is easily found, but premium priced. Collectors should choose examples with exceptional strikes: full feather tips and sharp diamond detail on the lower ribbon. Many coins are of a later die state with mushy details. While later-die-state coins may not be unattractive, a sharp early-die-state coin is worthy of a premium.

Collecting Circulated Pieces: The Optimal Collecting Grade is EF-40. These are easily found in most grades. Sharp strikes and crisp details are preferred but difficult to find.

Collecting Mint State Pieces: The Optimal Collecting Grade is MS-64. These can be found easily in moderate grades, but high-quality coins with crisp details are very hard to locate. Cherrypicking for quality is important for this date, since the prices are usually a bit more advanced than those of other dates of similar rarity, due to the type collector pressure.

Collecting Proof Issues: As a one-year design, it is under heavy demand. All are quite expensive for their rarity. Most are attractive, with cameo examples occasionally available. About 25% of gems show some cameo contrast. The recommended grade is PF-64 or PF-65. Collectors are advised to keep an eye out for coins with exceptional visual appeal.

Varieties: The Snow-1 has a full bold repunched date, and is a very rare and hotly contested variety. An MS-65 example sold for more than $12,000 at auction in 2001. Five other less-prominent repunched date varieties are known and bring moderate premiums.

1859 Snow-1

Patterns: An interesting pattern (Judd 228) was struck with the oak wreath and federal shield reverse first used for regular coinage in 1860. At least 300 pieces were struck in circulation-strike format, unusual for a pattern, which makes it common enough for collectors to be able to acquire one without extensive searching. Survivors tend to be MS-64 or higher. Prices for MS-65 and higher graded coins presently cost less than the regular issue! This may change if demand increases.

Judd 228

A Snapshot of the Year 1860

In 1860 cotton was the nation's main export, with $192 million destined for England's mills. Industry continued to develop as well as agriculture, for good and ill: in January the United States experienced its first major factory accident when 77 people were killed in a textile factory collapse in Lawrence, Massachusetts.

Late 1860 saw the election of Abraham Lincoln by more than twice the electoral votes of his main opponent, John C. Breckenridge. His old political foe from Illinois, Stephen A. Douglas, won 30% of the popular vote to Lincoln's 40%, but only 12 electoral votes compared to Honest Abe's 180.

In the South, Lincoln's election was met with shock and distaste. A few days before Christmas, South Carolina's legislature voted unanimously to secede from the Union.

Prior to this momentous severance, life went on in America with the usual advances and bright beginnings. John D. Rockefeller started business as an oilman despite his youthful 20 years' age. In April, the first rider of the Pony Express galloped into Sacramento—and into American history—carrying letters posted ten days earlier from St. Joseph, Missouri. In Washington, DC, the first Japanese envoys to the United States marveled at the strange American customs they witnessed at a dinner given by Secretary of State Lewis Cass. "The music commenced," commented vice-ambassador Muragaki, "and an officer in uniform with one arm round a lady's waist and the other holding one of hers, started moving round the room on his toes, many others following his example…. Our wonder at the strange performance became so great that we began to doubt whether we were not on another planet."

In numismatics, George Washington's birthday of February 22 was celebrated as the dedication day for the Mint Cabinet, with a display of Washington-related tokens and medals being its central focus. Through the 1860s "Washingtonia" would be a popular field for collectors. On the Indian Head cent, the laurel wreath was changed for an oak wreath surmounted by a federal shield. New designs were featured on the half dime and dime, with UNITED STATES OF AMERICA moved to the obverse of each.

Washingtonia
The hot collectibles of the 1860s, Washington tokens and medals celebrated the life and accomplishments of America's greatest hero.

1860, Pointed Bust Indian Head Cent

CIRCULATION MINTAGE:
EST. 1,000,000 POINTED BUST CENTS
(OF 20,566,000 TOTAL)

PROOF MINTAGE:
NOT MADE IN PROOF FORMAT

Enlarged 1.5x—Actual Size: 19mm

Market Values • Circulation Strikes

G-4	VG-8	F-12	VF-20	EF-40	AU-50	MS-60	MS-63
$18	$20	$25	$40	$85	$150	$275	$500
MS-64	MS-65	MS-66	PF-60	PF-63	PF-64	PF-65	PF-66
$2,000	$6,000	$10,000					

Certified Populations

G - VF	EF-40	EF-45	AU-50	AU-53	AU-55	AU-58	MS-60	MS-61	MS-62	MS-63	MS-64	MS-65	MS-66	MS-67	MS-68	MS-69	MS-70
2	0	2	0	0	0	2	1	2	7	220	290	50	20	0	0	0	0
<PF-60	PF-60	PF-61	PF-62	PF-63	PF-64	PF-65	PF-66	PF-67	PF-68	PF-69	PF-70						

Field populations: Circulation strike (<MS-60), 7,000; circulation strike (MS-60+), 500.

1860, Pointed Bust Cent Production: The Pointed Bust portrait is the design used for all Indian Head cents dated 1859. *Pointed Bust* refers to the pointed left tip of the neckline, as opposed to the later Broad Bust design. This bust was used on some 1860-dated cents, which could also be correctly called *1860, Type of 1859*. These were produced when as many as 10 undated obverse dies made in 1859 were dated with the 1860 date punch and put into production. They are possibly the first Indian Head cent issues with the new reverse. The long-over-looked design difference is as significant as the 1864 With L and 1864 No L design change.

Pointed Bust

The difference in the shape of the bust truncation may have been noted first in 1971 by Don Taxay, in *Scott's Comprehensive Catalogue and Encyclopedia of U.S. Coins*. In 1988 Walter Breen called it to collectors' attention in his popular *Complete Encyclopedia of U.S. and Colonial Coins*. Since then, there has been a steady increase in the number of pieces known as more and more collectors find them in dealers' inventories, priced as regular Broad Bust examples. Today they are priced similarly to the 1859 Indian Head cent in most grades.

Broad Bust

Perhaps because of its relatively recent popularization, the standard coin-collecting albums do not typically have openings for this design. If this changes, and if collector interest increases, demand should rise to absorb all examples found, with premiums rising if more fail to show up.

Survivability: These were not recognized as a separate design until the late 1980s, so surviving examples were not saved for this reason. Most might have been saved because they were the first coins of the new reverse design. Today most examples are well worn.

Collecting Challenges: This issue is usually well struck and when high-grade examples are found they can be very pretty. Collectors used to be able to find these unattributed, but that is getting more and more difficult.

Collecting Circulated Pieces: The Optimal Collecting Grade is EF-40. These are sometimes difficult to locate. Prices should presently be only a moderate premium over the Broad Bust design, about what 1859 Indian Head cents sell for. As demand increases, this may change. To reap a small reward, even if you do not need this date, be on the lookout for it being offered as the typically found Broad Bust cent.

Collecting Mint State Pieces: The Optimal Collecting Grade is MS-63. These are presently quite scarce in Mint State grades, with premiums rising from three to six times the price of a Broad Bust example. These are usually quite attractive.

Varieties: One very minor repunched date is known.

1860, BROAD BUST INDIAN HEAD CENT

CIRCULATION MINTAGE:
EST. 19,566,000 BROAD BUST CENTS
(OF 20,566,000 TOTAL)

PROOF MINTAGE:
EST. 1,000⁻

Enlarged 1.5x—Actual Size: 19mm

Market Values • Circulation Strikes and Proof Strikes

G-4	VG-8	F-12	VF-20	EF-40	AU-50	MS-60	MS-63
$12	$15	$20	$25	$55	$85	$150	$225
MS-64	**MS-65**	**MS-66**	**PF-60**	**PF-63**	**PF-64**	**PF-65**	**PF-66**
$400	$1,000	$2,750	$600	$800	$2,000	$4,000	$8,500

Certified Populations

G - VF	EF-40	EF-45	AU-50	AU-53	AU-55	AU-58	MS-60	MS-61	MS-62	MS-63	MS-64	MS-65	MS-66	MS-67	MS-68	MS-69	MS-70
49	74	64	114	23	112	135	68	103	233	1,740	3,180	1,382	304	38	0	0	0
<PF-60	**PF-60**	**PF-61**	**PF-62**	**PF-63**	**PF-64**	**PF-65**	**PF-66**	**PF-67**	**PF-68**	**PF-69**	**PF-70**						
0	0	2	6	42	192	161	76	10	10	0	0						

Field populations: Circulation strike (<MS-60), 100,000; circulation strike (MS-60+), 7,500; Proof, 250.

1860 Broad Bust Cent Production: Mintage levels lowered a bit this year, as the quantity of cents in circulation was becoming satisfactory.

Survivability: This issue saw only two years of circulation before being put away during the Civil War coinage crisis. By the 1870s the copper-nickel cents were being recalled and melted. Survivors either escaped retrieval from circulation at that time and are found well worn today, or were never returned to circulation after the war and are found in high grades.

Collecting Challenges: This issue is common. Selecting an attractive coin for the grade desired is important. Look for a sharp strike and an early die state.

Collecting Circulated Pieces: The Optimal Collecting Grade is AU-50. Look for well-struck pieces. Low-grade examples below Fine are readily available and should be purchased only if problem free.

Collecting Mint State Pieces: The Optimal Collecting Grade is MS-64. This date is readily found in most grades. Select a problem-free example.

Collecting Proof Issues: The mintage represents 1,000 Proof coins produced, with 450+ being melted, or released into circulation, due to poor sales. As such, these coins are much scarcer than their minted quantity would suggest.

This issue was poorly made, with a large percentage of examples seen struck only once. These will have average strikes and slightly rounded outer edges. Many examples described as prooflike were struck from the Proof dies and may have originally been part of the Proof issue. For this reason gems are very rare. Cameo contrast is virtually non-existent on this issue. The Optimal Collecting Grade is PF-64.

Varieties: There are three very minor repunched dates known for this year.

A Snapshot of the Year 1861

In February 1861, following South Carolina's December secession, the states of Mississippi, Florida, Alabama, Georgia, Louisiana, Texas, Virginia, Tennessee, Arkansas, and North Carolina split from the Union. Delegates from six of these states met in Montgomery, Alabama on February 4 to form the government of the Confederate States of America. Jefferson Davis, a moderate who many Northerners had hoped would give the Lincoln administration a chance, was provisionally selected as president. In October he was confirmed in a general election.

In early March Lincoln's army boasted only 13,024 officers and men. The president called for 75,000 volunteers to enlist in three-month terms. By July a force of 30,000 new soldiers in the Washington area was under the command of General Winfield Scott.

The War Begins
Lincoln ordered Union forces to relieve the federal garrison at Fort Sumter ... but help didn't arrive in time.

Hostilities began on April 12, 1861, with the Confederacy's massive bombardment of Fort Sumter in the harbor of Charleston, South Carolina. The city's high society gathered on the waterfront to watch the fireworks, women in their ball gowns and gentlemen in evening dress—not dreaming of the horrors that lay in wait with the rest of the war.

In the meantime, Kansas joined the Union as a free state on January 29. Colorado Territory was formed in late February, followed by Dakota Territory and Nevada Territory on March 2.

In mid-July, the first Battle of Bull Run ended in defeat for the Union. In August, in an effort to fund the war, Congress levied the first general income tax—3% on incomes over $800 per year. Northerners no longer felt confident that the Union would prevail quickly, and they began to hoard gold and silver. On December 30 banks suspended the payment of gold coins.

The federal mints at Dahlonega, Georgia; Charlotte, North Carolina; and New Orleans, Louisiana fell to rebel forces. At Charlotte, the Confederacy struck several hundred $5 gold pieces using worn coinage dies. At Dahlonega, they struck possibly as many as a thousand 1861-D gold dollars from unused Union dies. These brief bursts of minting activity made the entirety of Confederate coinage for these two mints, which were then closed, probably for an inability to produce new dies.

In Philadelphia, Robert Lovett Jr., an engraver and diesinker, received a commission through the jewelry firm of Bailey & Co. to make one-cent coins for the Confederacy. Lovett created dies for the coins, and struck a dozen pieces in copper-nickel alloy. He was too nervous to deliver the coins, however, fearing trial and execution for treason, so he hid the coins and their dies in his basement.

Confederate Cent and Half Dollar
The Confederate government was never able to strike enough coins for circulation, but did arrange for the creation of some interesting patterns.

1861 INDIAN HEAD CENT

CIRCULATION MINTAGE:
10,100,000

PROOF MINTAGE:
EST. 1,000⁻

Enlarged 1.5x—Actual Size: 19mm

Market Values • Circulation Strikes and Proof Strikes

G-4	VG-8	F-12	VF-20	EF-40	AU-50	MS-60	MS-63
$22	$35	$45	$60	$100	$175	$225	$275
MS-64	MS-65	MS-66	PF-60	PF-63	PF-64	PF-65	PF-66
$400	$1,000	$2,750	$700	$1,000	$4,000	$8,000	$15,000

Certified Populations

G - VF	EF-40	EF-45	AU-50	AU-53	AU-55	AU-58	MS-60	MS-61	MS-62	MS-63	MS-64	MS-65	MS-66	MS-67	MS-68	MS-69	MS-70
46	73	81	122	26	128	124	49	78	178	1,081	2,608	1,455	425	29	1	0	0
<PF-60	PF-60	PF-61	PF-62	PF-63	PF-64	PF-65	PF-66	PF-67	PF-68	PF-69	PF-70						
0	3	4	16	128	292	211	42	0	0	0	0						

Field populations: Circulation strike (<MS-60), 50,000; circulation strike (MS-60+), 8,000; Proof, 250.

1861 Cent Production: The 1861 cent had the lowest mintage of the copper-nickel series. It commands a higher premium over other dates because of this reported mintage, not actual scarcity, as these were widely saved during the Civil War coinage crisis. By 1860, the record production of copper-nickel cents had all but flooded commercial channels. The Mint produced the coins this year solely to replace old copper cents that were redeemed.

Survivability: The entire issue was essentially withdrawn from circulation in the summer of 1862. After the war, these circulated for a few more years before being redeemed by the Mint during the 1870s. Many high-grade examples are known due to the wartime hoarding.

Collecting Challenges: Collectors of Civil War memorabilia put added demand on the 1861 to 1865 cents. Still, the coins are relatively readily available and affordable. Seek out attractive and problem-free examples.

Collecting Circulated Pieces: The Optimal Collecting Grade is AU-50. Due to the survivability of this issue, Extremely Fine and Very Fine pieces are easily found but are of course typically priced higher than others of the era. The lower production seemed to affect the lowest grades the most, as their scarcity is more in line with the lower mintage. They are available, but at a higher premium.

Collecting Mint State Pieces: Due to the widespread hoarding during the Civil War, high-quality examples are widely available, although at a premium over the other dates.

A group of 15 to 30 pieces of exceptional quality, which came on the market many years ago, has made this one of the more common dates in the copper-nickel series in gem condition. One of these pieces, graded MS-68 by PCGS (still the only MS-68 for the copper-nickel series), sold at auction for $54,625 in January 2003.

Collecting Proof Issues: This is the key date in the Proof series, partly due to low mintage, but also because of poor quality of the dies and poor striking quality. The reverse die in particular had very shallow mirrors. Most have rounded outer edges. Gems with cameo contrast are nearly impossible to locate.

Most of the original mintage of 1,000 pieces remained unsold and might have been destroyed, or were simply released into circulation. It may be that only a few hundred pieces survived.

Varieties: There are only a few minor varieties of this year. On a few dies produced from a defective hub, the tops of the letters ES (in STATES) show some deterioration which progresses throughout the series until the design is reworked to the 1864 With L style. Some advanced collectors attempt to collect these for every year.

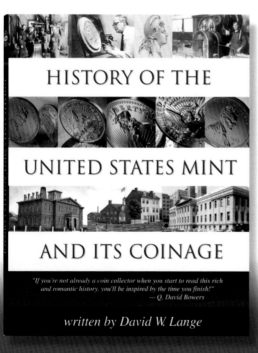

A Snapshot of the Year 1862

The second year of the Civil War saw notable successes for both sides, including the Union's first significant victory (General Ulysses Grant's capture of forts Henry and Donelson). In March the ironclad ships *Monitor* and *Merrimack* attacked each other off the Virginia coast, in an engagement that marked the decline of the wooden warship. President Lincoln shuffled commanders in an attempt to keep the Confederacy in check. In September he issued the Emancipation Proclamation, declaring that all slaves in the Confederate states would be free as of January 1, 1863.

In 1862 John D. Rockefeller invested $4,000 in his first oil refinery, and reporter Samuel Clemens took the pen name Mark Twain. Despite the war, waves of immigrants continued to flow into the United States, many of them laborers from Ireland, England, and Scotland, looking for work in the booming armament factories of the North. The Homestead Act was another enticing incentive, with its offer of a 160-acre farm free to any family who would claim it. Congress gave away even more land to the railroads: 100 million acres went to the Union Pacific, the Central Pacific, and others seeking to lay tracks to the West Coast.

Citizens in both the North and the South were hoarding all kinds of hard money by 1862: gold, silver, and copper-nickel were hidden away whenever it could be found. The federal government issued its first currency notes in April. These were the Legal Tender Notes, intended as a means to finance the war. Confidence in the paper money was so low that its value plummeted in relation to gold coin, and the notes often weren't even accepted outside of the Union (for example, in London's financial district).

"Our Little Monitor"
The famous ironclad was depicted on a Civil War token.

On the West Coast, hoarding was not a problem, and gold and silver coins continued to circulate freely. However, by the summer of 1862, in the East freshly minted silver coins from the three-cent piece to the half dollar went straight into storage or were exported—not to reappear in quantity for another decade after the war finally ended.

Undaunted by war and inflation, coin collectors continued with their hobby, and numismatic auctions started to grow in popularity (Philadelphia and New York being two centers of activity). The collection of William A. Lilliendahl was auctioned by W.H. Strobridge in May, featuring a quantity of rare silver dollars including Proof Liberty Seated coins of 1851 and 1852.

General Robert E. Lee
"It is well that war is so terrible—we should grow too fond of it."

1862 INDIAN HEAD CENT

CIRCULATION MINTAGE:
28,075,000

PROOF MINTAGE:
EST. 550

Enlarged 1.5x—Actual Size: 19mm

Market Values • Circulation Strikes and Proof Strikes

G-4	VG-8	F-12	VF-20	EF-40	AU-50	MS-60	MS-63
$10	$15	$20	$25	$45	$70	$100	$160
MS-64	MS-65	MS-66	PF-60	PF-63	PF-64	PF-65	PF-66
$375	$900	$2,750	$600	$700	$1,350	$2,750	$3,500

Certified Populations

G - VF	EF-40	EF-45	AU-50	AU-53	AU-55	AU-58	MS-60	MS-61	MS-62	MS-63	MS-64	MS-65	MS-66	MS-67	MS-68	MS-69	MS-70
45	59	46	116	9	148	228	97	166	500	2,531	4,775	1,734	339	56	0	0	0

<PF-60	PF-60	PF-61	PF-62	PF-63	PF-64	PF-65	PF-66	PF-67	PF-68	PF-69	PF-70
0	3	3	18	235	1,222	886	518	84	10	0	0

Field populations: Circulation strike (<MS-60), 200,000; circulation strike (MS-60+), 10,000; Proof, 500.

1862 Cent Production: With the hope of a quick end to the war diminishing, silver and gold coinage quickly vanished from general circulation. The only coin that circulated was the copper-nickel cent. Seeing demand for the cent increase, the Mint shifted most of its production from silver and gold coins to the cent. Speculators who sold them at a slight profit to merchants mostly bought up this large production.

Survivability: Most of this issue circulated briefly and then were removed from general circulation during the Civil War coinage crisis peaking in summer 1862. At the end of the war, these came out again and circulated until the redemption of the 1870s. Most examples are in higher than average condition.

Collecting Challenges: These are very popular as the predominant coin in use during the Civil War. Examples are plentiful, so collectors are advised to find problem-free pieces in as high a grade as their collecting parameters allow.

Collecting Circulated Pieces: The Optimal Collecting Grade is AU-50. Examples in all other grades are easily obtainable.

Collecting Mint State Pieces: The Optimal Collecting Grade is MS-65. These are widely available in all grades up to MS-65. They are difficult to find with early die states and full strikes. Full-strike pieces should have full feather tips as well as full diamonds on the lower ribbon.

Collecting Proof Issues: This is the most common date to find in the copper-nickel Proof series. One reason for this higher quality may be that all unsold examples were saved and resold to collectors at some later time, possibly after the war. Examples are of very high quality and collectors are advised to buy PF-64 and higher grades. Cameo examples exist, but not in great quantities.

Varieties: A few varieties with misplaced digits exist. There are no major varieties.

A SNAPSHOT OF THE YEAR 1863

President Lincoln's reelection campaign was dominated by the topic of slavery, but his signature on the Emancipation Proclamation, January 1 of 1863, had no real effect on freeing the nearly four million slaves in the rebellious states. The Civil War continued on several fronts, and in July saw a turning point in the Confederate defeat at the Battle of Gettysburg. With the surrender of Vicksburg, Mississippi, to federal troops on July 4, the Union effectively split the Confederacy in two. But the fighting was far from over.

Draft riots broke out in several Northern cities following the Conscription Act of March 3, which compelled citizens to report for duty or else pay a $300 exemption—a dual-edge stratagem to raise both troops and cash. In July hundreds of protestors were killed and injured in an anti-draft riot on Fifth Avenue in New York City.

Tobacco and Accoutrements
Armies on both sides of the Civil War supplied their men with plug tobacco for chewing. (Cigars and pipe tobacco had to be acquired privately.) In 1863 Congress mandated that cigars must be packaged in wooden boxes. This made it easy for Internal Revenue agents to affix stamps for an excise tax levied to raise war funds. With cigar boxes came cigar box *labels*, and with them a step forward in modern branding and advertising.

In March Congress supported the forced removal of all Indians from the state of Kansas. West Virginia joined the Union in June.

In the South, Confederate president Jefferson Davis, seeking solutions to a food shortage, suggested that plantation owners cultivate vegetables instead of cotton and tobacco. The previous year, Britain had decided not to recognize the Confederate States of America, despite doing business with the rebels.

By the middle of the year the federal government's Legal Tender Notes had depreciated so much that it took $140 to $150 in paper money to buy $100 worth of gold coins. Later it would take more than $200. Silver and gold coins struck in Philadelphia did not circulate, but were used to purchase goods in the export trade, or were stored in Treasury vaults.

◆

1863 Cent Production: Both the Union and the Confederacy were drained emotionally and financially due to the horrific battles of the Civil War, by 1863 entering its third year. The resulting fear had chased all federal silver and gold coinage into hiding, with the cent following in mid-1862. Still, the Mint pounded the cents out in record numbers. Eventually, with coinage substitutes (such as Fractional Currency notes) entering circulation, the cent lost its premium and started to be seen in commerce again.

Survivability: These survived in their original condition until the end of the war, when they reentered circulation. During the recoinage redemption of the 1870s a large percentage of the mintage was melted, but because the mintage was so great, even a small

1863 INDIAN HEAD CENT

CIRCULATION MINTAGE:
49,840,000

PROOF MINTAGE:
460+

Enlarged 1.5x—Actual Size: 19mm

Market Values • Circulation Strikes and Proof Strikes

G-4	VG-8	F-12	VF-20	EF-40	AU-50	MS-60	MS-63
$10	$15	$20	$25	$45	$70	$100	$160
MS-64	MS-65	MS-66	PF-60	PF-63	PF-64	PF-65	PF-66
$375	$950	$2,750	$600	$700	$1,400	$3,500	$8,500

Certified Populations

G - VF	EF-40	EF-45	AU-50	AU-53	AU-55	AU-58	MS-60	MS-61	MS-62	MS-63	MS-64	MS-65	MS-66	MS-67	MS-68	MS-69	MS-70
73	128	61	168	21	210	322	148	263	750	4,060	5,661	1,817	173	0	0	0	0
<PF-60		PF-60		PF-61		PF-62		PF-63		PF-64		PF-65		PF-66		PF-67	
0		2		4		12		187		638		354		114		21	
PF-68		PF-69		PF-70													
0		0		0													

Field populations: Circulation strike (<MS-60), 200,000; circulation strike (MS-60+), 10,000; Proof, 300.

percentage of survivors left a large quantity of coins for today's collectors. These are easily found today in excellent condition.

Collecting Challenges: Collectors are advised to search out well-struck examples from early-die-state dies. This issue is very easy to find otherwise.

Collecting Circulated Pieces: The Optimal Collecting Grade is AU-50. Examples in all the lower grades are very easy to locate. Avoid problem pieces.

Collecting Mint State Pieces: The Optimal Collecting Grade is MS-65. This date is easily found in all grades. Select coins with extra eye appeal. True gems with sharp details are slightly difficult to locate.

Collecting Proof Issues: Although similar in mintage to 1862, this issue is about twice as rare. Examples tend to be quite attractive with perhaps 40% qualifying for cameo status. The Optimal Collecting Grade is PF-65.

Bronze Tokens and Cents: This year saw the quantity of privately minted cent-sized copper tokens increase dramatically in major cities such as New York, Cincinnati, and Chicago. These Civil War tokens are collected extensively and offer an interesting sidelight to the federal coinage of the era.

The success of these tokens inspired the Mint to produce its own bronze cent. An interesting and historical pattern (Judd 299) was produced this year with the regular dies in bronze. These patterns make an affordable and interesting addition to collections as an early beginning to the full-scale production of bronze cents the next year.

Varieties: A few minor repunched dates are known for this date. The best variety is the reverse doubled die, Snow-10. This doubled die is popular, but not well known. This creates a possibility for cherrypicking overlooked varieties. Few dealers (or collectors for that matter) check the reverse dies for varieties.

A SNAPSHOT OF THE YEAR 1864

The Civil War continued through 1864, with both sides winning victories and suffering defeats in a series of violent battles and occupations. In August a Union fleet took Mobile Bay despite the Alabama harbor being mined with torpedoes, and in October Confederate troops were pushed out of Virginia's Shenandoah Valley. General William Tecumseh Sherman captured and burned Atlanta, after which he led 60,000 troops on a march through Georgia to the sea, cutting a path of destruction 30 to 60 miles wide. On Christmas Eve he took Savannah.

By that time Abraham Lincoln had won reelection with 55% of the popular vote, beating George McClellan (former commander of all Union forces, who had been relieved of that duty in 1862).

Nevada became the 36th state in the Union in 1864, and in May, Montana Territory was divided from Idaho Territory.

On the economic front, the value of the federal government's Legal Tender Notes continued to plummet; in mid-July, a $10 note would buy no more than $3.90 in silver coins. The situation was even worse for Confederate paper money, with a $10 note worth a mere 46¢ in coinage.

The Coinage Act of April 22, 1864 prohibited the private issue of any one- or two-cent coins, tokens, or devices for use as money; in June another law abolished private coinage of every kind. This marked the end of the Civil War tokens.

General William T. Sherman
"You might as well appeal against the thunderstorm as against the terrible hardships of war." (General Sherman to Atlanta's city leaders, who protested his order to evacuate)

IN GOD WE TRUST
Facing the horrors of war, many Americans turned to God for solace. A new motto was created for the nation's coins: IN GOD WE TRUST, placed on the two-cent piece in 1864 and on other coins soon after.

1864 Copper-Nickel Cent Production: Due to inaction on the part of Congress, the Mint was required to continue striking the copper-nickel cents in 1864. They were bought up by speculators and offered to the public only at a premium, even though their bullion value never reached a point where it was profitable to melt them down. These coins traded at a premium because the alternatives in circulation were worse. Merchants and their customers had to deal with paper money that seemed to lose value every week. Small change was made with postage stamps, Fractional Currency notes, and private copper tokens. When it came to silver and gold, any holder of federal coins could expect to get favorable discounts from merchants for using them instead of the alternatives. The copper-nickel cents were last struck in May.

1864, Copper-Nickel Indian Head Cent

CIRCULATION MINTAGE:
13,740,000

PROOF MINTAGE:
EST. 370

Enlarged 1.5x—Actual Size: 19mm

Market Values • Circulation Strikes and Proof Strikes

G-4	VG-8	F-12	VF-20	EF-40	AU-50	MS-60	MS-63
$20	$25	$35	$45	$75	$90	$160	$200
MS-64	MS-65	MS-66	PF-60	PF-63	PF-64	PF-65	PF-66
$500	$1,500	$5,500	$650	$750	$1,400	$3,500	$7,500

Certified Populations

G - VF	EF-40	EF-45	AU-50	AU-53	AU-55	AU-58	MS-60	MS-61	MS-62	MS-63	MS-64	MS-65	MS-66	MS-67	MS-68	MS-69	MS-70
743	375	222	334	52	331	332	225	239	597	2,929	4,359	1,454	197	2	0	0	0
<PF-60	PF-60	PF-61	PF-62	PF-63	PF-64	PF-65	PF-66	PF-67	PF-68	PF-69	PF-70						
0	0	0	4	190	520	330	171	10	0	0	0						

Field populations: Circulation strike (<MS-60), 60,000; circulation strike (MS-60+), 6,000; Proof, 325.

Survivability: Almost all 1864 cents were removed from circulation as soon as they were released. After the war, they came out and circulated extensively for about 10 more years. Examples that escaped the recoinage redemption of the 1870s may have circulated for another 20 more years. (For a record of minor coins redeemed from 1871 to 1881, see page 117.)

Collecting Challenges: This is one of the toughest dates in the copper-nickel series to find with attractive eye appeal. As such, collectors should put more effort into finding this date with a sharp strike and attractive luster.

Collecting Circulated Pieces: The Optimal Collecting Grade is EF-40. Examples are typically mushy with average strikes. Searching for early-die-state examples will take some patience.

Collecting Mint State Pieces: The Optimal Collecting Grade is MS-64. These typically lack eye appeal. Many are struck with worn dies and exhibit a grayish color. Search out examples with better luster and a sharp strike.

Collecting Proof Issues: These tend to be of a very high quality. They are a bit more common than the Proof cents of 1863, probably due to a higher survivability rate. High-grade coins usually come with deep mirrors. Cameo contrast is available on about 50% of these.

The year sets sold by the Mint were usually produced early in the year. Therefore most sets contained only one cent, the copper-nickel cent.

Varieties: There are only a few minor repunched dates known. A defective digit punch has what looks like repunching under the horizontal bar of the 4. Since the defect is on the punch, many dies show this feature.

1864, No L Indian Head Cent

Enlarged 1.5x—Actual Size: 19mm

CIRCULATION MINTAGE:
EST. 34,000,000

PROOF MINTAGE:
EST. 300

Market Values • Circulation Strikes and Proof Strikes

G-4	VG-8	F-12	VF-20	EF-40	AU-50	MS-60BN	MS-63RB	MS-64RB	MS-64RD
$10	$15	$25	$40	$70	$85	$100	$140	$250	$450

MS-65RB	MS-65RD	PF-66RD	PF-60RB	PF-63RB	PF-64RB	PF-64RD	PF-65RB	PF-65RD	PF-66RD
$350	$1,000	$3,000	$850	$1,500	$2,600	$5,000	$5,000	$15,000	—

Certified Populations

G - VF	EF-40	EF-45	AU-50	AU-53	AU-55	AU-58	MS-60	MS-61	MS-62	MS-63	MS-64	MS-65	MS-66	MS-67	MS-68	MS-69	MS-70
5	3	2	1	0	6	13	0	4	41	1,010	2,540	3,310	1,140	80	0	0	0

<PF-60	PF-60	PF-61	PF-62	PF-63	PF-64	PF-65	PF-66	PF-67	PF-68	PF-69	PF-70
0	0	0	1	90	370	240	251	40	0	0	0

Field populations: Circulation strike (<MS-60), 350,000; circulation strike (MS-60+), 10,000; Proof, 250.

Bronze **or** *No L*: These are typically called either 1864 No L or 1864 Bronze cents. Older collectors and grading services are accustomed to labeling this as *Bronze*. This separates these coins from the copper-nickel cents. The design change to the 1864 With L is assumed. In the past 10 years it has been also listed as the No L, which separates the coin from the With L issue. The change from the copper-nickel alloy is assumed.

1864 No L Cent Production: On April 22 a bill authorizing the change to a bronze cent was signed into law. This law also made the use of all private coinage illegal. The first bronze cents were produced on May 13 and released into circulation on May 20. There was no reason to make new dies for this coinage, as the Mint still had on hand many of the dies made at the beginning of the year for the copper-nickel cent coinage.

The coins were an immediate success. This cent composition remained basically unchanged, except for the emergency issues of World War II, until 1982, when it was changed to copper-coated zinc.

Survivability: These coins were released into circulation and stayed there for quite a while. They were only removed from circulation when they became too worn or damaged to be useful as coinage. Today they are mostly found in Very Good condition or lower.

Collecting Challenges: This issue is a one-year type, but this seems to be overlooked by most type collectors. As such, type collector demand is not a big factor in the pricing of these coins. These were mostly struck with dies used to strike the copper-nickel cents earlier in the year, and most coins show mushy details with numerous die clashes. Only about 1 in 30 coins was struck from fresh dies. The new dies produced crisp early-die-state pieces, which will have very sharp details. While many collectors will overlook die state when selecting coins, it may be important enough to spend the extra time to locate these. It may not cost much more, and the eye appeal of these pieces will more than make up for the time spent looking.

Collecting Circulated Pieces: The Optimal Collecting Grade is AU-50. The vast majority is found in low grade so it is important to buy the best you can for your budget. Early-die-state pieces may occasionally be found, and should be bought when encountered.

Collecting Mint State Pieces: The Optimal Collecting Grade is MS-65RB. This is one of the most common issues of the Civil War years. In Mint State this date is no more common than any of the copper-nickel issues, but it can be found at a much lower price. Finding examples with eye appeal is recommended. Common, early-die-state pieces are very hard to find, as are ones with even red-brown color. Pieces with full mint red color are hard to find with eye appeal. Trying to find an early-die-state example is quite a challenge.

Collecting Proof Issues: The typically reported mintage is 150, but this is unreasonably low. While this issue is quite scarce, it always seems to be available. More than 200 examples have been recorded graded by ANACS, NGC, and PCGS combined. Even with duplicate submissions it seems unlikely that the mintage is anywhere near 150. A more realistic estimate may be 300.

1864, No L, Snow-4

This issue is found mostly brown or with very little red present. Examples with even color with deep mirrors are most desirable for the issue. Full red examples are very difficult to find and are very expensive. Examples with cameo contrast are extremely rare and are usually priced with a significant premium.

1864 Two-Cent Clash
Composite

Varieties: The best variety is the Snow-4 doubled die, with the doubling most prominent on LIBERTY. It was discovered in 1991 and is widely known, yet few examples have turned up. Presently only seven examples are known. This is a coin that can make your day if you find one. There are only seven other varieties reported, mostly minor repunched dates.

An 1864 two-cent piece variety is known with clash marks from the obverse Indian Head cent die! This raises the question: does an 1864 Indian Head cent exist with the corresponding two-cent piece clash marks? None have yet been found.

1864 Two-Cent Clash (Detail)

1864, WITH L INDIAN HEAD CENT

Enlarged 1.5x—Actual Size: 19mm

CIRCULATION MINTAGE:
EST. 5,000,000

PROOF MINTAGE:
EST. 20

Market Values • Circulation Strikes and Proof Strikes

G-4	VG-8	F-12	VF-20	EF-40	AU-50	MS-60BN	MS-63RB	MS-64RB	MS-64RD
$60	$85	$150	$175	$275	$350	$400	$650	$850	$2,500
MS-65RB	MS-65RD	PF-66RD	PF-60RB	PF-63RB	PF-64RB	PF-64RD	PF-65RB	PF-65RD	PF-66RD
$1,750	$5,500	$30,000	$50,000	$75,000	$85,000	$125,000	$100,000	$175,000	—

Certified Populations

G - VF	EF-40	EF-45	AU-50	AU-53	AU-55	AU-58	MS-60	MS-61	MS-62	MS-63	MS-64	MS-65	MS-66	MS-67	MS-68	MS-69	MS-70
51	23	23	10	7	25	51	2	14	62	1,080	2,090	1,270	250	10	0	0	0

<PF-60	PF-60	PF-61	PF-62	PF-63	PF-64	PF-65	PF-66	PF-67	PF-68	PF-69	PF-70
0	0	0	0	0	40	10	0	0	0	0	0

Field populations: Circulation strike (<MS-60), 40,000; circulation strike (MS-60+), 2,000; Proof, 20.

1864, With L Cent Production: The new With L design is found on all Indian Head cents from this issue onwards. The redesign by Mint Engraver James B. Longacre is sharper than the No L design. Longacre added his initial L on the lower ribbon between the last feather and the hair curl. The bust point is narrow, similar to the 1859 issue. This feature may be used to attribute worn examples that no longer show the L; however, the premium is small in lower grades if the L does not show.

It is unknown when the design was put into production. It is likely that the new dies were made in time for the changeover to bronze in May and used side by side with the previously made No L dies. As such there is no way of knowing exactly how many coins were produced. The estimate of five million is based on the ratio of survivors compared to the No L pieces.

It is not known when this design change was reported to collectors. The rare Proof issue of this year was restruck for collectors sometime around 1870, so it is probable that it was known at that time. In the 1906 Leeds sale by Henry Chapman, lot #1213 was a single 1864 With L cent described as "Unc. Bright Red," which sold for $20. By this time they were considered rare.

Survivability: These were released into circulation alongside the No L issue and were not recognized as special by collectors for a very long time. Most are well worn.

Collecting Challenges: Many come sharp and pleasing, and it should not be too difficult to find attractive specimens.

Collecting Circulated Pieces: The Optimal Collecting Grade is EF-40. Date collectors did not retrieve these from circulation until many years after their issuance, so it is difficult to find examples above Very Good. Prices for choice pieces above Very Fine are high, but do not increase significantly between grades, so it may not cost a collector much more to purchase a higher-grade coin.

Collecting Mint State Pieces: The Optimal Collecting Grade is MS-64RB. These are usually available, but never cheap, unless the coin has problems. This issue offers a great value in full red, as long as the coin has no problems such as spots, or eye appeal issues such as streaky toning.

Collecting Proof Issues: This is the rarest date in the Proof series. Apparently 20 examples were struck and most are traced today. Two die pairs struck nine pieces in 1864. An additional 11 examples were struck with another die pair sometime around 1869. The attributes of the different dies are described fully in the *Flying Eagle and Indian Cent Attribution Guide, Volume 2 (1859–1869)*. For a summary, see page 94.

For many years, the only coins offered as Proofs were those described by Walter Breen in his *Encyclopedia of U.S. and Colonial Proof Coins*. In 1984 Breen announced the discovery of a new die pair. Ten years later, I first announced that the die pair Breen originally described as the true Proof were in fact struck much later than the date on the coins. The evidence came from the reverse dies, which were the same as those used on regular-issue Proofs and pattern cents from 1868 to 1871. Die-state analysis pinpointed production in 1869 or 1870. The second die discovered by Breen was found to have the same reverse as the regular 1864 copper-nickel Proofs. This confirmed that there were two striking periods: 1864, and 1869–1870. I discovered a third die pair in 1997, also from the first striking period.

The reason for their existence is not documented. The coins from the first striking period are found struck on both copper-nickel (unique in each die pair) and bronze planchets. They were probably struck at the same time, around the changeover to bronze planchets in May 1864. Perhaps they were struck as patterns of the new dies.

The second issuance came during the "Linderman" restriking period, 1867 to 1869, which was one of the times of active striking of collector issues at the Mint during the tenure of Mint Director Henry R. Linderman. Examples are known struck in aluminum, which was not regularly used until 1868. This issue was surely made to satisfy collector demand.

The 1864 With L Proof has excited collectors over the years. Two examples were in the estate of Mint Engraver James B. Longacre, which was sold by M. Thomas and Sons on January 21, 1870 (lot 247). The auctioneer described these as "thin die" (the No L style was conversely described as "thick die"). The pair brought $17. Prices have escalated ever since.

These coins seldom appear on the market, and usually set records when they do. In the 1960s prices were around $3,000. Sale prices in the 1970s were in the $5,000 to $10,000 range. In 1987, a superb red gem from the Norweb collection sold for $47,300. Soon after, in 1988, Breen's discovery piece sold for $44,000.

In Bowers and Merena's January 1999 Rarities sale, a PF-65RB from the first striking period set a record price for an Indian Head cent when it sold for $96,000. In the June 2002 Long Beach sale by Heritage Auctions, another example of the first striking period graded PF-64RD set another record when it sold for $132,000.

Varieties: There are many repunched dates known for this year. Presently 20 are described. Snow-1, -2, -3, and -7 show dramatic repunching on the 18 in various directions. The others are rather minor. Many collectors are interested in varieties of this year. A nearly full variety set was sold as part of the Larry R. Steve collection at the premier auction of American Numismatic Rarities (ANR), July 25, 2003. Larry R. Steve amassed the largest collection of Flying Eagle and Indian Head cent varieties in high grade ever assembled. In 1990, he co-founded the Flying Eagle and Indian Cent Collectors Society, serving as the first editor of its journal, *Longacre's Ledger*, and later, as president. Steve co-wrote a very useful book with Kevin Flynn: *Flying Eagle and Indian Cent Die Varieties*, in 1995. Selected sections of his collection were sold by American Numismatic Rarities in 2003. The balance of his collection was disbursed privately soon after.

1864 WITH L PROOF DIE PAIRS: A SUMMARY

Die Pair 1 (PR1)

Obv. 1: (B) The date numeral 1 is directly under the bust point. Thin denticles are at 3:00 and 9:00.

Rev. K: Nearly perfect dies. Only minute die lines in field at 1:00 confirm that these are from the same die as used on some 1864 No L Proofs.

Presently only seven examples are known. Examples from this die pair have occasionally been classified as pure copper die trials, Judd-358. It is now believed that most or all are actually struck in bronze. The difference between this obverse and Die Pair 3 is very minor. PR1 has the left edge of the base of the 1 between two denticles, while PR3 has it over the left half of a denticle. Some examples, known only through low-quality photographs in auction catalogs, may actually be PR3.

The dies are quite well made. The only identifying feature of the reverse are seemingly insignificant die-polish lines which were shown to match both this reverse and the 1864 No L PR2 only by direct comparison. In this case it is important in proving that the PR1 and PR3 were actually struck in the year of issue.

Additional examples from this die pair were also struck in aluminum, which was unavailable in quantity until 1868.

The ownership of the coin Breen mentions as being stolen has been settled. Some coins from different dies, which are not Proof, have been certified in the past.

Die Pair 2 (PR2)

Obv. 2: (B) A long, raised die line on the neck runs diagonally from NE to SW just under the jaw. The date is far to the right of the bust point.
Rev. 1868A: There are numerous light, crisscrossing die lines in the field. Heavy die lines off the olive leaves at 8:00 run towards the rim at 9:00.

This reverse die has very heavy and distinctive die-polishing lines. This reverse die is also found on the 1868 aluminum pattern and 1870–1871 Proofs. It is of a similar die state as some Proof issues of 1868 (Rev. A). The 1870 and 1871 issues are of a later die state. This reverse is also found on 1863 With L patterns and a minority of 1865 Proofs, all of which must have been produced on or after 1868.

Die Pair 3 (PR3)

Obv. 3: (LH) 864/864 (w). Minor repunching is visible under high magnification. Very similar to Obv. 1; compare the date position.
Rev. K: Same die as PR1, 1864 No L PR2. Minute die lines are in the field at 1:00.

This coin, presently thought unique, was discovered in the "Pennsylvania Estate," a collection assembled by a well-known numismatist in the 1930s to 1950s. The collection was incredible in that it had two gem Proof 1864 With L cents. This coin has set records every time it has changed hands.

A Snapshot of the Year 1865

In February Northern troops occupied Columbia, South Carolina. Charleston surrendered to the Union fleet the next day, and a few days later Wilmington, North Carolina—the last open Confederate port—fell to Union forces. On March 2 President Lincoln refused General Robert E. Lee's request for parlay, instead demanding unconditional surrender. Petersburg, Virginia, acquiesced on April 3 and the Confederate capital of Richmond, captured by General Ulysses Grant, was a smoldering ruin two days later. Within a week, General Lee surrendered his exhausted army to Grant at Appomattox Court House, Virginia. The Civil War was over—but not before more than a million men had been killed or injured in the nation's bloodiest war.

Seeking to avenge the South, on April 14 actor John Wilkes Booth shot President Lincoln while he watched a performance of *Our American Cousin* at Ford's Theatre in Washington. Before attending the play, Lincoln had told friends that the night before he dreamt he was moving quickly toward a dark, undefined shore—a dream he'd had on the eve of each of the war's major battles.

Booth was shot and killed in Virginia on April 27. On May 22 Jefferson Davis, attempting to escape Virginia (according to some reports disguised as a woman), was captured and imprisoned.

Lincoln's vice president, Andrew Johnson, succeeded to the presidency and began the era of Reconstruction. So-called carpetbaggers from the North went south to influence local and state governments, make money, and/or aid the region's newly liberated black citizens. Before war's end, in early March, the Bureau of Freed Slaves had been created to provide education, medical care,

The End
Four months into 1865, the Civil War was finally over. Both sides had far more orphans and widows than either had imagined four years earlier.

and financial aid to former slaves. After the war, in Tennessee, a group with decidedly different goals (mostly composed of Confederate veterans) created the Ku Klux Klan.

Three months before the surrender, in January, Confederate paper money had spiraled downward to a value of just $1.70 in gold for every $100, as exchanged on the London market. The Union's Legal Tender Notes fared better, but still brought only $46 in gold for each $100 of paper.

The U.S. Mint issued a new coin, authorized in March 1865: the nickel three-cent piece, designed to replace the Treasury's currency notes of the same denomination, which had been issued in great quantities.

1865 INDIAN HEAD CENT

CIRCULATION MINTAGE:
35,429,286

PROOF MINTAGE:
EST. 500+

Enlarged 1.5x—Actual Size: 19mm

Plain 5 • Market Values • Circulation Strikes and Proof Strikes

G-4	VG-8	F-12	VF-20	EF-40	AU-50	MS-60BN	MS-63RB	MS-64RB	MS-64RD
$10	$15	$20	$30	$45	$65	$90	$135	$275	$600
MS-65RB	MS-65RD	PF-66RD	PF-60RB	PF-63RB	PF-64RB	PF-64RD	PF-65RB	PF-65RD	PF-66RD
$500	$3,750	$20,000	$400	$475	$1,200	$3,500	$2,250	$9,500	$18,000

Fancy 5 • Market Values • Circulation Strikes

G-4	VG-8	F-12	VF-20	EF-40	AU-50	MS-60BN	MS-63RB	MS-64RB	MS-64RD
$10	$15	$20	$30	$45	$65	$90	$135	$250	$500
MS-65RB	MS-65RD	MS-66RD	PF-60RB	PF-63RB	PF-64RB	PF-64RD	PF-65RB	PF-65RD	PF-66RD
$450	$2,500	$8,000							

Certified Populations

G - VF	EF-40	EF-45	AU-50	AU-53	AU-55	AU-58	MS-60	MS-61	MS-62	MS-63	MS-64	MS-65	MS-66	MS-67	MS-68	MS-69	MS-70
90	76	65	87	20	89	80	67	59	205	1,285	2,997	2,045	245	10	0	0	0
<PF-60	PF-60	PF-61	PF-62	PF-63	PF-64	PF-65	PF-66	PF-67	PF-68	PF-69	PF-70						
3	3	5	23	320	1,177	828	205	10	0	0	0						

Field populations: Circulation strike (<MS-60), 300,000; circulation strike (MS-60+), 7,500; Proof, 350.

1865 Cent Production: In 1863, the older copper-nickel cents came out of hiding and circulated side by side with the new bronze cents, two-cent pieces, nickel three-cent pieces, nickel five-cent pieces, and paper Fractional Currency notes (in 3¢, 5¢, 10¢, 15¢, 25¢, and 50¢ denominations). This array of minor coinage and coinage substitutes was, to say the least, annoying to merchants and their customers. The redemption of out-dated coins and paper was an important reason for the issuance of the three- and five-cent nickel coinage this year and next.

The cents this year were struck in record numbers also to assist in replacing the non-current coinage and paper money. The entire issue stayed in circulation for as long as fifty years.

Two date varieties are known and are collected today as separate dates by many collectors. The Plain 5 date type has a banana-shaped top to the 5. The Fancy 5 date type has a sharp hook-shaped top to the 5. The Plain 5 is slightly scarcer, was produced first, and includes the Proof issue. The Fancy 5 was used on a slightly larger quantity of dies. No Fancy 5 Proofs were struck.

Plain 5 and Fancy 5 Styles

Survivability: This is the most readily available cent of the 1860s. These circulated for a long time, as there was not enough collector interest to save them until after the turn of the century. Most are in grades below Fine. Most high-grade survivors were saved by chance.

Collecting Challenges: Most specialists attempt to collect both the Plain 5 and Fancy 5 dates. Finding well-struck examples without problems should be the main focus for the collector.

Collecting Circulated Pieces: The Optimal Collecting Grade is AU-50 for both the Plain 5 and Fancy 5 date styles. These are usually available, so selecting visually appealing coins would be advised. Avoid coins with significant contact marks or scratches, or those that have been cleaned.

Collecting Mint State Pieces: The Optimal Collecting Grade is MS-65RB for both the Plain 5 and Fancy 5 date style. These are usually available, but finding an even-colored example with a good strike is difficult. Full red gems are very difficult to find without problems. The Plain 5 is much harder to find in gem full red.

Collecting Proof Issues: Proofs are available in the Plain 5 date style only. This is one of the tougher dates in the early Indian Head cent series. Its rarity is equal to that of the 1864 No L, but it is typically priced lower because it is not a one-year type. It usually is found with streaky red-brown colors. Full red examples are very hard to locate, especially without spots and problems. Cameos are very rare.

Varieties: The Plain 5 varieties are very popular. The Snow-2 variety has a very wide repunched date with a 1 digit visible under the 8! S-1 and S-3 are also bold repunched dates, which get good premiums. Six other more minor repunched dates are collected.

1865 Fancy 5 Snow-2

Among the Fancy 5 varieties is a very bold reverse doubled die, Snow-2. This is very rare and worth a very significant premium. Many dealers overlook this variety because it is on the reverse. This creates an opportunity for collectors. S-1 used to be known as an 1865/4 overdate, but its overdate feature was discovered to be a digit punch defect, which shows up on two-cent pieces as well. Eight other repunched dates are known. One variety has a concentric raised die line through the feathers, which is puzzling to collectors and experts alike. Such varieties make collecting fun!

A SNAPSHOT OF THE YEAR 1866

On April 9, 1866, Congress passed a Civil Rights Act that made most native-born people citizens—Indians excepted. Meanwhile, Reconstruction continued in the South, with carpetbaggers and scalawags (white Southerners who supported or worked for the federal government) remaining influential in many local and state government activities. Graft and corruption were endemic.

With the Civil War over, the American economy was sound, but the year saw a general decline in prices and the onset of a recession, influenced by London's financial panic of May 11.

American business saw the acquisition of two telegraph companies by Western Union, which would hold the first significant industrial monopoly in the United States. Meanwhile, the Washburn-Crosby Company saw its start in Wisconsin; over the next hundred years it would expand and transform into the commercial giant General Mills.

The American Society for the Prevention of Cruelty to Animals was established in New York City, its main goal to prevent the mistreatment of horses.

The motto IN GOD WE TRUST, introduced on the two-cent piece in 1864, appeared on circulating silver quarters, half dollars, and dollars in 1866, as well as on the gold $5, $10, and $20 coins. The year's mintages for lower-denomination silver coins (three-cent pieces, half dimes, and dimes) were remarkably low; the silver three-cent piece would continue to be struck in small numbers until its termination in 1873. The Shield nickel made its debut this year. The Mint produced pattern five-cent coins with a portrait of Abraham Lincoln, but the latter design was never translated to circulation. The martyred president, although a frequent subject of the nation's paper money, would not appear on a circulating coin until 1909.

1866 Pattern "Lincoln Nickel"
The design would be tested in nickel, copper, brass, and bronze.

1866 INDIAN HEAD CENT

CIRCULATION MINTAGE:
9,826,500

PROOF MINTAGE:
EST. 725+

Enlarged 1.5x—Actual Size: 19mm

Market Values • Circulation Strikes and Proof Strikes

G-4	VG-8	F-12	VF-20	EF-40	AU-50	MS-60BN	MS-63RB	MS-64RB	MS-64RD
$50	$60	$75	$100	$185	$240	$275	$330	$750	$3,000
MS-65RB	MS-65RD	MS-66RD	PF-60RB	PF-63RB	PF-64RB	PF-64RD	PF-65RB	PF-65RD	PF-66RD
$1,300	$12,500	$21,000	$400	$475	$800	$3,000	$1,200	$6,500	$10,000

Certified Populations

G - VF	EF-40	EF-45	AU-50	AU-53	AU-55	AU-58	MS-60	MS-61	MS-62	MS-63	MS-64	MS-65	MS-66	MS-67	MS-68	MS-69	MS-70
183	124	126	101	29	90	85	49	34	124	980	2,025	1,451	277	0	0	0	0
<PF-60	PF-60	PF-61	PF-62	PF-63	PF-64	PF-65	PF-66	PF-67	PF-68	PF-69	PF-70						
0	1	1	12	160	331	569	141	10	0	0	0						

Field populations: Circulation strike (<MS-60), 25,000; circulation strike (MS-60+), 2,000; Proof, 400.

1866 Cent Production: By 1866, the bronze cents were becoming well entrenched in commercial channels. The large production of the new three-cent nickel and five-cent nickel coins helped replace these denominations of Fractional Currency notes and the old copper-nickel cents in circulation. The need for cents diminished to the point that the Mint could direct its efforts to producing the new nickel coins.

Survivability: Collectors did not save this cent at the time of issue, except for Proofs. Between 1871 and 1875 most of the issue was turned in and melted at the Mint, making it scarce afterwards (see further discussion under 1871). This date is not widely available except in well-worn condition. High-grade examples that did survive the 1870s meltdown did so only by chance.

Collecting Challenges: This is the first in a series of scarcer dates that runs until 1878. A collector requiring a challenge can attempt to collect the 1866 to 1878 dates in what could be called a "Reconstruction era" set.

It is very difficult to find problem-free examples. Many attractive coins in the Very Fine to About Uncirculated grades have been processed (wire-brushed, called *whizzing*) to simulate mint luster. This was a common practice by dishonest elements of the hobby in the 1960s and 1970s. Collectors should learn how to spot the strange luster pattern on these whizzed coins and avoid them at all costs. (See appendix B for more on altered coins.)

Collecting Circulated Pieces: The Optimal Collecting Grade is VF-20. Examples with full detail on the feather tips and diamond area are worth premium prices. Depending on the price, some minor problems such as hits and scratches may be acceptable. Expect to pay a premium for a problem-free example.

Collecting Mint State Pieces: The Optimal Collecting Grade is MS-64RB. Many of these coins come with streaky toning, which may not be a problem for red-brown coins, but for full red coins it may be a reason for rejection. Well-struck examples are not particularly tough to find. Coins with great eye appeal are worth their price. Full red coins are very tough and in high demand. Beware of chemically brightened coins, especially coins that are not certified by a top-tier grading service.

Collecting Proof Issues: The 1866 Proof issue is very scarce. Only one die pair struck this issue. The cheek area of the portrait always shows some roughness, which may have been caused by the obverse die being allowed to rust slightly. This is not a grade-limiting feature. Full red examples are very rare and will attract serious competition if problem free. Gem examples are usually available, for a price. Many may have been undergraded in the past due to the facial roughness.

Varieties: One of the top varieties in the Indian Head cent series is the Snow-1, an obverse doubled die that has a bold doubled LIBERTY. In addition to the doubled die, it has a base of a numeral 1 boldly sticking out of the necklace, and the tops of other digits in the denticles. This is a great variety with strong collector demand. Another very minor doubled die is known. There are 13 repunched dates known for this date, some very pronounced. Due to the high premiums this date receives, some varieties may not be worthy of an additional premium.

1866 Snow-1

A Snapshot of the Year 1867

In 1867 Secretary of State William Henry Seward negotiated the purchase of Alaska from Russia for $7,200,000, or less than two cents per acre. His detractors would belittle the massive northern land tract as "Seward's Icebox."

Nebraska was admitted to the Union as the 37th state.

The railroad industry was booming, and the directors of the Union Pacific Railroad did everything they could to hide the outrageous personal profits they made from government contracts. George Pullman and Andrew Carnegie—the latter well on his way to becoming one of America's wealthiest industrialists—established the Pullman Palace Car Company.

In October, William Cody set out on an eight-month hunting spree in which he killed 4,300 American bison, inspiring his nickname, *Buffalo Bill*.

1867 was the year Henry Linderman first took the post of director of the U.S. Mint. The now-infamous Linderman would use his two terms in that office, into the late 1870s, to create numerous pattern and fantasy coins for his own personal gain.

In 1867 the nation's money supply was a chaotic mixture of small coins and paper currency. Several new coins were floating around: two-cent pieces and nickel three- and five-cent coins were still relatively new to the American scene. Silver and gold were in very short supply, and the public remained wary of the paper

Secretary of State William Seward
His efforts to acquire millions of acres of Alaskan territory from Russia would be lampooned as "Seward's Folly."

money issued to finance the war. The Treasury Department continued to release an array of Fractional Currency notes in denominations as low as 3¢ and as high as 50¢. Sizes and colors varied. In addition, hundreds of federally chartered National Banks issued their own paper currency.

Various Fractional Currency Notes of the 1860s
Never popular, these small notes were inconvenient to count, and quickly became dirty and tattered from use. (shown reduced)

1867 INDIAN HEAD CENT

CIRCULATION MINTAGE:
9,821,000

PROOF MINTAGE:
EST. 625+

Enlarged 1.5x—Actual Size: 19mm

Market Values • Circulation Strikes and Proof Strikes

G-4	VG-8	F-12	VF-20	EF-40	AU-50	MS-60BN	MS-63RB	MS-64RB	MS-64RD
$50	$60	$80	$135	$225	$265	$290	$350	$750	$3,000
MS-65RB	MS-65RD	MS-66RD	PF-60RB	PF-63RB	PF-64RB	PF-64RD	PF-65RB	PF-65RD	PF-66RD
$1,300	$12,500	$25,000	$400	$475	$500	$2,250	$950	$6,500	$10,000

Certified Populations

G - VF	EF-40	EF-45	AU-50	AU-53	AU-55	AU-58	MS-60	MS-61	MS-62	MS-63	MS-64	MS-65	MS-66	MS-67	MS-68	MS-69	MS-70
138	112	85	84	20	83	75	39	39	114	910	2,074	1,324	172	0	0	0	0
<PF-60	PF-60	PF-61	PF-62	PF-63	PF-64	PF-65	PF-66	PF-67	PF-68	PF-69	PF-70						
4	4	1	13	195	738	580	156	0	0	0	0						

Field populations: Circulation strike (<MS-60), 25,000; circulation strike (MS-60+), 2,000; Proof, 400.

1867 Cent Production: This is another lower-mintage date, similar in rarity to the 1866. The Mint put most of its resources into the production of the new nickel five-cent piece. The nickels' mintage was nearly three times the mintage of cents in 1867. Together with the dwindling production of two-cent and three-cent pieces, the Mint was producing mostly minor coinage this year in an effort to replace tattered Fractional Currency notes issued during the Civil War (although new notes were still being made in large quantities).

Survivability: These were minted in a high enough quantity that they did not initially attract collector interest, except for the Proof issue. Starting in 1871, the cent coinage in circulation began to be recalled and melted by the Mint (see the discussion under 1871). The targets were the old copper-nickel cents, but even freshly minted bronze cents were taken in and melted. The lower-mintage dates 1866 to 1870 were among the hardest hit in this recoinage effort. The Mint continued redeeming bronze cents up until 1875. Any in high grade today survived purely by chance.

When premiums of Mint State coins soared in the 1960s, this date was a target of processors who would wire brush, or *whiz*, Very Fine to About Uncirculated coins to make them look Mint State. A large percentage of available examples in these grades were destroyed.

Collecting Challenges: Searching for problem-free examples will be difficult. Most collectors tend to settle on pieces in a grade lower than average for their set, with the hope of finding the right coin later. Be prepared to pay a good premium for attractive examples in any grade.

Collecting Circulated Pieces: The Optimal Collecting Grade is VF-20. Most collections that started with Grandma's box of old coins will have a bent or corroded example to represent this date. Selecting a problem-free coin with adequate detail is important. Collectors soon realize that extra money spent on an attractive coin is money well spent. When it comes time to sell, nice coins will sell easily, perhaps for a healthy profit.

Collecting Mint State Pieces: The Optimal Collecting Grade is MS-64RB. Many coins are found struck on planchets which have lighter and darker patterns, similar to the look of woodgrain. This is caused when the tin and zinc alloy in the ingot is not fully mixed. When the ingot is rolled out, the small pockets of alloy get stretched into streaks, which quickly turn dark after the planchets are cut out and struck. This type of toning is acceptable for red-brown coins, but it will prevent a coin from staying full red. For this reason, the already scarce Mint State example of this date is very rare in full red.

1867/67 Snow-1

Collecting Proof Issues: Proofs of this year typically show good mirrors and average quality. Gems are very hard to find, especially with full red color. Cameo contrast is very hard to find on this issue. Perhaps only 5% of Proofs PF-64 and higher might qualify as cameo.

Varieties: The 1867/67 (Snow-1) is a very bold repunched date that is widely collected by date-set collectors. It is worthy of a very good premium. There are other minor varieties known for this date, but these have much weaker collector interest. Varieties on scarce-date issues have to be very bold and interesting for collectors to be willing to pay an additional premium over an already pricey coin.

1867/67 • Market Values • Circulation Strikes

G-4	VG-8	F-12	VF-20	EF-40	AU-50	MS-60BN	MS-63RB	MS-64RB	MS-64RD
$100	$150	$325	$400	$500	$650	$800	$1,200	$2,000	$10,000
MS-65RB	MS-65RD	MS-66RD	PF-60RB	PF-63RB	PF-64RB	PF-64RD	PF-65RB	PF-65RD	PF-66RD
$3,500	—	—							

A Snapshot of the Year 1868

In early 1868 President Andrew Johnson dismissed his secretary of war, Edwin M. Stanton, a supporter of retribution against the South. Several days later, on February 21, the House of Representatives voted to impeach the president of "high crimes and misdemeanors," launching a lengthy trial. In May a Senate ballot failed to impeach Johnson by only one vote. Many felt the impeachment failed only because people disliked Johnson's next in line: the radical Lincoln critic Benjamin Wade, president pro tempore of the Senate. (Wade, meantime, had been so confident that Johnson would be ousted that he had already selected his cabinet.)

That summer, Congress voted to readmit to the Union the states of the defeated Confederacy—provided that their black citizens be allowed to vote.

In the year's presidential contest, Ulysses Grant defeated his Democratic opponent. Grant was supported by bankers and creditors who wanted their bonds repaid in gold, instead of in lower-valued paper money (as proposed by the Democrats).

Specie payments remained in suspension, and Fractional Currency notes took the place of silver coins in commerce. Large quantities of silver began flowing into the Philadelphia Mint beginning in 1868, as bullion dealers learned of a loophole in the Coinage Act of 1853 that permitted silver deposits to be converted into silver dollars. However, these dollars, being worth more than face value, were mainly used in the export trade.

Ulysses S. Grant
The Civil War hero was elected to the White House three and a half years after accepting the Confederate surrender in Virginia.

1868 INDIAN HEAD CENT

Enlarged 1.5x—Actual Size: 19mm

CIRCULATION MINTAGE:
10,266,500

PROOF MINTAGE:
EST. 600+

Market Values • Circulation Strikes and Proof Strikes

G-4	VG-8	F-12	VF-20	EF-40	AU-50	MS-60BN	MS-63RB	MS-64RB	MS-64RD
$45	$50	$70	$100	$170	$220	$250	$300	$600	$1,750
MS-65RB	MS-65RD	MS-66RD	PF-60RB	PF-63RB	PF-64RB	PF-64RD	PF-65RB	PF-65RD	PF-66RD
$1,100	$5,500	$15,000	$400	$475	$500	$2,250	$950	$6,500	$9,000

Certified Populations

G - VF	EF-40	EF-45	AU-50	AU-53	AU-55	AU-58	MS-60	MS-61	MS-62	MS-63	MS-64	MS-65	MS-66	MS-67	MS-68	MS-69	MS-70
107	90	85	69	13	75	57	34	36	125	827	2,057	1,362	218	10	0	0	0

<PF-60	PF-60	PF-61	PF-62	PF-63	PF-64	PF-65	PF-66	PF-67	PF-68	PF-69	PF-70
0	2	1	13	173	502	348	148	10	0	0	0

Field populations: Circulation strike (<MS-60), 30,000; circulation strike (MS-60+), 2,500; Proof, 350.

1868 Cent Production: The Mint continued to put most of its attention on producing the five-cent nickel and the one-cent piece. The two-and three-cent pieces were still being made in sizable quantities, but their totals were nowhere near the amount minted for the one- and five-cent coins. The coinage of cents was not much greater in quantity than in 1866 and 1867.

In Congress this year, Mint Director Linderman promoted a bill that called for the abolishment of all other coinage below 25 cents, to be replaced by nickel coinage in one-cent, three-cent, and five-cent denominations. The three-cent piece and five-cent nickel were already established, but the idea of changing the cent to nickel failed in the Senate and lost favor when James Pollock replaced Linderman the next year.

Survivability: This issue was not considered scarce until well after the coinage melts of 1871 to 1875 (see the discussion under 1871). Any high-grade survivors were kept from being melted only by chance. Most of this mintage today is in grades lower than Fine. Many surviving Very Fine to About Uncirculated coins were destroyed during the 1960s when unscrupulous people took these coins and wire-brushed them to simulate mint luster.

Collecting Challenges: Selecting problem-free coins will be difficult. Search for well-struck pieces with good eye appeal and expect to pay a premium for these coins.

Collecting Circulated Pieces: The Optimal Collecting Grade is VF-20. These are mostly found in grades below Fine. Finding attractive well-struck coins in choice circulated condition is difficult. Stay away from problem coins with heavy scratches or corrosion, unless they are offered at a gift price.

Collecting Mint State Pieces: The Optimal Collecting Grade is MS-64RB. These are available in quantities similar to those of the 1866 and 1867 coins. All three dates should be priced similarly, except in grades MS-65RD or higher, as more 1868 pieces are available in this grade. Selecting quality pieces is difficult, as many of these suffer from poor strikes. Expect to pay a premium for very attractive examples.

Collecting Proof Issues: These are found in similar quantities as the 1866, 1867, and 1869 issues. Examples tend to be red-brown in color, as many planchets have streaky toning due to improperly mixed alloy.

About 15% of this issue is found with the reverse rotated 170 degrees from normal. These are possibly from a group of Proofs struck a year or two after the date on the coin. This was a period when the Mint was striking many collector coins of earlier dates.

Varieties: There are three doubled dies known for this year. Snow-1, with doubling on the lower ribbon and the designer's initial, L, receives the highest premium, but is relatively unknown outside of specialist collectors. Five varieties featuring repunched dates are known as well, but all are rather minor.

A Snapshot of the Year 1869

James B. Longacre, chief engraver of the U.S. Mint since 1844 and the designer of the Flying Eagle and Indian Head cents, died on New Year's Day, 1869. His successor was William Barber, who would serve until 1879.

On May 10, tracks from the Union Pacific and Central Pacific railroads met at Promontory Summit, Utah, completing a transcontinental rail link after six years of labor. Travelers finally had an overland train route from New York to California, and no longer needed to make the long journey by way of Panama.

In the newly formed Wyoming Territory, women enjoyed the rare privileges of voting and holding public office. Striving to make such rights universal, Susan B. Anthony started the Woman's Suffrage Association, rallying her followers with the motto "Men, their rights and nothing more; women, their rights and nothing less."

Wall Street saw its first financial "black day" on Black Friday, September 24. Many speculators were ruined. Jay Gould, James Fisk, and others (including President Grant's brother-in-law) attempted to corner the gold market, driving the metal's price up to $162 per ounce; in response, Secretary of the Treasury George Boutwell flooded the market with government-held gold in order to push the price back down.

In October a massive petrified figure, said to be the fossil of an ancient human being, was unearthed behind a farmer's barn in Cardiff, New York. The Cardiff Giant, as it came to be known, was pronounced genuine by various authorities— either as the remains of one of the "giants" mentioned in the Book of Genesis, or as a 17th-century sculpture. A robust sightseeing trade was set up (despite the protests of scientists who labeled it a silly fraud), with

Transcontinental Railroad Commemorative
Issued in 1944, this stamp honors the 75-year anniversary of the completion of the nation's first coast-to-coast rail.

Railroad Travelers
With the new transcontinental train route, a trip from New York City to San Francisco could be made in just eight days (instead of two months).

thousands paying 50¢ apiece to look at it for 15 minutes. When the "giant" was moved to Syracuse, New York, it was finally revealed to be a modern humbug. This didn't stop the curious, who still paid eagerly to get a glimpse of the hoax. The Giant's unstoppable popularity encouraged P.T. Barnum to make an offer of $60,000 for a three-month lease; when he was rebuffed, he had his own replica carved—a fake of a fraud—and went on to make even more money than the original.

1869 INDIAN HEAD CENT

CIRCULATION MINTAGE:
6,420,000

PROOF MINTAGE:
EST. 600+

Enlarged 1.5x—Actual Size: 19mm

Market Values • Circulation Strikes and Proof Strikes

G-4	VG-8	F-12	VF-20	EF-40	AU-50	MS-60BN	MS-63RB	MS-64RB	MS-64RD
$65	$85	$220	$275	$375	$475	$480	$600	$1,000	$2,200
MS-65RB	MS-65RD	MS-66RD	PF-60RB	PF-63RB	PF-64RB	PF-64RD	PF-65RB	PF-65RD	PF-66RD
$1,500	$7,000	$20,000	$350	$625	$725	$2,000	$1,100	$6,500	$9,000

Certified Populations

G - VF	EF-40	EF-45	AU-50	AU-53	AU-55	AU-58	MS-60	MS-61	MS-62	MS-63	MS-64	MS-65	MS-66	MS-67	MS-68	MS-69	MS-70
366	107	102	101	17	63	70	32	29	92	785	1,830	1,398	263	0	0	0	0
<PF-60	PF-60	PF-61	PF-62	PF-63	PF-64	PF-65	PF-66	PF-67	PF-68	PF-69	PF-70						
1	5	4	17	141	606	571	138	10	0	0	0						

Field populations: Circulation strike (<MS-60), 20,000; circulation strike (MS-60+), 2,500; Proof, 350.

1869 Cent Production: With an original mintage lower than those of the 1866 to 1868 cents, the 1869 issue is obviously rarer. Mintages for the cent, two-cent piece, nickel three-cent piece, and nickel five-cent piece all drop this year and continued to drop over the next few years.

Survivability: Between 1868 and 1869, more than three million bronze cents and two-cent pieces were turned in to the Mint for melting. A flaw in the Mint Act of April 22, 1864 failed to give any redemption clause for the coins. At that time the cent was given a 10¢ legal tender limit, and that was lowered to only 4¢ the next year. The banks could refuse to take the cents in from merchants and, as Carothers notes, many likely did. As a result, the Mint was the buyer of last resort and obliged itself to buy and melt the coins. This was done without any authorization from Congress, but it helped to solve the oversight.

The effect of this was the wholesale melting of all the bronze issues. Many of the recently issued coins went straight back to the Mint to be melted. Over the next 10 years, more than 55 million bronze cents were melted; these mass meltings have had a great impact on the availability of this date as well as all others of the era.

Collecting Challenges: This is a very tough date to find, in all grades. Few collectors realize how rare this date really is. Its price has climbed steadily over the years. With little supply of quality pieces available, it will probably continue to appreciate. Expect to always pay a premium for attractive pieces.

Collecting Circulated Pieces: The Optimal Collecting Grade is F-12. Most examples are a very low grade. Finding problem-free examples in Very Fine condition or better is very difficult. Examples with problems such as scratches, cleaning, and rim dents are mostly what collectors will encounter. Try and hold out for original coins without serious problems.

Collecting Mint State Pieces: The Optimal Collecting Grade is MS-64RB. Although this grade is very scarce, there are usually examples available in the same proportion as for the 1866 to 1868 dates. These coins were saved only by chance, and in very small quantities. On such small scale, the chance survival of even a 50-piece roll would alter the pricing structure between these dates. However, such an occurrence is very unlikely for coins of this era. Full red examples, although scarce, are a bit more readily available than earlier dates.

Collecting Proof Issues: This issue was struck in the same mintage range as the 1866 to 1868 issues. Most have a mottled red-brown look, with average mirrors. Gem red examples are difficult to find. Most of this issue comes with light die-polishing lines in the fields. Die-polishing lines, sometimes confused with *hairlines*, are transferred to every coin struck from that die and are raised on the coin. Hairlines are fine scratches on the surface of a coin and are remnants of some kind of cleaning or wiping of the coin after it is struck.

Varieties: The so-called 1869/8 issue was believed to be an actual overdate in the 1950s and 1960s. As overdates receive great demand from collectors, it soared in value more than the regular non-overdate coins. It was added to coin albums and reported in pricing guides. However, this changed in 1970 when researchers at the American Numismatic Association reported that the overdate was actually only a repunched date, 1869/9. The makers of coin albums have since relabeled their product with 1869/9.

Collectors still search for an example of this coin, and fill the void with the Snow-3 variety, which has a bold 69/69 repunching. S-3 is common enough in high grades of Mint State to satisfy collector demand, but it is very difficult to find in circulated grades, especially in Extremely Fine or About Uncirculated.

There are 15 other repunched date varieties known for this date, some of which show doubling on the 9 only. The Snow-1 variety has a boldly repunched 18 and is quite scarce. Most of the other repunched dates are minor and attract little premium.

1869/69 Snow-3

1869/69 • Market Values • Circulation Strikes

G-4	VG-8	F-12	VF-20	EF-40	AU-50	MS-60BN	MS-63RB	MS-64RB	MS-64RD
$120	$165	$275	$375	$550	$650	$700	$850	$1,500	$3,000
MS-65RB	MS-65RD	MS-66RD	PF-60RB	PF-63RB	PF-64RB	PF-64RD	PF-65RB	PF-65RD	PF-66RD
$2,000	$7,500	$22,500							

A SNAPSHOT OF THE YEAR 1870

The ninth United States census reported the country's population as 38.6 million, including about three million immigrants who had arrived in the preceding decade. The census results made evident how the immigration surge from Europe to the Northern states had tilted congressional powers prior to, during, and after the Civil War.

On the technological front, July 24 marked the arrival of the first through railway cars from San Francisco to New York City. In politics, the donkey symbol denoting the Democratic Party appeared for the first time in the January 15 issue of *Harper's Weekly*.

In 1870 the 15th Amendment to the U.S. Constitution was ratified, forbidding denial of the right to vote "on account of race, color, or previous condition of servitude." Women were not included in this protection, much to the chagrin of the National Woman Suffrage Association (NWSA). In the view of the organization's leaders (including Susan B. Anthony and Elizabeth Cady Stanton), the 15th Amendment should not have been supported until women's right to vote was included.

Even with the amendment's passage, black Americans had a difficult time registering to vote in parts of the South. In spite of the barriers, the first black members of Congress were elected. The Rev'd Hiram Rhoades Revels, a freeborn black man of African and Native-American origins, was elected as a Mississippi senator. In an ironic Reconstruction-era twist, he was chosen to fill what had been Jefferson Davis's pre-war seat. Later that year, Joseph H. Rainey—born a slave—was elected to fill a House vacancy.

In New York City, the Metropolitan Museum of Art was chartered on April 13, and later in the year the F.A.O. Schwarz toy store opened for business. Also in that city, the first apartment building was constructed—a five-story walk-up. John D. Rockefeller's Standard Oil Company of Ohio (Sohio) was incorporated.

Susan B. Anthony
Her belief that the 15th Amendment didn't go far enough contributed to a schism in the NWSA.

The U.S. Mint experimented with "Standard Silver" patterns this year. The year's Proof coins (except for silver dollars) were struck from carelessly polished dies, as was typical for that era. This was a banner year for branch mint activity, with the cornerstone laid for a new mint in San Francisco, and, in Nevada, the first gold and silver coins struck in the new Carson City Mint.

1870 Indian Head Cent

Enlarged 1.5x—Actual Size: 19mm

CIRCULATION MINTAGE:
5,275,000

PROOF MINTAGE:
EST. 1,000+

Market Values • Circulation Strikes and Proof Strikes

G-4	VG-8	F-12	VF-20	EF-40	AU-50	MS-60BN	MS-63RB	MS-64RB	MS-64RD
$55	$75	$200	$260	$350	$400	$450	$565	$850	$2,000

MS-65RB	MS-65RD	MS-66RD	PF-60RB	PF-63RB	PF-64RB	PF-64RD	PF-65RB	PF-65RD	PF-66RD
$1,500	$5,500	$18,000	$400	$575	$625	$1,500	$1,100	$3,500	$7,000

Certified Populations

G - VF	EF-40	EF-45	AU-50	AU-53	AU-55	AU-58	MS-60	MS-61	MS-62	MS-63	MS-64	MS-65	MS-66	MS-67	MS-68	MS-69	MS-70
303	140	126	96	18	77	87	41	43	107	640	1,688	1,039	167	0	0	0	0

<PF-60	PF-60	PF-61	PF-62	PF-63	PF-64	PF-65	PF-66	PF-67	PF-68	PF-69	PF-70
1	7	5	16	206	747	562	170	0	0	0	0

Field populations: Circulation strike (<MS-60), 20,000; circulation strike (MS-60+), 1,800; Proof, 450.

1870 Cent Production: In 1870 the reverse design was changed slightly. The new design features a bold ONE CENT denomination. The previous design had a shallower denomination, with the N in ONE being especially shallow. A growing number of collectors seek both reverse designs for this year as well as for 1871 and 1872.

Since reverse dies do not have dates, the Mint had a number of Shallow N dies on hand at the time, perhaps from the prior year. The Mint reworked many of these dies with the Bold N design, creating numerous doubled-die reverse varieties—a situation similar to the 1878, 7 Over 8 Clear Doubled Feathers Morgan dollar.

The production of all minor coinage was in a decreasing trend during this era. The main reason for this cutback was the lack of a redemption clause in any of the issuing legislation. The nickel and bronze coinage was beginning to accumulate in commercial channels.

Survivability: This issue was not saved to a great extent. Most of the coins were returned to the Mint over the next few years, during the 1870s recoinage (see 1871 for further discussion). Without any authority from Congress, the Mint accepted nickel and bronze issues, which had been jammed in bank vaults in ever growing numbers, and melted them

Shallow N (Type of 1869)

Bold N / Shallow N

Bold N (Type of 1870)

down to make new coins. The 1870 cents were most likely at the top of the heap of coins being returned to the Mint. Any that survived in circulation are today found in mostly very low grades. The few high-grade examples that are available survived mainly by chance.

Collecting Challenges: As with all dates of this era, finding attractive problem-free coins will be difficult, though most are well struck. Shallow N reverse coins are slightly scarcer than those with the Bold N reverse, but not enough to warrant a premium.

Collecting Circulated Pieces: The Optimal Collecting Grade is VF-20. Higher grades will be very difficult to find. Lower grades are usually available. Avoid problem pieces, such as cleaned, scratched, or corroded coins. These are discounted in general, but usually not enough to make them good buys.

Collecting Mint State Pieces: The Optimal Collecting Grade is MS-64RB. These coins are typically red-brown, with even-colored pieces particularly difficult to find. Many come with streaky toning due to an improperly mixed alloy in the planchets. Full red coins are rare, and collectors should beware of chemically altered pieces impersonating original full red coins.

When originally struck, all bronze coins are full red. The heat of striking creates a molecular shell, which somehow blocks any change in the color. When the acids in your hands come in contact with the surface of the coin, this layer is destroyed and the coin will start to turn brown. When a coin is cleaned, it is also susceptible to turning a brown color within a short period of time. For this reason, it is very important that any full red coin not have any indication of having been cleaned in the past.

Collecting Proof Issues: Proofs are usually found with medium mirrors. It seems that the dies were not polished very deeply to begin with. Any deep-mirror examples should be worthy of a significant premium. Cameo examples are rare; perhaps only 5% of high-quality examples qualify.

This date in Proof is found with the Shallow N reverse, in use from 1868, as well as a new Bold N reverse. There is a growing general collector interest in the reverse types.

Varieties: Due to the reverse design change, and the subsequent reworking of the dies, there are at least 23 reverse doubled dies known. Some are very dramatic, but most are very minor. The most dramatic varieties are the misplaced dates (MPD). Snow-5 shows a bold 0 digit sticking into the field under the date. S-8 shows the remnants of multiple digits above the denticles, possibly as many as eight. Both garner premiums greater than five times normal value.

One popular variety, dubbed the *Pickaxe*, has die damage by the last feather, which looks like a miner's axe. It is relatively common, being paired with at least five different dies.

Above all these in significance are the reverse design varieties: the Shallow N and Bold N. These are gaining in popularity with date collectors, as their existence becomes more widely known.

An 1870 Shield nickel variety is known with clash marks from the obverse Indian Head cent die! This gives rise to the question: does an 1870 Indian Head cent exist with the corresponding Shield nickel clash marks? None have yet been found.

A Snapshot of the Year 1871

The 1870s opened a new chapter for the Native American population as westward expansionism once again took hold over the national mindset. Congress declared, under the Indian Appropriation Act (March 3, 1871), that Indians were now wards of the government and from then on, tribes would not be recognized as separate nations—no further treaties would be made with them. This marked a pivotal moment in Native-white relations that began in 1768 when Britain signed a treaty at Fort Stanwix recognizing the Indian Nation. From March 1871 onward, each Native American was considered an individual in the eyes of the U.S. government.

With the ensuing land expropriation, railroad magnates expanded their dominion west of the Mississippi. The Pennsylvania Railroad extended service to New York City, Chicago, and St. Louis, among other cities. In Wall Street, the firm of Drexel, Morgan & Co. was organized. J.P Morgan would later become a coin collector and assemble a cabinet containing runs of U.S. gold Proof sets—a collection later given to the American Numismatic Society.

The Chicago fire raged on October 8 and 9, destroying more than three square miles of the city, killing 300 people, causing an estimated $200 million worth of damage, and leaving about 90 thousand homeless.

The year 1871 changed the course of New York City politics when accusations of the corruption of William "Boss" Tweed and his group of "forty thieves" heated to the boiling point. Tweed, the undisputed czar of New York City, was long known for controlling the Democratic Party, swindling city coffers, and rigging elections. He was challenged by a group of citizens incensed by a cartoon by Thomas Nast and the evidence against the corrupt police force unearthed by *The New York Times*.

The Great Chicago Fire
According to legend, the fire was sparked when Mrs. O'Leary's cow kicked over a lantern.

If New York City wanted more historical presence, it certainly got it when in July of 1871 fighting broke out between the Presbyterian and Catholic Irishmen living there. The skirmish that began during a Scotch-Irish parade claimed 33 lives. Later that month, a Staten Island ferry was rocked by an explosion that killed 72 passengers and caused many injuries.

During this year, there were several mints in operation, including those of Philadelphia, Carson City, and San Francisco. The coinage of the Carson City Mint would, in time, be distinguished for its rarity.

CIRCULATION MINTAGE:
3,929,500

PROOF MINTAGE:
EST. 960+

Enlarged 1.5x—Actual Size: 19mm

Shallow N • Market Values • Circulation Strikes and Proof Strikes

G-4	VG-8	F-12	VF-20	EF-40	AU-50	MS-60BN	MS-63RB	MS-64RB	MS-64RD
$250	$300	$500	$750	$1,200	$1,750	$2,500	$5,000	$7,000	$15,000
MS-65RB	MS-65RD	PF-66RD	PF-60RB	PF-63RB	PF-64RB	PF-64RD	PF-65RB	PF-65RD	PF-66RD
$12,500	$45,000	—	$500	$625	$725	$1,500	$1,100	$3,500	$8,500

Bold N • Market Values • Circulation Strikes

G-4	VG-8	F-12	VF-20	EF-40	AU-50	MS-60BN	MS-63RB	MS-64RB	MS-64RD
$65	$80	$260	$300	$375	$435	$480	$600	$1,300	$5,000
MS-65RB	MS-65RD	MS-66RD	PF-60RB	PF-63RB	PF-64RB	PF-64RD	PF-65RB	PF-65RD	PF-66RD
$3,000	$22,500	—							

Certified Populations

G - VF	EF-40	EF-45	AU-50	AU-53	AU-55	AU-58	MS-60	MS-61	MS-62	MS-63	MS-64	MS-65	MS-66	MS-67	MS-68	MS-69	MS-70
285	126	117	87	24	68	79	42	34	121	732	1,666	1,127	92	0	0	0	0
<PF-60	PF-60	PF-61		PF-62		PF-63		PF-64		PF-65		PF-66		PF-67	PF-68	PF-69	PF-70
7	7	3		27		275		661		717		124		0	0	0	0

Field populations: Circulation strike (<MS-60), 10,000; circulation strike (MS-60+), 1,200; Proof, 600.

1871 Cent Production: The Mint Act of March 3, 1871, provided much-needed authorization for the Mint to redeem the nickel and bronze coinage that was clogging up commercial channels. Because these coins didn't have a bullion value close to their face value, and because their legal-tender status was limited, banks had had nowhere to go to turn in excess coinage. Now the Mint was given the legal authorization to do what it had been doing for the past few years anyway.

In the decade following, more than 31 million copper-nickel cents from 1857 to 1864 were melted. By 1909, about half the original mintage of copper-nickel cents was turned in and destroyed.

More than 55 million bronze cents were melted in the years following 1871. The metal was reused to make more cents. This seemingly wasteful cycle of redeeming older coins and recoining the metal into new coins went on until 1874, when the Mint started reissuing older coins alongside the new pieces.

The Shallow N reverse is found on a small number of coins from this date. As collector appreciation increases, this is becoming a very high–premium coin.

Bold N

Shallow N

Survivability: This is one of the rarest dates in the series. Most new 1871 cents went though a quick round trip from the Mint, to the banks, and then back to the Mint for recoinage. As a result, most survivors are coins that escaped into circulation and stayed there for a long time. Most are in very low grades.

Collecting Challenges: Problem-free examples are very difficult to locate; however, a majority of this issue is found well struck. Select attractive examples. The Shallow N reverse is very scarce, but dealer awareness is presently low. This may offer an opportunity for collectors.

Collecting Circulated Pieces: The Optimal Collecting Grade is F-12. Most examples are in very low grades. Searching for quality within the grade desired is important. Examples in Extremely Fine and About Uncirculated are very hard to locate and are always in demand. Avoid problem pieces with pitted surfaces, heavy scratches, or dents. Don't forget to check for the very scarce Shallow N reverse.

Collecting Mint State Pieces: The Optimal Collecting Grade is MS-63. These are typically well struck, but attractive examples are particularly elusive. Most are dull red-brown, with more brown than red. Coins with even color and vibrant luster, regardless of color, are very desirable. Many collectors prefer solid brown coins compared to streaky red-brown pieces.

Collecting Proof Issues: These typically come with moderate mirrors and red-brown coloration. It seems that no example of this date comes with the crisp, early-die-state detail that can be found on other dates in previous years. The coins always have an over-polished look rather than the fine polishing and sharp contrast seen on Proofs of other years. As a result, Proofs of this date are very rare with cameo contrast.

Both Shallow N and Bold N reverses are found for this date in Proof format. Neither is worth a premium, as collector awareness is very low. Also, there is a scarce date variation with the numerals 7 and 1 touching. These are usually poorly made and may be mistaken for circulation strikes.

Varieties: The scarce Shallow N reverse offers a challenge for collectors, and the premium for these has been increasing as collector awareness increases. An MS-65RB example sold for $13,000 in 2005. The Shallow N dies are given variety designations Snow-4 or Snow-5. The S-5 has a misplaced digit variety on the obverse. There are only a few other die varieties. The variety with the 7 and 1 touching, S-2, is very rare.

THE RECOINAGE OF THE 1870S

When the cent was changed to bronze in 1864 it was deemed necessary to add a legal-tender limit to the authorizing legislation. At first it was 10¢, but shortly after it was dropped to only 4¢. This did little to ensure the cent's circulation—necessity and convenience alone made the new coins successful. However, by actually stating a legal-tender limit, rather than just releasing them into circulation, the banking establishments could point to a reason to refuse them in larger quantities. As the Mint's production of cents exceeded the demand in the late 1860s the coins started to accumulate with no legal outlet.

To remedy this situation, the Mint Act of 1871 authorized the Mint to redeem minor coinage (all coins previously minted in copper and nickel alloy, five cents and below) and to reissue the cents. Accordingly, the Mint took in millions of these minor coins and melted them all. The reissued coinage up until 1874 was in the form of newly minted cents.

Below is the record of bronze cents redeemed and reissued, including the quantity of copper-nickel cents redeemed and melted. It seems that in 1874 someone decided that the redeemed cents could just as easily be reissued without being melted and recoined. The coinage of cents during the 1870s was heavily influenced by this decision. In 1877 alone, enough cents were redeemed and reissued to make the mintage of new coins almost unnecessary.

Record of Minor Coins Redeemed 1871–1881

Year	Copper-Nickel Cents Redeemed	Bronze Cents Redeemed	Bronze Cents Reissued
1871	8,569,848	7,275,091	
1872	5,751,073	5,635,999	
1873	2,641,157	2,661,362	
1874	3,015,870	4,051,908	372,500
1875	2,204,701	3,937,872	3,926,000
1876	3,106,895	5,932,723	5,599,500
1877	2,870,433	9,908,148	9,821,500
1878	1,993,125	8,213,999	8,242,500
1879	870,342	3,515,327	3,357,500
1880	577,130	3,626,501	3,342,000
1881	81,393	765,395	1,132,500
Totals	31,681,967	55,524,325	35,794,000

Source: National Archives; reprinted in Steve/Flynn 1995

A Snapshot of the Year 1872

The U.S. economy's dependency on horsepower became evident when the nation was struck by the Great Epizootic of 1872, cause of the deaths of four million horses. The virus wreaked havoc on urban transportation systems. In Philadelphia and New York City, men were hitched to streetcars and carts to haul passengers and cargo. To make matters worse, a fire in Boston devastated more than 750 buildings and caused an estimated $75 million in damages, in part because most of the horses used to pull steam fire engines were incapacitated. Commerce suffered and the epizootic was recognized as a factor in the Panic of '73.

John D. Rockefeller's Standard Oil Trust was refining 10,000 barrels of kerosene daily, while Commodore Cornelius Vanderbilt, known for his own monopolies, endowed funds to establish Vanderbilt University in Nashville, Tennessee.

In a pivotal moment in the suffrage movement, Susan B. Anthony and other advocates of women's rights attempted to vote in the presidential election in Rochester, New York, and were subsequently arrested. During that election, Ulysses S. Grant won his second term on the Republican ticket, despite allegations that his administration was corrupt and poorly led.

Much legislation came to pass this year, including the act for the creation of the Yellowstone National Park and the law making it illegal to use the U.S. mail to defraud. Concurrently, mail-order services began to prosper, and one could order virtually anything by simply sending a check—from a pint of rum to a parlor reed organ. One of the biggest mail-order companies, Montgomery Ward, was founded this year in Chicago.

"Amazonian" Pattern Design
This design by William Barber was used on pattern quarter, half dollar, and dollar coins of 1872.

Meanwhile, specie payments continued in suspension, and Fractional Currency notes, most of which grew dirty and tattered in circulation, took the place of coins in many small transactions. Indian Head cents, two-cent pieces, nickel three-cent pieces, and nickel five-cent pieces circulated actively, although by this time the two-cent piece had fallen out of favor.

1872 INDIAN HEAD CENT

CIRCULATION MINTAGE:
4,042,000

PROOF MINTAGE:
EST. 950+

Enlarged 1.5x—Actual Size: 19mm

Shallow N • Market Values • Circulation Strikes and Proof Strikes

G-4	VG-8	F-12	VF-20	EF-40	AU-50	MS-60BN	MS-63RB	MS-64RB	MS-64RD
$150	$200	$350	$550	$750	$1,000	$1,200	$1,750	$3,000	$18,000
MS-65RB	MS-65RD	PF-66RD	PF-60RB	PF-63RB	PF-64RB	PF-64RD	PF-65RB	PF-65RD	PF-66RD
$7,000	—	—	$500	$550	$650	$2,250	$1,100	$5,500	$8,500

Bold N • Market Values • Circulation Strikes

G-4	VG-8	F-12	VF-20	EF-40	AU-50	MS-60BN	MS-63RB	MS-64RB	MS-64RD
$80	$100	$300	$340	$450	$550	$600	$925	$2,000	$12,500
MS-65RB	MS-65RD	MS-66RD	PF-60RB	PF-63RB	PF-64RD	PF-64RD	PF-65RB	PF-65RD	PF-66RD
$4,250	$35,000	—							

Certified Populations

G - VF	EF-40	EF-45	AU-50	AU-53	AU-55	AU-58	MS-60	MS-61	MS-62	MS-63	MS-64	MS-65	MS-66	MS-67	MS-68	MS-69	MS-70
567	189	123	115	21	91	77	19	39	114	696	1,508	980	116	0	0	0	0
<PF-60	PF-60	PF-61	PF-62	PF-63	PF-64	PF-65	PF-66	PF-67	PF-68	PF-69	PF-70						
4	6	3	26	270	843	746	234	0	0	0	0						

Field populations: Circulation strike (<MS-60), 300,000; circulation strike (MS-60+), 7,500; Proof, 350.

1872 Cent Production: These cents were struck in quantities similar to those of 1871. Aside from the 1877, this is the toughest date to find today. The planchets made from the recoinage melt were not of a consistent quality. Most coins of this date are streaky due to uneven alloy mixes. Many examples were poorly struck or are found with missing detail due to some liquid, such as machine oil or water, getting on the planchet or dies.

A minority of these coins was struck with the Shallow N reverse (see 1871). This is becoming a well-known design change that is increasing in value as specialists become more familiar with its existence.

Survivability: The ongoing recoinage effort created a crazy situation where the recently issued coinage was being sent back to the Mint to be melted and struck into new coins. As soon as the new coins reached the banks, many may have been piled on top of older coins that were scheduled to be shipped back to the Mint. As a result, most of this issue was melted soon after its production.

Examples that survived are usually very low-grade pieces. It is very difficult to find problem-free coins. In the past, many examples in the Very Fine to Extremely Fine grades were wire-brushed to simulate mint luster. These whizzed coins were dangerous to collectors until the advent of certified grading. Many coins were ruined in the process of being whizzed.

Collecting Challenges: It is very difficult to find attractive, problem-free examples. Most are poorly struck, or are struck through machine oil. Any attractive problem-free example should be considered for your collection. Some collectors target this date for investment potential. One Detroit collector, Carl Herkowitz, spent 25 years buying problem-free examples of this date. Even so, he had a difficult time finding more than

200 pieces. His hoard contained 22 Mint State examples, 20 About Uncirculated, 50 Extremely Fine, 50 Very Fine, 50 Fine, and 20 Very Good. His hoard was sold from 2003 to 2005. Only one example in this group had a Shallow N reverse, and it was bought already attributed as such. Hoards of high-quality pieces like these do not cause concern about price drops if they were to be sold—on the contrary, if large groups of rare coins enter the market at once, they excite collectors and prices may actually rise.

Collecting Circulated Pieces: The Optimal Collecting Grade is F-12. This is one of the toughest dates in the series to find in attractive shape, without any problems. Consider dropping strict standards on strike and light hits to acquire this date. These are very rare when properly graded in Extremely Fine and About Uncirculated.

Some collectors attempt to find the Shallow N reverse as well as the typically found Bold N reverse.

Collecting Mint State Pieces: The Optimal Collecting Grade is MS-63RB. It is very difficult to locate with a full strike. Many are missing detail, usually on the reverse, due to machine oil or water resting on the planchet or on the dies. Coins that were struck through liquid will have good strikes on one side and missing details on the other. Weakly struck coins will have missing detail on both sides.

This issue will be mostly streaky red-brown, due to improperly mixed alloy. Full red coins are very rare. This is the toughest date to find in MS-65R D.

A growing number of collectors attempt to acquire both reverse types. The Shallow N is about 10 times rarer than the Bold N.

Collecting Proof Issues: Proofs of 1872 are much more readily available than high-grade Mint State coins. As a result, many substitute the less expensive Proof in their collections of Uncirculated coins, although the different texture may be distracting to most collectors.

These are a bit more readily available than 1871 and earlier dates, but because of date collector pressure they receive similar prices. While they tend to be red-brown, they are not as streaky as other dates. This makes finding attractive examples a bit easier. Proofs of this date are quite scarce in full red, and gems are very tough.

It is difficult to find deep mirrors on this issue and examples with full cameo contrast are rare.

A new Bold N reverse die with a distinctive bulging right pennant of the T in CENT is found on all Proof issues. This die was used intermittently until 1878.

1872 Bulging T

Varieties: At least three different Shallow N dies were used this year. The die pairs without obverse varieties are listed as Snow-4. Shallow N dies paired with obverse varieties are listed as S-13 (repunched date) and S-14 (bold misplaced digit). There are a number of minor repunched dates, but because of the high price of this date, premiums are small.

A small part of the D in UNITED started to deteriorate on the hub starting this year. (The hub is the undated steel positive used to make dies for coinage. A hub can be used over many years since it does not carry the date.) This hub deterioration, resulting in a "broken D," is an interesting aspect to trace over the next few years, but its coins do not warrant a premium.

A Snapshot of the Year 1873

Life in the U.S. in 1873 was heavily impacted by the stock market's weakness. A farmers' reaction against railroad tariffs, in addition to weather-related harvest disasters, caused many railroad stocks and bonds to drop. European investors, who had been a major force in the U.S. stock market and major investors in Western mines, withdrew capital, causing a pronounced drop in prices. In September, Jay Cooke & Company, agent for the Northern Pacific Railroad, collapsed. This single financial failure sparked the legendary Black Friday. Stocks fell precipitously across the board. Numerous banks and brokerages failed, primarily in New York City. Although the stock exchange closed for 10 days, the damage was done; by the end of the year an estimated 5,100 businesses had dissolved and millions were unemployed. The consequent depression lasted through 1877. Wages dropped 20% to 25% and a period of deflation began.

In Nevada the Comstock Lode was going strong, but optimism did not prevail, as the price of silver continued to decline on worldwide markets. In the same state a new silver strike was made in the Panamint Mountains. The more silver was mined, the lower its price fell in terms of gold, contributing to the era's economic hardship.

As this depression took hold in the coming years, some of the blame was diverted to what would become known as the Crime of '73—the Mint Act of February 12, 1873. Originally written as a report by Deputy Comptroller of the Currency John Jay Knox in 1869, the Mint Bill was designed to be merely a restatement of past laws as well as a vehicle to push for an all-nickel minor coinage system. One of the core ideas in this report was to change the cent's composition to nickel (when the bill was finally written this idea was dropped).

1873 Liberty Seated Dollar
The denomination would be shelved by the Mint Act of February 12, 1873.

Another idea Knox had written into his report was a simple lowering of the weight of the silver dollar to correspond to the weights of fractional silver coinage from the Act of 1853. The silver dollar didn't circulate and it was thought that this would make it more practical to produce. No one seemed to realize that by doing this the United States would go on a de facto gold standard.

In late 1872, as the Mint Bill was being reviewed in the Senate Finance Committee, a dramatic change was made without much debate or notice. The reduced-weight silver dollar (or standard dollar, as it was to be known) was dropped completely. A new bullion coin called a trade dollar was to be struck for use in trade with China. A big mistake in the bill was granting the trade dollar legal-tender status up to $5. It was not supposed to circulate domestically, yet the lawmakers in effect said it could.

The "Crime of '73" was actually a cry from politicians for an expanding money supply. The gold standard tightened money and credit at a time when there was a deep national depression. Although this was not caused by the Mint Act of 1873, it was an easy target for blame, coming seven months prior to the collapse of the credit system.

The Mint Act did stop production of the half dime and three-cent silver piece. This assured continued use of the nickel coinage. The Indian Head cent's big brother, the two-cent piece, also passed into history. The remaining silver coins were brought up to metric weights and arrows were added to their designs to show this change.

1873, CLOSE 3 INDIAN HEAD CENT

CIRCULATION MINTAGE:
EST. 2,500,000 CLOSE 3 CENTS
(OF 11,676,500 TOTAL)

PROOF MINTAGE:
EST. 1,100+

Enlarged 1.5x—Actual Size: 19mm

Market Values • Circulation Strikes and Proof Strikes

G-4	VG-8	F-12	VF-20	EF-40	AU-50	MS-60BN	MS-63RB	MS-64RB	MS-64RD
$25	$35	$60	$120	$180	$225	$425	$550	$1,250	$4,000
MS-65RB	MS-65RD	MS-66RD	PF-60RB	PF-63RB	PF-64RB	PF-64RD	PF-65RB	PF-65RD	PF-66RD
$3,000	$12,500	$30,000	$400	$575	$625	$1,250	$850	$4,000	$7,500

Certified Populations

G - VF	EF-40	EF-45	AU-50	AU-53	AU-55	AU-58	MS-60	MS-61	MS-62	MS-63	MS-64	MS-65	MS-66	MS-67	MS-68	MS-69	MS-70
18	7	10	4	2	7	13	1	1	15	290	600	430	50	0	0	0	0
<PF-60	PF-60	PF-61	PF-62	PF-63	PF-64	PF-65	PF-66	PF-67	PF-68	PF-69	PF-70						
5	5	5	23	62	185	64	8	0	0	0	0						

Field populations: Circulation strike (<MS-60), 8,000; circulation strike (MS-60+), 1,000; Proof, 700.

Closed or *Close*: The label *Closed 3* was popularized by Harry X Boosel, whose affection for this date translated into a series of articles called "1873–1873." These were published in book form in 1960. Today, through the published works of Q. David Bowers in Whitman's Bowers Series, and because the naming convention is used in the Red Book, this has shifted slightly to *Close 3*. Rightly so, as the "closed" 3 is not really closed, but nearly so. *Close* is a more accurate term.

1873, Close 3 Cent Production: On January 18, Chief Coiner A.L. Snowden submitted a formal complaint that the 3 in the dates on all the coinage dies was too close and could easily be confused for an 8. New date punches with a more open 3 were made and put into use on all the remaining dies to be made. There is no way to accurately record how many coins were struck from the dies made prior to the change. After the Open 3 dies were prepared, it is probable that both date styles were struck simultaneously. The mintage given here is estimated from the surviving percentage of Close 3 coins compared to Open 3 examples.

1873, Close 3

Survivability: About 25% of all 1873 Indian Head cents have the Close 3 date style. These seem to be about as readily available as the 1872 issue, which has a higher mintage. The pace of the redemption of cents slowed a bit in 1873 and 1874, so more of this issue survived. These pieces stayed in circulation for a long time.

1873, Open 3

Collecting Challenges: The 1873 Close 3 cent is very difficult to find unattributed, as its desirability has been known for many years. Expect to pay a premium about double the price of the Open 3. Look for attractive problem-free pieces. Many collectors add both the Close 3 and Open 3 digit styles to their collections; however, if only one example is desired, collectors usually choose the less expensive Open 3. This keeps demand a bit lower than it would otherwise be.

Collecting Circulated Pieces: The Optimal Collecting Grade is VF-20. Most are well struck. Avoid problem pieces with corroded surfaces or with aggressive cleaning. Most coin albums label a hole for this coin, so demand is moderately strong.

Collecting Mint State Pieces: The Optimal Collecting Grade is MS-63RB. These are very scarce, but the premium over the Open 3 style is lower due to weaker demand from date collectors. Most are found with streaky red-brown colors. Full red examples are very scarce. Beware of cleaned examples offered as gem full red.

Collecting Proof Issues: Proofs were struck in Close 3 style only. These are moderately scarce, though much more common than the Mint State format. The dies seem to have been heavily polished prior to use. None are known from what numismatists call an early die state. Mirrors are usually medium. Cameo examples are rare.

Varieties: The main variety for this year is the Doubled LIBERTY, Snow-1. This variety is very popular. There is a second, less dramatic doubled LIBERTY, S-2. It has doubling on just the BERTY of LIBERTY. All known examples are struck with the Bold N reverse. A Shallow N reverse may exist on the S-2 as well as others, but none have been authenticated yet.

1873, Doubled Liberty Indian Head Cent

CIRCULATION MINTAGE:
EST. 100,000 DOUBLED LIBERTY CENTS
(OF 11,676,500 TOTAL)

PROOF MINTAGE:
NOT MADE IN PROOF FORMAT

Enlarged 1.5x—Actual Size: 19mm

Market Values • Circulation Strikes

G-4	VG-8	F-12	VF-20	EF-40	AU-50	MS-60BN	MS-63RB	MS-64RB	MS-64RD
$200	$325	$700	$1,200	$2,400	$4,200	$7,500	$13,000	$20,000	$100,000
MS-65RB	MS-65RB	MS-66RD	PF-60RB	PF-63RB	PF-64RB	PF-64RD	PF-65RB	PF-65RD	PF-66RD
$70,000	—	—							

Certified Populations

G - VF	EF-40	EF-45	AU-50	AU-53	AU-55	AU-58	MS-60	MS-61	MS-62	MS-63	MS-64	MS-65	MS-66	MS-67	MS-68	MS-69	MS-70
15	4	9	3	2	3	6	2	0	11	81	154	65	0	0	0	0	0
<PF-60	PF-60	PF-61	PF-62	PF-63	PF-64	PF-65	PF-66	PF-67	PF-68	PF-69	PF-70						

Field populations: Circulation strike (<MS-60), 250; circulation strike (MS-60+), 25.

1873, Doubled LIBERTY Cent Production: This is the boldest doubled die in the series. It is commonly referred to as the *Doubled LIBERTY*, classified as Snow-1. The doubling is boldest on the headband and feathers. There is little or no doubling on the legend UNITED STATES OF AMERICA. This is due to the nature of the die-making process at the time. A blank die is given a shallow conical head when first turned down. The first impression of the hub into the die did not impress the entire design, only the central portion. The next impression of the hub filled out the design, but at a slightly rotated position. Thus, only the central portion of the design got doubled impressions. The date did not get doubled because it was added to the die after the portrait and legend.

1873 Snow-1

Survivability: Walter Breen first described this variety in 1953. (At the time there was little knowledge regarding doubled dies. Collector interest in doubled dies grew after the discovery of the 1955 doubled-die Lincoln cent.) Few have turned up over the years. In Breen's 1988 *Complete Encyclopedia of U.S. and Colonial Coins* he proclaimed the possible finest known to be an MS-60 cleaned piece in the 1983 Roy Harte III sale. Today, about 150 examples of the Doubled LIBERTY are known, about 20 of which are in Mint State.

Collecting Challenges: These are highly sought after. It is very rare to find one unattributed, although it still happens. One of the greatest cherrypicks on record involved this coin. In 2000, a collection of Mint State Indian Head cents was offered to Indian Head cent collector Dr. Tom Turissini by a local dealer. The set contained many beautiful high-grade coins in an old-time holder. The 1873 cent was an unattributed example of the famed Doubled LIBERTY. It later was graded MS-64RD by PCGS, and sold for nearly double the record price for the variety at the time. Later still, it surfaced in the Stewart Blay Collection (the example pictured on page 125); this is still the only example graded full red.

The finest graded piece, a nearly full red MS-65RB graded by PCGS, was initially bought as a generic "BU" (Brilliant Uncirculated) from a seller on the Internet for $5,000 in 1996. It later sold at auction for $69,000 in 2005.

At the 1990 ANA show in Seattle, Brian Wagner walked into the show, and at the first table he stopped at, bought an 1873 cent in About Uncirculated for $60. It was not even labeled as a Close 3, let alone the Doubled LIBERTY. He sold it right away for $1,800. He probably should have held on to the coin, as it has advanced considerably in value since then. The coin was featured on the cover of the premier issue of *Longacre's Ledger* in 1990.

Buying an already attributed Doubled LIBERTY is the route most collectors have to go to get this famous coin. Most examples will have problems such as heavy or numerous marks. The high-quality pieces usually do not have to wait too long to find ready buyers, unless grossly overpriced.

Collecting Circulated Pieces: The Optimal Collecting Grade for these is VF-20 or F-12, below which the details of interest will be worn away. On Very Good and lower examples, the doubling is visible on the nose and the ES of STATES. Problems such as scratches and nicks may be acceptable if they are reflected in the price. There usually are large price jumps between grades, so be careful about overgraded pieces.

Collecting Mint State Pieces: Mint State examples are very rare and as such, very expensive. Most are dark red-brown or brown. Presently only one full red example is known. Only about 20 other Mint State examples exist. Most are well struck. One example has a machine oil strike-through on the ERTY, leaving only the feathers and LIB showing doubling—an unfortunate situation.

One famous example of this coin is an MS-65RB example, which was featured on the cover of my book *Flying Eagle and Indian Cents* (1992). This coin was graded MS-65RB by NGC in 1993, after being photographed for the book; however, NGC failed to designate its Doubled LIBERTY status on the holder. Elliott Goldman, proprietor of Allstate Coin Co. of Tucson, Arizona, owned the coin. Elliott sent the coin back to NGC and it was stolen en route. Although it was insured, it was a loss to the numismatic community. Since this was the cover plate coin on my book as well as being the first 1873 Doubled LIBERTY cent to receive the MS-65RB grade, it was very difficult for the insurance company to figure out what it was worth. Eventually a $35,000 settlement was arrived at.

In 1998, this coin surfaced. A dealer member of the Professional Numismatists Guild was offered the coin. He held it until the rightful owner could be found. Elliott Goldman had passed away in 1995, and the insurance case was difficult to track down. Finally, after much research and legal wrangling, the coin was returned to the insurance company and sold back to the numismatic community. As it turned out, the thief did not know what he had, as it was unattributed in its NGC holder. He sold the coin soon after the theft for $200, to the person who later tried to sell it in 1998. The buyer forfeited ownership when he discovered it was stolen. There were no prosecutions in the case.

1873, OPEN 3 INDIAN HEAD CENT

CIRCULATION MINTAGE:
EST. 9,000,000 OPEN 3 CENTS
(OF 11,676,500 TOTAL)

PROOF MINTAGE:
NOT MADE IN PROOF FORMAT

Enlarged 1.5x—Actual Size: 19mm

Market Values • Circulation Strikes

G-4	VG-8	F-12	VF-20	EF-40	AU-50	MS-60BN	MS-63RB	MS-64RB	MS-64RD
$20	$30	$50	$85	$160	$190	$250	$325	$425	$3,000
MS-65RB	MS-65RD	MS-66RD	PF-60RB	PF-63RB	PF-64RB	PF-64RD	PF-65RB	PF-65RD	PF-66RD
$1,350	$10,000	—							

Certified Populations

G - VF	EF-40	EF-45	AU-50	AU-53	AU-55	AU-58	MS-60	MS-61	MS-62	MS-63	MS-64	MS-65	MS-66	MS-67	MS-68	MS-69	MS-70
208	166	124	126	30	91	86	50	54	130	756	1,952	1,276	140	1	0	0	0
<PF-60	PF-60		PF-61		PF-62		PF-63		PF-64		PF-65		PF-66		PF-67	PF-68	PF-69	PF-70

Field populations: Circulation strike (<MS-60), 25,000; circulation strike (MS-60+), 2,000.

1873, Open 3 Cent Production: The new dies with the Open 3 were made as soon as it was practicable. It seems that the Close 3 digit punch was reworked to make the balls of the 3 smaller. Coins from these new dies were apparently struck alongside those of the Close 3 dies.

Survivability: Although this date is scarce, examples survived the 1870s recoinage a bit better than earlier dates. A little more than six million coins, mostly early cents, were redeemed during the 1873 and 1874 fiscal years. After 1874, coins were no longer melted unless they were unfit for circulation. This saved many coins from this date onward from the melting pot. This date is mostly found in very low grades.

1873, Open 3

Collecting Challenges: This date is more readily available than earlier dates, but is still scarce enough to be difficult to find problem free.

Collecting Circulated Pieces: The Optimal Collecting Grade is EF-40. As with most issues of this era, finding problem-free examples is very difficult.

Collecting Mint State Pieces: The Optimal Collecting Grade is MS-64RB. This coin is much more readily avail-

1873, Close 3

able than the Close 3 digit style. It is similar in rarity to the 1874 and 1875 issues. Most examples have streaky red-brown toning, as the source of the metal for this issue was a mixture of melted-down bronze cents and virgin metal. Full red examples are scarce.

Varieties: A minor doubled die exists with doubling only on the L in LIBERTY. More interesting is a bold repunched date, Snow-1, which looks like a Close 3 date style due to the multiple threes.

A Snapshot of the Year 1874

This year marked a beginning of literary antagonism against America's upper class. Mark Twain's *The Gilded Age* was published as an affront to the increasing materialism of the well-to-do.

The Women's Christian Temperance Union was founded with the sole objective of fighting the growing dependence of Americans on alcohol. The group would later be credited with the passage of the 18th Amendment to the Constitution.

This same year, silver was discovered in Oro City, Colorado (renamed Leadville in 1878), leading to several fortunes, including that of H.A.W. Tabor (whose wife, Baby Doe, would later be the foundation for the play *The Unsinkable Mollie Brown*).

On the shore of Lake Chautauqua, near Jamestown, New York, the Chautauqua Movement began as a summer training program for Sunday school instructors. As time went on, traveling tent shows and permanent locales were established (such as that which survives today in Boulder, Colorado), providing a lyceum for public speakers and other entertainment—some of which included lengthy oral dissertations on religion, politics, science, travel, and other subjects.

The year 1874 brought to New York City the first electrically propelled streetcar; however, horsepower continued to provide most of its transportation services. Barnum's Hippodrome opened in that same city; it would later became known as Madison Square Garden.

On the labor front, Massachusetts enacted a law that limited the daily working hours of women to 10. There were no effective child labor laws in the United States, so it was not unusual to see six- to ten-year-old children working from dawn to dusk in textile mills, coal mines, and other hazardous occupations.

1874 also brought to the world the Remington typewriter. The backers of the typewriter later paid an astounding $10,000 for the first publicly distributed 1892 Columbian commemorative half dollar.

At the Philadelphia Mint, patterns were made for a new denomination, the 20-cent piece, and for Dana Bickford's international $10 gold piece. The latter was one of a string of poorly conceived proposals for a coin readily interchangeable across international borders. The concept was doomed to fail because it didn't take into account constantly changing exchange rates.

1874 Bickford $10 Gold Pattern

1874 INDIAN HEAD CENT

CIRCULATION MINTAGE:
14,187,500

PROOF MINTAGE:
EST. 700+

Enlarged 1.5x—Actual Size: 19mm

Market Values • Circulation Strikes and Proof Strikes

G-4	VG-8	F-12	VF-20	EF-40	AU-50	MS-60BN	MS-63RB	MS-64RB	MS-64RD
$18	$20	$40	$50	$100	$140	$225	$250	$425	$2,000
MS-65RB	MS-65RD	MS-66RD	PF-60RB	PF-63RB	PF-64RB	PF-64RD	PF-65RB	PF-65RD	PF-66RD
$800	$5,000	$8,000	$275	$425	$500	$1,350	$900	$5,500	$7,500

Certified Populations

G - VF	EF-40	EF-45	AU-50	AU-53	AU-55	AU-58	MS-60	MS-61	MS-62	MS-63	MS-64	MS-65	MS-66	MS-67	MS-68	MS-69	MS-70
61	85	79	89	20	88	52	44	32	115	772	2,198	1,551	267	0	0	0	0
<PF-60	PF-60	PF-61	PF-62	PF-63	PF-64	PF-65	PF-66	PF-67	PF-68	PF-69	PF-70						
3	5	3	12	165	516	541	195	11	0	0	0						

Field populations: Circulation strike (<MS-60), 40,000; circulation strike (MS-60+), 2,500; Proof, 400.

1874 Cent Production: Obviously, with mintages climbing slightly this year, this date is more readily available than the earlier dates in the 1870s.

Survivability: Beginning this year, the Mint began to reissue cents redeemed under the provisions set in the Mint Act of 1871. The Mint was required to buy base-metal coins in quantities no smaller than $20 and melt them down only if there were too many in circulation. Of the four million older bronze cents redeemed this year, 372,500 were released back into circulation. The 1874 cent is available in most grades, but it is not common by any comparison.

Collecting Challenges: These come well struck. The planchets tend to be rather streaky, due to a variable alloy mix. Many have been cleaned over the years. As with other dates, search for problem-free examples.

Collecting Circulated Pieces: The Optimal Collecting Grade is EF-40. These should not be very difficult to find, though problem-free examples are elusive.

Collecting Mint State Pieces: The Optimal Collecting Grade is MS-64RB. It is difficult to find evenly colored red-brown examples. Most have streaky colorations. This issue is typically found well struck.

Collecting Proof Issues: All examples are from a single die pair with a defect on the date numeral 4, which has in the past been erroneously described as a repunched date. The reverse die used is the same die as is found on the 1872 and 1873 Proof issues, with a bulging right pennant on the T in CENT.

These typically have streaky red-brown toning. As the mintage suggests, they are a bit scarcer than 1873 Proofs. Mirrors are usually medium, but deeply mirrored examples do exist. Full red examples are rare, as are cameo examples.

Varieties: A minor, but elusive doubled die is known, Snow-1. A few repunched dates are known, but these are all minor.

A Snapshot of the Year 1875

In 1875 the New York City Court House was finished to the final tune of $13 million—more than 50 times its pre-construction estimate, thanks to bill-padding by William Marcy Tweed, the notorious "Boss" of Tammany Hall. Among the project's bills was $361,000 for a month's work by one carpenter. Editorial cartoonist Thomas Nast created many scathing caricatures of Tweed and his cronies. The corrupt politician would later blame his downfall and imprisonment on Nast's cartoons, complaining that his constituents couldn't read, but they could understand the pictures.

In 1875 Alexander Graham Bell conducted experiments that would lead to the creation of the telephone.

November 12 brought the first Harvard-Yale football game and the start of one of the nation's most famous gridiron rivalries. And in the sport of horse racing, the Kentucky Derby was run for the first time.

In the nearly abandoned town of Butte, in Montana Territory, the Anaconda Company was formed; it would grow into one of the world's most prolific producers of copper. Meanwhile, a glut of silver continued on the world markets, due to massive quantities dumped by the German Empire and other European nations, as well as continued mining.

It was a slim year for gold coins at the Philadelphia Mint; with the exception of the double eagle, quantities struck were small. The $3 gold piece of 1875, minted only in Proof format, had a coinage of just 20 pieces. Meanwhile, James Pollock and other Mint officers busily created rare "patterns" (actually, private oddities) for Director Henry Linderman and other insiders.

"THAT'S WHAT'S THE MATTER."
Boss Tweed. "As long as I count the Votes, what are you going to do about it? say?"

An Unsavory View of "Boss" Tweed, by Thomas Nast
"As long as I count the votes, what are you going to do about it?"
(*Harper's Weekly*, 1871)

◆

1875 Cent Production: The mintage is moderately low, similar to those of 1873 and 1874. The Mint Act of 1871 required the Mint to melt down old base-metal coins if they were redundant in circulation. Apparently, the cent backlog in commerce was easing, as the Mint released back to circulation the nearly four million bronze cents it took in this year. Thus, the Mint actually sent out more than 17 million cents in 1875. During the early 1870s much of the bronze used for cents came from the melting of redeemed cents and two-cent pieces of earlier years. Now, most of the bronze used was produced from new copper.

Survivability: This issue is scarce overall, about on the same level as the 1874. These coins stayed in circulation for a long time and are available in lower grades.

1875 INDIAN HEAD CENT

CIRCULATION MINTAGE:
13,528,000

PROOF MINTAGE:
EST. 700+

Enlarged 1.5x—Actual Size: 19mm

Market Values • Circulation Strikes and Proof Strikes

G-4	VG-8	F-12	VF-20	EF-40	AU-50	MS-60BN	MS-63RB	MS-64RB	MS-64RD
$18	$20	$40	$50	$100	$140	$225	$275	$425	$2,000
MS-65RB	MS-65RD	MS-66RD	PF-60RB	PF-63RB	PF-64RB	PF-64RD	PF-65RB	PF-65RD	PF-66RD
$800	$5,000	$8,000	$250	$425	$500	$2,000	$900	$8,500	$12,500

Certified Populations

G - VF	EF-40	EF-45	AU-50	AU-53	AU-55	AU-58	MS-60	MS-61	MS-62	MS-63	MS-64	MS-65	MS-66	MS-67	MS-68	MS-69	MS-70
80	71	58	72	14	72	54	37	32	105	840	2,390	1,434	249	0	0	0	0
<PF-60	PF-60	PF-61	PF-62	PF-63	PF-64	PF-65	PF-66	PF-67	PF-68	PF-69	PF-70						
1	1	5	23	248	744	546	79	10	0	0	0						

Field populations: Circulation strike (<MS-60), 40,000; circulation strike (MS-60+), 2,500; Proof, 350.

Collecting Challenges: These come rather well struck, so it should not be difficult to find well-struck examples. Many are struck on streaky planchets. This is due to improperly mixed tin and zinc in the bronze.

Collecting Circulated Pieces: The Optimal Collecting Grade is EF-40. Search out even-colored examples. In circulated grades naturally colored cents should be a chocolate brown. Corroded coins tend to be dark, close to black. Cleaned coins tend to be bright. There are fewer variations for original coins, so if you know what an original coin looks like, you should have little trouble determining which coins have been cleaned.

Collecting Mint State Pieces: The Optimal Collecting Grade is MS-64RB. Search out attractive coins without problems. Many have a woodgrain type of toning, which may be acceptable; personal preference plays a part here. This type of toning will hinder a coin's ability to stay full red, but does not effect the desirability of coins graded red-brown.

Collecting Proof Issues: For some reason, the Proofs of this year were made fairly carelessly. This applies not only to cents but to all denominations. As a result, high-grade examples are very difficult to find. Many have streaky red-brown toning. Full red examples are rare. Cameo examples are prohibitively rare.

Some of the Proofs were struck with the 1872 reverse die, with the bulging right pennant of the T.

Varieties: A few repunched dates are known for this year. None are particularly scarce and none gain a substantial premium. Most examples show deterioration on the top of the D in UNITED. This was caused by hub deterioration progressing over the 1873 to 1875 years. The hub is an exact image of the coin, without the date, on a steel die. It is used to impress the design into any number of coinage dies over a period of years.

A Snapshot of the Year 1876

This was the year of the nation's 100th anniversary of independence. The Centennial Exhibition was mounted on 236 acres in Fairmount Park, in Philadelphia. President Ulysses Grant addressed the crowd on opening day, May 10. At his side was Dom Pedro, emperor of Brazil—the first major foreign head of state to visit the United States. The Exhibition was attended by 37 nations and 26 states, with displays of art, industry, agriculture, and other accomplishments.

The Battle of Little Big Horn on June 25 ended in an unusually swift and decisive victory for the Indians led by Sioux Chief Sitting Bull. In less than an hour of battle, Civil War hero George Armstrong Custer was killed along with his contingent of more than 260 men.

By 1876 most of the California gold deposits mined since 1849 had been depleted, but a new star was rising: the Homestake Mining Company was formed this year in a town called Lead, in the Black Hills of the Dakota Territory. It would grow into the most productive single source of United States gold ever.

"Wild Bill" Hickock was murdered in Deadwood, Dakota Territory, on August 2. He was shot from behind by Jack McCall in Saloon No. 10, while playing poker. The cards he'd been dealt—two black aces and two black eights (plus a jack of diamonds)—would become known as *the dead man's hand.*

General George A. Custer
Expecting a handful of opponents, he instead encountered an entire army of Sioux, Cheyenne, and Crow warriors.

The presidential election of 1876 was not resolved until early 1877; neither candidate (Republican Rutherford B. Hayes vs. Democrat Samuel J. Tilden) had enough electoral votes to win the White House. Votes from several Southern states and Oregon were in dispute. Different numbers were reported by different sources, and backroom agreements were bandied about. Finally, the election was solved by commission, with five senators, five representatives, and five Supreme Court justices weighing in. Each judged the matter in favor of his political party's candidate, and since there were eight Republicans on the commission, Hayes won the presidency. In the words of numismatist and historian Q. David Bowers, "The Republicans stole the election from the Democrats, who had stolen it from the Republicans in the first place."

In Baltimore, The Johns Hopkins University was established by bequest of the late Johns Hopkins. In 1942, the University would receive the gift of the Garrett Collection of United States coins.

In Carson City this year, 10,000 twenty-cent pieces were minted. All but about 20 of the coins were melted, and a rarity was born.

1876 INDIAN HEAD CENT

CIRCULATION MINTAGE:
7,944,000

PROOF MINTAGE:
EST. 1,150+

Enlarged 1.5x—Actual Size: 19mm

Market Values • Circulation Strikes and Proof Strikes

G-4	VG-8	F-12	VF-20	EF-40	AU-50	MS-60BN	MS-63RB	MS-64RB	MS-64RD
$35	$40	$55	$80	$160	$225	$300	$380	$700	$2,000
MS-65RB	MS-65RD	MS-66RD	PF-60RB	PF-63RB	PF-64RB	PF-64RD	PF-65RB	PF-65RD	PF-66RD
$1,200	$6,000	$10,000	$300	$450	$600	$1,350	$900	$4,500	$6,500

Certified Populations

G - VF	EF-40	EF-45	AU-50	AU-53	AU-55	AU-58	MS-60	MS-61	MS-62	MS-63	MS-64	MS-65	MS-66	MS-67	MS-68	MS-69	MS-70
78	87	74	67	14	50	46	43	40	86	618	1,903	1,320	225	21	0	0	0
<PF-60	PF-60	PF-61	PF-62	PF-63	PF-64	PF-65	PF-66	PF-67	PF-68	PF-69	PF-70						
3	10	1	13	280	786	664	236	40	0	0	0						

Field populations: Circulation strike (<MS-60), 30,000; circulation strike (MS-60+), 2,000; Proof, 550.

1876 Cent Production: Cent mintage dipped quite a bit in 1876. This was not due to lack of demand. On the contrary, the issuance of cents from the Mint was more than 13 million pieces. In addition to the nearly eight million *new* cents produced, 5,599,500 older cents were released back into circulation. The older coins had been redeemed under the Mint Act of 1871.

Survivability: 1876 cents stayed in circulation and are usually found well worn. This is a popular date with collectors and is one of the tougher dates to find in most grades.

Collecting Challenges: These are very scarce and desirable. It is difficult to locate problem-free examples. Coins of this era are frequently found with oil or water strike-throughs, resulting in missing detail on otherwise well-struck coins, or depressions in the field.

Collecting Circulated Pieces: The Optimal Collecting Grade is VF-20. Problem-free examples are very difficult to locate. Most are in very low grades. Search out coins with smooth, chocolate-brown-colored surfaces.

Collecting Mint State Pieces: The Optimal Collecting Grade is MS-64RB. Many of these have average strikes. It might be a challenge to locate an example with all the qualities you desire. Full red examples are more readily available than might be expected. Many come from an original roll that surfaced in the 1970s.

Collecting Proof Issues: This issue is more readily available than the scarce 1875, about equal to the 1873 Proof. A small percentage of these are one-sided Proofs. These are similar to other Proofs in their striking qualities and obverse surface quality. However, the reverse die was roughly polished, leaving numerous heavy die striations in the field.

Overall, the quality of this issue is quite good. Gems are easily found, as are full red examples. Cameo gems are very scarce.

Varieties: There are no varieties known for this year. A Shallow N example was reported but has been verified to be counterfeit (see page 238).

A Snapshot of the Year 1877

On January 4 Commodore Cornelius Vanderbilt died, leaving a fortune in excess of $100 million to his 38-year-old widow and 10 children, with his 56-year-old-son William Henry Vanderbilt being the chief beneficiary.

On March 4 Rutherford B. Hayes took office as president, voted in by commission over Samuel Tilden, who had won the popular vote. The *Washington Post*, founded later in the year, would refer to Hayes as "His Fraudulency" when discussing "the crime of 1876." Meanwhile, the nation's economic slump, which had commenced in 1873, continued.

The first Bell telephone was sold in May, and by August there were 778 instruments in use. The first commercial telephone switchboard was installed on May 17 in the Boston office of the Holmes Burglar Alarm Service.

The Chase National Bank was founded on September 12, taking its name from the late Salmon P. Chase, secretary of the Treasury under Abraham Lincoln. Years later in a merger it would become the Chase-Manhattan Bank. The bank would eventually acquire and exhibit (in a special museum) the Money of the World Collection, previously owned by numismatist Farran Zerbe, later donating the coins to the Smithsonian Institution.

In Hartford, Connecticut, Augustus Pope opened the first bicycle factory in the United States, manufacturing velocipedes in the penny-farthing style. Years later he would produce automobiles. In the meantime, bicycling would become a fad in America, particularly during the 1890s, when numerous clubs were formed.

In late November Thomas Edison demonstrated a hand-cranked tinfoil-covered phonograph, regaling listeners with a recording of "Mary Had a Little Lamb." Seeing the phonograph as an office machine and not an entertainment device, the inventor would spend the next 15 years or so marketing it as a dictation technology.

With the continuing slump in the national economy, activity was slow at the U.S. Mint. Only 20 Proof specimens were struck of each of the gold denominations in 1877, and likely some went unpurchased. Nickel three-cent pieces, Shield nickels, and twenty-cent pieces were not minted for circulation, and the only specimens made were Proofs for collectors. This was the first full year of silver coins in circulation since 1861.

1877 INDIAN HEAD CENT

CIRCULATION MINTAGE:
852,500

PROOF MINTAGE:
EST. 900+

Enlarged 1.5x—Actual Size: 19mm

Market Values • Circulation Strikes and Proof Strikes

G-4	VG-8	F-12	VF-20	EF-40	AU-50	MS-60BN	MS-63RB	MS-64RB	MS-64RD
$625	$800	$1,200	$1,600	$2,200	$2,600	$3,400	$4,000	$7,500	$17,500
MS-65RB	MS-65RD	MS-66RD	PF-60RB	PF-63RB	PF-64RB	PF-64RD	PF-65RB	PF-65RD	PF-66RD
$13,500	$45,000	$125,000	$3,500	$4,000	$4,500	$5,000	$5,000	$12,500	$17,500

Certified Populations

G - VF	EF-40	EF-45	AU-50	AU-53	AU-55	AU-58	MS-60	MS-61	MS-62	MS-63	MS-64	MS-65	MS-66	MS-67	MS-68	MS-69	MS-70
3,050	401	301	153	49	128	127	34	26	87	487	1,133	954	98	0	0	0	0
<PF-60	PF-60		PF-61		PF-62		PF-63		PF-64		PF-65		PF-66	PF-67	PF-68	PF-69	PF-70
1	7		8		36		341		998		918		208	22	0	0	0

Field populations: Circulation strike (<MS-60), 5,000; circulation strike (MS-60+), 500; Proof, 600.

1877 Cent Production: This is the rarest date in the Indian Head cent series. The low mintage of 852,500 accounts for its relative rarity, but the real reason for its scarcity is tied to the economy of the time and its effects on the redemption program called for in the Mint Act of 1871.

Since 1873 the country had been suffering from a severe depression. By 1877, 27% of the working population was jobless, and those who did have jobs saw their wages cut, in many cases nearly in half.

Other major events made this one of the toughest years, economically, since the Civil War. The reconstruction of the South was terminated as a bargaining chip in the controversial election of Rutherford B. Hayes. A nationwide railroad strike crippled the economy further and brought with it the birth of the modern labor movement.

This had a very important impact on the redemption of the minor coinage. Huge amounts of these coins flooded back to the Mint. Enough nickel three-cent and five-cent pieces were turned in that, except for Proofs, the Mint stopped production of those denominations. Nearly 10 million cents were turned in to the Mint this year, of which 9,821,500 were reissued (see further discussion under 1871). In addition to the reissues, the number of cents minted was the smallest since 1823.

Survivability: Even with a mintage close to one million pieces, the number of surviving 1877 cents is unusually low. Only two obverse dies and a single reverse die are known on circulation-strike examples. The single reverse die is of the Shallow N style last used in 1872. It suffered only a minor die clash, and no die cracks, over its lifetime striking of 1877 cents. The average die life during this era has been calculated to be 150,000 to 250,000 pieces. This "miracle die" could not possibly have struck all the cents minted this year without totally deteriorating or busting into pieces. There might have been more than one reverse die used but presently no others are known. The 1878 Mint report says that three obverse and six reverse dies were in stock for coinage of cents, but then says that only two reverse dies were used, and the four remaining dies were used in 1878. This additional die may be one of the Proof dies.

There are a few possibilities for the missing coins, including:

1. Perhaps the Mint record shows examples struck with 1876 dies early in 1877. This practice was common in the early 1800s but was not standard procedure in 1877.

2. Perhaps three-fourths of the original mintage was destroyed, leaving not one coin from additional die pairs as evidence of their existence.

The fact remains that the purported original mintage of this date appears to be way too high compared to the number of observed surviving examples. An upper estimate of 200,000 coins struck seems more accurate. Very few of these were saved at the time. Taken with the 10 million reissued cents, this estimated mintage amounts to only 5% of the total released by the Mint this year. This coin was scarce from the day it was issued.

Collecting Challenges: This is the top coin on every Indian Head cent collector's list. Due to the high cost and difficulty in finding acceptable coins, many collectors reduce their standards and buy anything to fill the void. I suggest waiting until the right coin becomes available. Cost should be a secondary consideration. Attractive coins will serve their owners very well when it comes time to sell. This date is always expensive.

Collecting Circulated Pieces: The Optimal Collecting Grade is F-12. It is very difficult to find accurately graded examples, especially in Extremely Fine or About Uncirculated grades. Dealers and grading services tend to grade this date liberally because of its rarity. Properly graded coins often carry a significant premium over pieces reported in pricing guides.

The diamond detail on the lower ribbon is usually shallow and is quickly worn down to only three diamonds. It is very difficult to find full-diamond examples in circulated condition. When found they command an added premium.

Problems such as rim dents, scratches, and unnatural color may be acceptable if the price reflects the problem. If fully priced, wait for a problem-free example. Many coins, actually Fine or Very Fine, have been wire-brushed to simulate mint luster. These are dangerous to buy, as they have a very low resale value.

Counterfeits: Counterfeits are numerous for this date. Luckily, there are only two obverse dies and one reverse die known on authentic pieces. If the diagnostics for these are known, the counterfeits will be easy to spot. Coins with altered dates are typically altered from 1879- or 1875-dated coins. Both these dates always have the Bold N reverse. False-die counterfeits are typically seen with a reverse die that was transferred from a common-date coin, also with the Bold N reverse. Even though the majority of counterfeits are found with the Bold N reverse, this should not condemn all 1877 cents found with this style reverse. The Proofs of this year all have the Bold N reverse, so it is possible that a circulated Proof might be mistaken for a fake. The best protection is to buy coins certified and authenticated by a major grading service. It is strongly recommended that you purchase this date from a reputable dealer who offers a guarantee, has a return policy, and is easy to locate. This will protect your investment.

Collecting Mint State Pieces: The Optimal Collecting Grade is MS-63RB. Look for well-struck examples with even coloration. Although the diamond detail for this issue is typically shallow, it is usually fully visible on well-struck Uncirculated coins. The best indicator for a full strike is full feather tips. Minor problems are acceptable if they are reflected in the price. Problem-free examples are highly sought after and will generally get higher premiums than expected.

Although the 1872 and 1871 cents are rarer in full red condition, this date is much pricier due to higher collector demand. Beware of cleaned examples. Because of the great difference between red-brown and full red examples, there is a temptation for unscrupulous individuals to lighten the color in an attempt to get a higher premium.

Perhaps the finest 1877 Indian Head cent is the example pictured on page 135 from the collection of Stewart Blay. This coin set a record price when it sold uncertified for $71,300 in Stack's Americana sale, January 1999. Today it is graded MS-66RD by PCGS. Stewart Blay can easily boast of having the finest collection of small cents (Flying Eagle, Indian Head, and Lincoln) ever assembled.

Collecting Proof Issues: All Proofs of this year are struck with Bold N reverse dies. Three obverse dies were used along with three reverse dies. One of the reverse dies has a bulging right pennant of the T in CENT. This is a die first used in 1872 and is found on some examples from all dates from that year until 1878.

The actual mintage of Proof cents for this year (and all years prior to 1878, for that matter) is unknown. Walter Breen in his 1977 *Complete Encyclopedia of U.S. and Colonial Proof Coins* gave a figure of 510+ coins as the mintage. Research by R.W. Julian revised the estimate to 900. The 510 figure is the quantity of complete sets sold, not including gold issues. At least 400 smaller sets of only the nickel and copper coins were also distributed. These numbers represent coins sold, not produced. It is likely that at least 1,500 coins were produced, with the remaining unsold pieces being destroyed or released into circulation. The quantity of survivors in population reports is similar to the 1876 issue.

Examples are usually readily available, and these are priced much higher than other Proof issues of similar rarity due to date-collector demand. However, prices are much lower than the Mint State circulation-strike issue. Some collectors will substitute a Proof 1877 for a circulation strike if the price differential is too great.

The issue is typically found with slightly subdued mirrors. One of the die pairings is weak on the right side. Some are found singly struck; these will have rounded edges. (Proofs are normally double struck, giving them very sharp edges.) Enough coins are usually available for collectors to be able to find a suitable example, without problems. Gems are also available, but cameo examples are quite scarce.

Varieties: There are no varieties known for this year. Collectors might want to acquire both the Proof and circulation-strike issue as an example of the Bold N and Shallow N reverse-design styles.

An example is known struck on a copper-nickel one-centavo piece from Venezuela. It is graded MS-61 by NGC. In 1876, 10 million one-centavo coins were struck for the Venezuelan government at the Philadelphia Mint.

A SNAPSHOT OF THE YEAR 1878

American business remained in a slump in 1878, still feeling the after-effects of the Panic of 1873. More than 10,000 businesses failed this year.

On Wall Street, the value of gas company stocks fell in reaction to Thomas Edison's development of cheap methods to produce and transmit electricity. Edison tinkered with more than 500 potential materials for a practical incandescent bulb filament (finally settling on carbon in 1879).

White Soap—later to be renamed as *Ivory Soap*—was introduced by Procter & Gamble in Cincinnati. Later, its ability to float in water would result by accident: a workman left a machine on through his lunch break, frothing the soap mixture and adding air to it.

The South and West were hit by two epidemics this year. One swept through Deadwood, in Dakota Territory, where smallpox beleaguered the population. Martha Jane Canary nursed the sick—no shrinking violet, her "Wild West" reputation would bring her the nickname Calamity Jane. Elsewhere, in the Gulf Coast, yellow fever raged, killing an estimated 15,000 people, including 4,500 in New Orleans.

On the market on December 17, 1878, greenback Legal Tender Notes achieved par with gold and silver (this would have happened soon anyway, by a law mandated to take place on January 1, 1879). For the first time in American history, paper dollars, gold dollars, and silver dollars all had the same real value.

At the Philadelphia Mint, production of nickel three-cent pieces, Shield nickels, and twenty-cent pieces was limited to Proofs for collectors. None of these coins were made for circulation in 1878. The trade dollar—a commercial coin intended, since its introduction in 1873, for trade with the Orient—was struck in San Francisco and Carson City this year, with Proofs made in Philadelphia.

Since 1873, no silver dollars had been struck for domestic commerce. The gold dollar had become the nation's unit coin. Resumption of coinage of the silver dollar was authorized by the Act of February 28, 1878, known as the Bland-Allison Act. George T. Morgan designed the new silver dollar, which would be struck from 1878 through 1904, and then again in 1921.

Calamity Jane
Known for her riding and shooting skills, Calamity Jane would eventually join Buffalo Bill's Wild West traveling show. In 1903 she died and was buried next to her old companion, Wild Bill Hickock.

1878 Morgan Dollar
George Morgan's famous silver dollar is one of the most popular of all United States coins. It debuted in 1878.

1878 INDIAN HEAD CENT

CIRCULATION MINTAGE:
5,797,500

PROOF MINTAGE:
2,350

Enlarged 1.5x—Actual Size: 19mm

Market Values • Circulation Strikes and Proof Strikes

G-4	VG-8	F-12	VF-20	EF-40	AU-50	MS-60BN	MS-63RB	MS-64RB	MS-64RD
$32	$40	$55	$80	$160	$225	$300	$380	$550	$1,200
MS-65RB	MS-65RD	MS-66RD	PF-60RB	PF-63RB	PF-64RB	PF-64RD	PF-65RB	PF-65RD	PF-66RD
$1,000	$2,750	$6,000	$350	$450	$500	$750	$500	$1,500	$3,500

Certified Populations

G - VF	EF-40	EF-45	AU-50	AU-53	AU-55	AU-58	MS-60	MS-61	MS-62	MS-63	MS-64	MS-65	MS-66	MS-67	MS-68	MS-69	MS-70
68	63	54	46	10	38	48	41	32	80	726	2,113	1,208	214	1	0	0	0
<PF-60	PF-60	PF-61	PF-62	PF-63	PF-64	PF-65	PF-66	PF-67	PF-68	PF-69	PF-70						
1	4	4	30	330	1365	1045	157	11	0	0	0						

Field populations: Circulation strike (<MS-60), 50,000; circulation strike (MS-60+), 3,500; Proof, 1,200.

1878 Cent Production: The quality of cents improved in 1878. Since 1864, the Mint had been purchasing all its copper planchets from private businesses (usually Scovill Manufacturing in Waterbury, Connecticut, although they were not the sole provider). Yearly bids were asked for the planchet contract. Competition came from Benedict & Burnham Brass & Copper Co., also of Waterbury. This year more than eight million older cents were redeemed and issued alongside the nearly six million new cents.

Survivability: This is a very difficult date to locate in the upper circulated grades. Apparently the coins were released into circulation and stayed there well into the 20th century. However, enough of the coins escaped circulation that finding this date in Mint State is relatively easy.

Collecting Challenges: This is one of the last dates many collectors locate for their Extremely Fine and About Uncirculated sets. Collectors need to target this date to ensure finding a problem-free example.

Collecting Circulated Pieces: The Optimal Collecting Grade is EF-40, with full diamond detail on the lower ribbon. Examples in grades below Fine are easy to locate; however, finding examples in About Uncirculated is very difficult.

Collecting Mint State Pieces: The Optimal Collecting Grade is MS-64RB. These are usually available in all grades and are well struck. Search for examples with attractive eye appeal.

Collecting Proof Issues: The typical Proof from this year is well made; this is one of the more readily available dates in gem full red. Cameo examples are easier to find for 1878 than for most other dates.

From this date on, mintage figures are of actual coins produced as accounted in the report of the director of the Mint. Earlier, mintages of Proof minor coins were calculated from sales records of minor coin sets plus the production of silver sets (which had been recorded since 1859), or simply guessed at.

Starting about 1878, coin dealer David U. Proskey began a practice of purchasing the unsold cent, nickel three-cent, and five-cent Proof coinage from the Mint. This eventually grew into a vast hoard, which probably contained hundreds of each date of Proof cents from 1878 onward. In the 1920s these were sold to F.C.C. Boyd, who later sold them to Howard MacIntosh of Tatham Coin Co. in Springfield, Massachusetts. By this time many of the coins had toned to vivid iridescent blue colors. Apparently the coins were kept in original Mint paper wrappers, which imparted this unusual tone. The Tatham Coin Co. marketed these in their advertisements as iridescent Proofs. These coins are encountered occasionally today and are very hotly contested when they are found.

Varieties: The three varieties known include a repunched date (Snow-1), misplaced date (Snow-2), and reverse doubled die (Snow-3). None of these are under any great collector demand.

A Snapshot of the Year 1879

Midwest United States farmers prospered in 1879 as a crop failure in Europe brought high demand for American wheat. In Brooklyn, the Echo Farms Dairy introduced an innovation to the domestic scene: the milk bottle. Before this year, milk had been poured into customers' pitchers.

The artificial sweetener saccharine was discovered by accident at The Johns Hopkins University in Baltimore this year.

Under the Bland-Allison Act the federal government continued to purchase millions of ounces of unneeded silver from American mines, and Colorado saw big growth in its mining boom towns, including Central City, Black Hawk, Georgetown, and Leadville.

George B. Selden filed a patent this year (it would not be granted until 1895) for a road machine powered by an internal combustion engine. At the turn of the century he would hobble the infant automobile industry in the United States by demanding royalties from manufacturers.

1879 Flowing Hair Stella

Frank Winfield Woolworth laid the cornerstone in empire of five-and-dime stores when he established a counter at which all merchandise cost five cents. "Twenty nickels make a dollar, you know," he said. Woolworth borrowed $400 to open a store in Utica, New York, but it failed in three months. Undaunted, he opened a similar store in Lancaster, Pennsylvania—and went on to change the face of retail sales in America.

1879 Coiled Hair Stella

The pattern Stella or $4 gold coin was first struck in 1879 as a proposal for international coinage. A few more than a dozen Proofs were made of Charles E. Barber's Flowing Hair design, followed by a supplemental coinage of 400 to 600 more of the same date in 1880. Stellas were also struck of George T. Morgan's Coiled Hair design, but in smaller numbers (probably fewer than 20).

Almost 20 years after being shut down during the Civil War (in 1861), the New Orleans Mint finally struck coins again in 1879.

◆

1879 Cent Production: The mintage during this period increased significantly. In addition, more than three million redeemed coins were reissued alongside the new coins. Starting this year, the Mint cut back on the production of all coinage except cents, silver dollars, and gold issues. The coinage crisis from the Civil War was over. The paper greenback was now fully redeemable in gold. The massive amounts of silver coinage struck the previous five years, together with large quantities of coins struck between 1853 and 1860, were now available in excessive quantities in commerce. After December 17, 1878, gold coinage circulated for the first time since 1861.

1879 INDIAN HEAD CENT

CIRCULATION MINTAGE:
16,228,000

PROOF MINTAGE:
3,200

Enlarged 1.5x—Actual Size: 19mm

Market Values • Circulation Strikes and Proof Strikes

G-4	VG-8	F-12	VF-20	EF-40	AU-50	MS-60BN	MS-63RB	MS-64RB	MS-64RD
$8	$12	$18	$38	$70	$80	$90	$120	$250	$400
MS-65RB	MS-65RD	MS-66RD	PF-60RB	PF-63RB	PF-64RB	PF-64RD	PF-65RB	PF-65RD	PF-66RD
$500	$1,250	$3,750	$225	$375	$450	$600	$500	$1,350	$3,000

Certified Populations

G - VF	EF-40	EF-45	AU-50	AU-53	AU-55	AU-58	MS-60	MS-61	MS-62	MS-63	MS-64	MS-65	MS-66	MS-67	MS-68	MS-69	MS-70
31	37	35	47	5	33	24	59	20	106	1,024	2,623	1,790	300	12	0	0	0
<PF-60	PF-60	PF-61	PF-62	PF-63	PF-64	PF-65	PF-66	PF-67	PF-68	PF-69	PF-70
6	8	10	39	377	1163	1203	571	71	10	0	0

Field populations: Circulation strike (<MS-60), 250,000; circulation strike (MS-60+), 7,000; Proof, 1,300.

Survivability: 1879 is the first of the semi-common dates in the series. Examples are widely available in all grades, as are all dates from here on, with the exception of the San Francisco Mint coinage at the end of the series.

Collecting Challenges: Coins are readily available with minimal searching. These are typically well struck. Finding attractive coins with minimal problems should be the goal here.

Collecting Circulated Pieces: The Optimal Collecting Grade is AU-50. Problem-free examples can be difficult to locate, as dealers can find them very easy to sell, leaving only the "second tier" of quality coins to choose from. Waiting for the right coin is advised.

Collecting Mint State Pieces: The Optimal Collecting Grade is MS-65RB. These are quite easy to locate in all grades. When buying certified coins, select coins with good eye appeal and few problems. Uncertified coins above MS-63 should be carefully inspected for original color.

Collecting Proof Issues: Mintage figures escalated during this period. This issue is the highest-mintage Proof up until this date; this and many of the dates in the next decade are the common dates in the Proof series. Full red gem 1879 Indian Head cents are about as common as any date in the series.

Two of the three known Proof dies show repunching on the date. One of these, with wide repunching on the 8 and 9 to the right, is also found on regular-production coins (Snow-1). It was not unusual for Proof dies of this era to later be put into use for regular-production coins. After a very short time at the regular-production speed the dies lost their mirrored finish and produced coins that look like normal Mint State pieces.

Varieties: There are three repunched dates known for this date. Snow-1 is struck from dies earlier used on Proof issues.

A SNAPSHOT OF THE YEAR 1880

According to the decennial census, in 1890 the United States' population stood at 50,155,783. The nation boasted 87,800 miles of railway in operation. Canned fruits and meats began to appear in stores. Thomas A. Edison and Joseph W. Swan independently developed the first practical electric lights.

After a Republican deadlock over nominating President Ulysses S. Grant to run for an unprecedented third term, convention delegates selected James Abram Garfield to represent the party on the 36th ballot. Garfield defeated Democrat Winfield Scott Hancock, a military officer with no political experience, in the November election with one of the smallest popular vote margins in history (10,000 votes). However, Garfield won the *electoral* vote easily, perhaps due to Hancock's lack of political savvy.

Many newspapers adopted the halftone photographic illustration process, using pictures composed of tiny dots. In time, this method would replace steel engravings and other processes. Singer sewing machines and McCormick reapers began to dominate their respective markets, and Andrew Carnegie developed the first large steel furnace.

Popular books published in 1880 included *Ben-Hur*, by General Lew Wallace, governor of the New Mexico Territory; and *Five Little Peppers and How They Grew*, by Margaret Sidney (nom de plume of Harriet Mulford Stone Lothrop). Folktales earlier published in the *Atlanta Constitution* were compiled into *Uncle Remus: Legends of the Old Plantation*, the first of many books of the popular stories. The author, a young copyeditor at the newspaper named Joel Chandler Harris, sought only to document the folklore and did not believe the tales would have lasting historical value.

The United States Mint continued to produce numerous metric patterns in 1880, as well as Flowing Hair and Coiled Hair $4 Stellas.

Cyrus McCormick
The inventor's reaper would revolutionize farming in America.

◆

1880 Cent Production: The mintage of cents for 1880 more than doubled compared to the previous year. This was the highest-production year since 1863. Quality was very high, for the most part. Many of the date punches used had broken elements that imparted digits with missing sections; the majority of these were later corrected.

Survivability: Although one of the largest production years of the 1880s, this issue circulated widely. The vast majority of coins wore down to low grades before being withdrawn from circulation and melted during the early 1900s; however, enough pieces survived to satisfy collector needs in all grades.

Collecting Challenges: Search out problem-free coins regardless of the grade level desired.

Collecting Circulated Pieces: The Optimal Collecting Grade is AU-50. Select pieces with a full strike and even, natural color.

1880 INDIAN HEAD CENT

CIRCULATION MINTAGE:
38,961,000

PROOF MINTAGE:
3,955

Enlarged 1.5x—Actual Size: 19mm

Market Values • Circulation Strikes and Proof Strikes

G-4	VG-8	F-12	VF-20	EF-40	AU-50	MS-60BN	MS-63RB	MS-64RB	MS-64RD
$5	$7	$8	$11	$26	$90	$110	$130	$175	$350
MS-65RB	MS-65RD	MS-66RD	PF-60RB	PF-63RB	PF-64RB	PF-64RD	PF-65RB	PF-65RD	PF-66RD
$450	$1,100	$3,750	$250	$325	$400	$600	$500	$1,350	$3,000

Certified Populations

G - VF	EF-40	EF-45	AU-50	AU-53	AU-55	AU-58	MS-60	MS-61	MS-62	MS-63	MS-64	MS-65	MS-66	MS-67	MS-68	MS-69	MS-70
21	31	18	55	6	31	23	62	22	99	925	2,592	1,604	285	1	0	0	0
<PF-60	PF-60	PF-61	PF-62	PF-63	PF-64	PF-65	PF-66	PF-67	PF-68	PF-69	PF-70						
5	9	10	53	517	1,402	1,180	500	82	0	0	0						

Field populations: Circulation strike (<MS-60), 300,000; circulation strike (MS-60+), 8,000; Proof, 1,500.

Collecting Mint State Pieces: The Optimal Collecting Grade is MS-65RB. Find an example with exceptional eye appeal. Examples with vibrant luster and a high percentage of red color are usually in high demand.

Collecting Proof Issues: As one of the higher mintages of the series, this issue should be classified and priced at the common "type" price. Vividly toned examples are in high demand and sometimes garner exceptional prices. These are usually a deep cobalt blue or purple. Although these coins are typically graded with a BN (for *brown*) designation, they trade at RB to RD price levels or even greater if the toning is exceptional.

The 1880 Proof Indian Head cent is occasionally available with a cameo contrast. Such pieces are highly sought after and usually get good premiums over non-cameo examples.

Varieties: The Snow-1 variety has a very wide off-center clash mark on the reverse. A semi-circular impression from an obverse die is seen curving from the N in CENT through the E in ONE, towards the upper-right wreath. Apparently, this interesting and rare variety was caused by an obverse die that possibly fell out of the hammer position of the press onto the face of the reverse die. This variety also features a slight doubled LIBERTY on the obverse. This is one of the most interesting and popular varieties of the Indian Head cent series.

1880 Snow-1
(Off-Center Clash)
Enlarged 2x—Actual Size: 19mm

A SNAPSHOT OF THE YEAR 1881

Three different presidents lived in the White House in 1881, the only year to hold that distinction. Rutherford B. Hayes stepped down on March 4, the day James A. Garfield took the oath of office. On July 2 Garfield was wounded by a gunshot from a rejected office-seeker; the president died on September 19 after weeks of poor medical care resulting in infection. Succeeding him in office was his vice president, Chester Alan Arthur.

In this year the Wharton School of Finance was established at the University of Pennsylvania by a gift from businessman Joseph Wharton, who for years had been the sole refiner of nickel in the United States. A close friend of politicians and Mint officials, it was Wharton who had successfully lobbied for the creation of the nickel five-cent coin in 1866.

On the entertainment front, the Barnum & Bailey Circus was created by a merger between Phineas T. Barnum's traveling show and that of John Anthony Bailey. Big business in the United States, 19th-century circuses usually moved from city to city in special railroad cars.

Because earlier silver coins were still abundant in circulation and in the Treasury's vaults, the U.S. Mint struck relatively few new dimes, quarters, and half dollars in 1881. The Mint created a new pattern design that would eventually be used on the Liberty Head nickel.

P.T. Barnum
The famous showman would be immortalized on the 1936 Bridgeport, Connecticut, Centennial half dollar.

1881 Cent Production: The 1881 issue is very similar in mintage quantity and production quality to the 1880 issue. The date shape seemed to be in a transition phase this year. Between 1872 and 1880 the date punch had a straight base, but after 1881 the dates were curved. In 1881 only, the date punch had the first pair of digits straight and horizontal while the second pair of digits were straight but at an angle to the horizontal digits.

Survivability: This issue was placed into circulation and stayed there for many years. Most examples that survived are in very low grades. The odd original roll or long-time accumulation (yes, they had "penny jars" back then) is the main source of high-grade examples today.

Collecting Challenges: Selecting a problem-free and eye-appealing example is the main goal of collectors. The 1881 cent is normally well struck, but many pieces have mushy details. This is caused by extreme die wear. Die wear results as the dies strike thousands of coins. The friction of the planchets against the face of the die causes the

1881 INDIAN HEAD CENT

CIRCULATION MINTAGE:
39,208,000

PROOF MINTAGE:
3,575

Enlarged 1.5x—Actual Size: 19mm

Market Values • Circulation Strikes and Proof Strikes

G-4	VG-8	F-12	VF-20	EF-40	AU-50	MS-60BN	MS-63RB	MS-64RB	MS-64RD
$5	$6	$7	$10	$20	$30	$60	$90	$200	$350
MS-65RB	MS-65RD	MS-66RD	PF-60RB	PF-63RB	PF-64RB	PF-64RD	PF-65RB	PF-65RD	PF-66RD
$425	$1,100	$3,750	$250	$325	$375	$600	$500	$1,350	$3,000

Certified Populations

G - VF	EF-40	EF-45	AU-50	AU-53	AU-55	AU-58	MS-60	MS-61	MS-62	MS-63	MS-64	MS-65	MS-66	MS-67	MS-68	MS-69	MS-70
20	18	14	28	4	19	19	47	15	72	802	2,700	1,768	364	25	0	0	0

<PF-60	PF-60	PF-61	PF-62	PF-63	PF-64	PF-65	PF-66	PF-67	PF-68	PF-69	PF-70
9	15	8	38	316	1,138	1,333	666	97	10	0	0

Field populations: Circulation strike (<MS-60), 300,000; circulation strike (MS-60+), 8,000; Proof, 1,500.

surface to abrade. This constant abrasion causes minute radial grooves called *flow lines*, which create a cartwheel effect when the coin is slowly turned in a strong light source. This is desirable, as it contributes to the eye appeal of the coin, but too much die wear will cause design elements to disappear. For many collectors, die state is as important as strike and condition.

Collecting Circulated Pieces: The Optimal Collecting Grade is AU-50. Select problem-free examples. Collectors tend to discount problems (such as corrosion, large hits, and scratches) much less than dealers do. As a result, a "bargain"-priced coin with corrosion might in fact be priced much higher than one can ever hope of recovering when the time comes to sell.

Collecting Mint State Pieces: The Optimal Collecting Grade is MS-65RB. As with other dates in the early 1880s, it is possible (with patience) to find attractive eye-appealing coins without too much trouble.

Collecting Proof Issues: 1881 was another high-mintage year. This is a common date and is typically priced with no premium. It makes an affordable date for type collectors who want only one example to show off the design. Examples are usually attractive, with above-average mirrors. Cameos are a bit tougher to find than in earlier dates. Spots are a problem with this issue, as many 1881 cents were not stored carefully over the years. This applies in general to many of the Proofs of this era. Vivid toning is occasionally seen and is worth a substantial premium.

Varieties: Only seven minor repunched dates are known for this year. No major varieties exist.

A SNAPSHOT OF THE YEAR 1882

In 1882 Congress passed a new Immigration Act placing a tax of 50 cents on all aliens landing at U.S. ports. The money was collected to defray expenses associated with immigration and the care of new immigrants. Authorities were also given the right to deny entry to "convicts (except those convicted of political offences), lunatics, idiots and persons likely to become public charges." The Chinese Exclusion Act, passed by Congress in 1880, took effect in 1882 and remained in force for 10 years. Prejudice against the Chinese would continue for several decades.

On October 2, William H. Vanderbilt made the undiplomatic remark of "The public be damned" to a reporter of the *Chicago Daily News*, adding fuel to the fire of widespread antagonism against the "robber barons" of industry. The Standard Oil Trust was incorporated by John D. Rockefeller and his associates, bringing 95% of the American petroleum industry under one roof.

P.T. Barnum brought the elephant Jumbo to Madison Square Garden. Barnum had purchased the pachyderm, "the largest elephant in or out of captivity," from the Royal Zoological Gardens for $10,000. While the British weren't happy about this development, Americans flocked to see the elephant until he met an untimely demise, hit by a freight train in Ontario in 1885. To this day, Jumbo's name is an adjective for unusually large size.

On September 4, electricity was used for the first time to illuminate large sections of New York City. Power was generated by the Edison Illuminating Company, financed by J.P. Morgan. However, urban conditions were crude by today's standards. In 1882, only 2% of the homes in New York were connected to a water main, and nearly all private houses had privies in their backyards.

Jesse James, the notorious outlaw who was then living under the name of Thomas Howard, was shot and killed by a friend who sought to claim a large cash reward for James, "dead or alive."

In sports, the American Baseball Association was founded and the last bareknuckle championship boxing match took place.

General Tom Thumb
Decades before Barnum made Jumbo famous for his great mass, the impresario had made a household name of General Tom Thumb, billed as the world's smallest man. By 1882 Tom Thumb was wealthy and retired from show business. He would pass away the following year at the age of 46.

1882 Indian Head Cent

CIRCULATION MINTAGE:
38,578,000

PROOF MINTAGE:
3,100

Enlarged 1.5x—Actual Size: 19mm

Market Values • Circulation Strikes and Proof Strikes

G-4	VG-8	F-12	VF-20	EF-40	AU-50	MS-60BN	MS-63RB	MS-64RB	MS-64RD
$5	$6	$7	$10	$20	$30	$60	$90	$175	$350
MS-65RB	MS-65RD	MS-66RD	PF-60RB	PF-63RB	PF-64RB	PF-64RD	PF-65RB	PF-65RD	PF-66RD
$350	$1,100	$3,750	$250	$325	$375	$1,000	$500	$2,500	$5,000

Certified Populations

G - VF	EF-40	EF-45	AU-50	AU-53	AU-55	AU-58	MS-60	MS-61	MS-62	MS-63	MS-64	MS-65	MS-66	MS-67	MS-68	MS-69	MS-70
19	26	16	39	3	23	21	36	31	100	741	2,717	1,883	391	2	0	0	0

<PF-60	PF-60	PF-61	PF-62	PF-63	PF-64	PF-65	PF-66	PF-67	PF-68	PF-69	PF-70
2	8	10	34	285	1,241	1,163	603	120	0	0	0

Field populations: Circulation strike (<MS-60), 300,000; circulation strike (MS-60+), 8,000; Proof, 1,000.

1882 Cent Production: This is another high-mintage date of the 1880s; the quality of these coins is usually high.

By this time new issues from the last few years dominated the cents in circulation. The redemption program started in 1871 was essentially ended. Many of the older bronze cents had been redeemed and melted or reissued. Now only spoiled cents were being turned in. Copper-nickel cents still in circulation continued to be redeemed and melted.

Survivability: Much of this issue went into circulation and remained there. Most wore down to low grades before being removed from commerce. The few that survived by chance are typically above average for this era.

Collecting Challenges: Seek out problem-free and attractive examples.

Collecting Circulated Pieces: The Optimal Collecting Grade is AU-50. This date should easily be found in most grades. Most are well struck. Finding problem-free examples should be the main concern.

Collecting Mint State Pieces: The Optimal Collecting Grade is MS-65RB. This issue can easily be found in most grades. Full red examples may be difficult to find without spots or detracting problems. True gems are very tough to locate. Prices for this date in all grades are similar to those of the 1880 through 1883 issues.

Collecting Proof Issues: 1882 is another high-mintage Proof issue, one of the easiest dates to find. However, examples graded PF-65RD and higher are very difficult to find. On the other hand, this is the most available date with vivid blue toning. Perhaps a larger percentage of this date remained in the Proskey hoard compared to other dates. (See 1878 for details on this hoard.)

Varieties: Snow-6 is a very popular and rare variety, with the bases of numerous 1 digits in the neck and pearl necklace. Of all the major varieties, this is one of the most elusive.

A Snapshot of the Year 1883

On March 3, 1883, Congress voted to build three new warships, the first constructed since the Civil War. In the intervening years, America had fallen to 12th place among sea powers of the world.

On May 24 the Brooklyn Bridge opened in a special ceremony, linking Brooklyn and Manhattan through one of the engineering wonders of the world. At the time, it was the longest suspension bridge in the world (half again as long as any previously built), took 14 years to complete, and cost 27 lives. One hundred years later it was designated a National Historic Engineering Landmark.

William Cody, a.k.a. Buffalo Bill
His popular traveling show glorified the American West.

On the entertainment scene, William H. Vanderbilt, age 34, son of Commodore Vanderbilt, threw a $250,000 party at his Fifth Avenue mansion to the delight of the social set, perhaps a precursor to other lavish spending in the coming years. William Cody's traveling entourage, "Buffalo Bill's Wild West Show," opened at Omaha, Nebraska and went on to achieve great fame, enchanting Americans with dramatizations of the rough and ready cowboy life. Two years later, 25-year-old Annie Oakley joined the show and earned renown for her sharpshooting prowess, including shooting holes in cards and tickets. For many years, admission tickets punched by theater owners as free passes would be known as *Annie Oakleys*.

Liberty Head Nickel
In 1883 the Shield nickel design was replaced by Charles Barber's Liberty Head motif.

The first vaudeville theater opened in Boston, Massachusetts, and the first rodeo was held in Pecos, Texas.

Robert Louis Stevenson's *Treasure Island* saw print in book form, and Mark Twain's *Life on the Mississippi* was published from the world's first significant book manuscript submitted typewritten.

In 1883, in Roselle, New Jersey, the first standardized incandescent electric lighting system employing overhead wires began service, built by Edison Electric Light Company. Canadian and U.S. railroads instituted five standard continental time zones, ending the confusion of hundreds of local times.

In Philadelphia, *Dye's Coin Encyclopædia* was published: an immense volume of 1,152 pages and more than 1,500 illustrations. With its wide distribution, the book promoted the hobby of coin collecting in an era in which few textbooks or price guides were available.

1883 INDIAN HEAD CENT

CIRCULATION MINTAGE:
45,591,500

PROOF MINTAGE:
6,609

Enlarged 1.5x—Actual Size: 19 mm

Market Values • Circulation Strikes and Proof Strikes

G-4	VG-8	F-12	VF-20	EF-40	AU-50	MS-60BN	MS-63RB	MS-64RB	MS-64RD
$5	$6	$7	$10	$20	$30	$60	$90	$175	$350
MS-65RB	MS-65RD	MS-66RD	PF-60RB	PF-63RB	PF-64RB	PF-64RD	PF-65RB	PF-65RD	PF-66RD
$350	$1,100	$3,750	$250	$325	$375	$1,000	$500	$3,000	$5,500

Certified Populations

G - VF	EF-40	EF-45	AU-50	AU-53	AU-55	AU-58	MS-60	MS-61	MS-62	MS-63	MS-64	MS-65	MS-66	MS-67	MS-68	MS-69	MS-70
31	28	26	37	3	38	26	47	24	89	717	2,581	1,909	483	47	0	0	0
<PF-60		PF-60		PF-61		PF-62		PF-63		PF-64		PF-65		PF-66		PF-67	
8		25		14		65		569		1,686		1,969		716		206	

<PF-60	PF-60	PF-61	PF-62	PF-63	PF-64	PF-65	PF-66	PF-67	PF-68	PF-69	PF-70
8	25	14	65	569	1,686	1,969	716	206	0	0	0

Field populations: Circulation strike (<MS-60), 350,000; circulation strike (MS-60+), 8,000; Proof, 1,700.

1883 Cent Production: This is the highest-mintage date of the 1880s for both Proof and circulation-strike formats. The circulation-strike production continued the record mintages of the previous three years. The high Proof production was due to the increased sales of minor coinage sets. These sets included, along with the cent and nickel three-cent piece, one of three types of five-cent nickel designs. Collectors who ordered their sets early in the year got a four-piece minor Proof set with both the old Shield design and the new Liberty Head design. The new nickel lacked the word CENTS, which was added to a revised design included in the Proof sets by June. Collectors who ordered early had to reapply to get the five-piece set containing the nickel with the word CENTS. A number of dealers speculated on the popularity of the nickel five-cent pieces and bought many coins of this issue.

Survivability: 1883 Indian Head cents mostly went into circulation and stayed there. Most of the remaining examples are in very low grades. Mint State survivors are plentiful, but many were not cared for properly over the years. Gem survivors are difficult to find.

Collecting Challenges: Search out attractive problem-free examples. Many of these will have mushy details due to extended die wear. Examples with crisp details are always preferred.

Collecting Circulated Pieces: The Optimal Collecting Grade is AU-50. While the large mintage ensures plenty of examples in all grades, finding attractive examples in Extremely Fine and About Uncirculated is rather difficult.

Collecting Mint State Pieces: The Optimal Collecting Grade is MS-65RB. The 1883 issue is similar in rarity to the 1880 to 1882 dates. On all high-grade examples of this era, beware of uncertified coins offered at premium prices. The practice of artificially lightening the color of a coin to full red is seen more and more often as the values escalate.

Collecting Proof Issues: As the high-mintage date of the 1880s, 1883 holds the banner as being the common coin. However, survivability of the cents is quite low, as many buyers of the day were more interested in the nickel five-cent coinage. Dealers who had bought large quantities of the minor sets for the nickel five-cent pieces had quantities of the cent for decades. Many of these were stored in envelopes or mint wrappers, and over the years the coins toned to red-brown or brown. Some of these toned to the highly desirable wild iridescent-blue. Examples in full red are quite difficult to find. Due to the higher mintage, early-die-state examples with cameo contrast form a smaller percentage and are a bit harder to find.

Varieties: The best variety of this year is the Snow-1, which shows the base of a numeral 1 sticking out of the neck, below the first pearl. On a few other dies, a defective digit punch shows a bit of an extra 3 above the digit. Since this defective digit punch was pressed into a number of dies, it is not considered an important variety.

A SNAPSHOT OF THE YEAR 1884

Like that of 1880, the 1884 presidential election saw a close race in popular votes (only 20,000 votes separated the top candidates) and a decisive electoral victory. New York Governor Grover Cleveland led the Democrats to their first victory since 1856, defeating contender James G. Blaine, long-term congressman from Maine.

The Washington Monument was completed after 36 years. When the capstone was set in December, it was the tallest structure in the world, holding that title until 1889, when the Eiffel Tower was finished in Paris. In 1884 the cornerstone of another monument, the Statue of Liberty, arrived in New York Harbor.

A severe earthquake occurred off the northeast Atlantic coast. Estimated today at 5.5 on the Richter scale, the quake's effects extended from southern Maine to central Virginia and west to Cleveland, Ohio. In other environmental news, the water hyacinth was first introduced in the United States. The free-floating aquatic perennial, native to South America, quickly became an invasive species when unchecked.

Moxie Nerve Food was compounded in Lowell, Massachusetts by Augustion Thompson, M.D., a native of Maine. Later, Dr. Thompson carbonated the "cure-all" and marketed it as a drink simply named Moxie. The claims of wonder-drug status remained until federal laws forced the removal of such extravagant declarations. By the 1930s, "moxie" had become slang for strength, energy, courage, and mental sharpness. Moxie outsold Coca-Cola (first formulated in 1886) in its primary trading area, New England, until the 1920s.

The Federation of Organized Trades and Labor Unions made the first U.S. proclamation for eight-hour workdays on May 1, now designated International Workers' Day. While the proclamation led to labor unrest in the years to follow, it eventually succeeded in gaining official sanction of the shorter workday.

In the field of entertainment, visitors to the New York seaside resort at Coney Island were enchanted by the new roller coaster.

In August, *Mason's Monthly Illustrated Coin Collector's Magazine* offered for sale a group of 200 Proof sets dated from 1860 to 1883, containing between one and 45 sets (the latter from 1878) of each year, the lot costing $800.

The Adventures of Huckleberry Finn
Mark Twain's popular novel was published in 1884. (Painting by Tom Newsom)

◆

1884 Cent Production: For four years the Mint had pumped out record numbers of cents. Now it slowed production to about half the previous year's emission.

Survivability: These coins were mostly placed in circulation, and stayed there for long periods. Most are lower-grade circulated pieces. Examples that escaped circulation or destruction are slightly scarce in comparison to the earlier four years. In fact, the

1884 Indian Head Cent

CIRCULATION MINTAGE:
23,257,800

PROOF MINTAGE:
3,942

Enlarged 1.5x—Actual Size: 19mm

Market Values • Circulation Strikes and Proof Strikes

G-4	VG-8	F-12	VF-20	EF-40	AU-50	MS-60BN	MS-63RB	MS-64RB	MS-64RD
$5.50	$6.50	$9	$14	$27	$38	$75	$120	$200	$600
MS-65RB	MS-65RD	MS-66RD	PF-60RB	PF-63RB	PF-64RB	PF-64RD	PF-65RB	PF-65RD	PF-66RD
$450	$2,250	$5,000	$250	$325	$375	$600	$500	$1,350	$3,000

Certified Populations

G - VF	EF-40	EF-45	AU-50	AU-53	AU-55	AU-58	MS-60	MS-61	MS-62	MS-63	MS-64	MS-65	MS-66	MS-67	MS-68	MS-69	MS-70
12	25	17	34	3	25	26	41	23	71	599	2,315	1,781	433	13	0	0	0
<PF-60	PF-60	PF-61	PF-62	PF-63	PF-64	PF-65	PF-66	PF-67	PF-68	PF-69	PF-70						
5	9	3	41	290	1,306	1,551	974	209	0	0	0						

Field populations: Circulation strike (<MS-60), 200,000; circulation strike (MS-60+), 8,000; Proof, 1,700.

percentage of Mint State survivors of any date of the 1880s is very small compared to the number of coins minted.

Collecting Challenges: Search for attractive examples with sharp details. Avoid problems such as corrosion and heavy spots. Toning should be even and attractive.

Collecting Circulated Pieces: The Optimal Collecting Grade is AU-50. Search out attractive, problem-free examples. Avoid cleaned coins at full price. Many collectors attempt to color-match their sets—striving to get all the coins in a chocolate brown color, for instance. A cleaned coin will usually not blend in well with original coins.

Collecting Mint State Pieces: The Optimal Collecting Grade is MS-65RB. Choose attractive coins with even coloration. These will usually come well struck, so the main problem is selecting the right eye appeal. Although a tougher date to find than those of 1880 to 1883, the survivors are nearly as plentiful as those dates. The rarity of these coins in high grades depends more on the chance survival of even as small a quantity as a few rolls.

Collecting Proof Issues: This is another high-mintage date. It is one of the easiest dates to locate in PF-63RB to PF-65RD. Full red gems are plentiful. Cameo examples may be a bit difficult to find but not prohibitively so. Carbon spotting plagues many coins from this decade. The size and placement of spots is usually the determining factor between one that is attractive or unattractive. Copper is a highly reactive metal and care should always be taken to handle these coins very carefully. Prior to modern plastic encapsulation these coins could easily develop spots by careless collectors talking over their exposed collections.

Varieties: There are only a few minor varieties known for this year: one misplaced date and two repunched dates.

A Snapshot of the Year 1885

In the autumn of 1885, Chicago's first skyscraper, the Home Insurance Company building, opened to the public, creating a sensation. The Statue of Liberty, reduced to 350 individual pieces in 214 crates, arrived in New York Harbor. It took four months to reassemble her.

The premier issue of *Good Housekeeping* was published this year. Parker Brothers was founded in Salem, Massachusetts. Its first game, *Banking*, was released without thought that 50 years later another game, *Monopoly*, would make the company a fortune. The United States Playing Card Company manufactured Bicycle Playing Cards for the first time. George Eastman invented and manufactured flexible photographic film designed to load on roll holders.

By 1885 nickel three-cent pieces were still being minted but were fading in popularity, as were gold dollars and $3 gold pieces. The famous 1885 trade dollar was struck not as part of the year's regular coinage, but for collectors; none were listed in the Mint director's annual report.

Bald Eagle
In 1885 the National Audubon Society was formed. The group would go on to attract countless bird lovers, including, years later, President Theodore Roosevelt. (Vignette from a $3 note of 1853, Mechanics Bank, Georgetown, DC)

1885 Cent Production: Planchets this year were ordered from the firm of James Watson & Son. Their last shipment arrived on February 20; no new planchet deliveries were made until 1887. Coinage for both the cent and five-cent denominations was halted on February 16 and did not resume until late 1886. As a result it is probable that the planchets on hand were used for two years of cent production. Mintages for 1885 and 1886 fell to roughly half the normal amount, a low for the decade.

Survivability: Although today 1885 is recognized as a relatively scarcer date, this was not recognized until the coins were in circulation for many years. Most cents of this year are well worn. Any examples that survived extensive circulation were likely originally saved by happenstance. Numerous treasures could be found in the bottom of a 50-year-old "penny jar." Most of the Uncirculated pieces are from random accumulations.

Collecting Challenges: Since the 1885 date will be slightly more difficult to locate than others of the era, you should target it early in your search. These usually come well struck, so avoid weak and problem pieces.

1885 Indian Head Cent

CIRCULATION MINTAGE:
11,761,594

PROOF MINTAGE:
3,790

Enlarged 1.5x—Actual Size: 19mm

Market Values • Circulation Strikes and Proof Strikes

G-4	VG-8	F-12	VF-20	EF-40	AU-50	MS-60BN	MS-63RB	MS-64RB	MS-64RD
$8	$9	$15	$28	$65	$75	$110	$200	$300	$750
MS-65RB	MS-65RD	MS-66RD	PF-60RB	PF-63RB	PF-64RB	PF-64RD	PF-65RB	PF-65RD	PF-66RD
$700	$2,250	$5,500	$250	$325	$400	$750	$500	$3,000	$6,500

Certified Populations

G - VF	EF-40	EF-45	AU-50	AU-53	AU-55	AU-58	MS-60	MS-61	MS-62	MS-63	MS-64	MS-65	MS-66	MS-67	MS-68	MS-69	MS-70
9	27	22	37	3	36	37	31	24	71	705	2,066	1,470	326	20	0	0	0
<PF-60	PF-60	PF-61	PF-62		PF-63		PF-64		PF-65		PF-66		PF-67		PF-68	PF-69	PF-70
8	8	8	36		231		1,159		1,356		916		193		30	0	0

Field populations: Circulation strike (<MS-60), 150,000; circulation strike (MS-60+), 5,000; Proof, 1,200.

Collecting Circulated Pieces: The Optimal Collecting Grade is AU-50. Search for well-struck, problem-free pieces. Due to its higher demand, some dealers may find it easy to push their grading on this date. Make sure you don't get overexcited about finding a bargain-priced coin of this date. Chances are it is not as great a deal as you may think. An overgraded coin is likely an overpriced coin.

Collecting Mint State Pieces: The Optimal Collecting Grade is MS-64RB. Full red gems are very hard to locate. It is not the most difficult date of the decade to find—that honor goes to 1888 and 1889. Many 1885 cents come with vibrant luster and a sharp strike. Most examples are red-brown.

Collecting Proof Issues: Although this is another high-mintage date, they have not survived the decades very well. Most collectors of the time sought the Proof issues only to satisfy their date collections. Many old-time collections with intact Proof sets may have vibrant gems in all other denominations, but the cent will have toned dark brown. In fact, the majority of this issue is found with a deep, even, brown color (sometimes with vivid blue toning). It is very difficult to find full red examples, and examples with deep cameo contrast are very tough to find.

Varieties: Only a few minor varieties are known.

A Snapshot of the Year 1886

In 1886 the United States' labor movement received worldwide attention and gained its first martyrs in Chicago's Haymarket Massacre. The disaster began with a May 1 strike calling for an eight-hour workday. On May 3, police fired into a crowd of striking laborers, killing four and wounding others. The next day, at a peaceful mass meeting held to protest police brutality, an unidentified person threw a bomb, police fired into the crowd, and more casualties were added to the list. In the trial that followed, seven labor leaders were condemned to death.

This was the year that B.F. Keith and Edward F. Albee joined together to form a vaudeville circuit. During the next three decades, the Keith, Orpheum, and other circuits would book traveling troupes into theaters they owned in cities large and small. Albee gained control of the enterprise and ruled the virtual monopoly with an iron fist, earning him dislike from many in the industry. Vaudeville entertainment varied and usu-

A Monumental Gift

On October 28, 1886, the Statue of Liberty (a gift from France more formally known as *Liberty Enlightening the World*) was dedicated on Bedloe's Island, renamed Liberty Island, in New York Harbor. She would be featured on a commemorative silver dollar 100 years later.

ally consisted of musical and magic acts, skits, comedy, and other antics. The typical patron paid 10¢ to 30¢ to attend, depending upon seat location.

Richard Warren Sears entered the merchandising business in Minnesota by buying a group of watches that had been refused by a local jeweler, thus setting the stage for Sears, Roebuck & Co., and the soft drink Coca-Cola was sold for the first time in Atlanta, Georgia.

1886, TYPE I INDIAN HEAD CENT

CIRCULATION MINTAGE:
EST. 14,000,000 TYPE I CENTS
(OF 17,650,000 TOTAL)

PROOF MINTAGE:
EST. 2,500 TYPE I CENTS (OF 4,290 TOTAL)

Enlarged 1.5x—Actual Size: 19mm

Market Values • Circulation Strikes and Proof Strikes

G-4	VG-8	F-12	VF-20	EF-40	AU-50	MS-60BN	MS-63RB	MS-64RB	MS-64RD
$6	$8	$20	$55	$140	$160	$200	$225	$450	$1,150
MS-65RB	MS-65RD	MS-66RD	PF-60RB	PF-63RB	PF-64RB	PF-64RD	PF-65RB	PF-65RD	PF-66RD
$1,150	$4,500	$7,500	$250	$325	$425	$950	$500	$3,500	$6,500

Certified Populations

G - VF	EF-40	EF-45	AU-50	AU-53	AU-55	AU-58	MS-60	MS-61	MS-62	MS-63	MS-64	MS-65	MS-66	MS-67	MS-68	MS-69	MS-70
31	56	37	55	8	42	45	35	24	80	335	1,038	562	114	15	0	0	0
<PF-60	PF-60	PF-61	PF-62		PF-63		PF-64		PF-65		PF-66		PF-67		PF-68	PF-69	PF-70
0	0	0	4		60		170		170		120		20		0	0	0

Field populations: Circulation strike (<MS-60), 200,000; circulation strike (MS-60+), 6,000; Proof, 1,000.

Type I and Type II identification: The change in the design this year was not noticed by collectors until 1954. The redesign by Charles Barber only slightly altered the shape of the portrait, and slightly lowered the relief. The reason for the change may have been the elimination of the extra outlines found on Longacre's master die since the 1864 With L design was introduced. Extra outlines are found on many of Longacre's designs. They are light shelves around the devices and letters. As a master die artifact, these were transferred to each hub that was made. The dies made from these hubs did not always have this detail. It depended on whether the dies were sunk deep enough to show it clearly.

Collectors usually call the different styles *Type I* (or *Type 1*) and *Type II* (or *Type 2*). The use of the Roman numeral rather than the Arabic numeral is more custom than convention. A seldom used, but more accurate, way to describe the difference would be *Type of 1885* and *Type of 1887*. Some grading services and collector-album makers use *Variety 1* and *Variety 2*, as does the Red Book. In my opinion this might confuse collectors, as the difference is considered to be not an individual *die* variety, but a minor design change.

Extra Outlines

The easiest way to determine the difference is the placement of the last feather in relation to the ICA in AMERICA. On a Type I coin, the feather points between I and C. On a Type II coin, the feather points between C and A. While these differences are well known, many collectors have trouble remembering which definition fits which design. I would recommend thinking of the feather as a clock hand, with the Type I being an earlier "time" than the Type II. Comparison with earlier and later dates will also help.

1886, Type I Cent Production: Overall this is a scarcer date in the context of the decade. The further division of this date between the two design styles raises their scarcity even more. The estimated division of the mintage is based on the survivor ratio rather than actual pieces produced.

Although coin production ceased in early 1885, die production did not. Records show 44 dies being made in 1885, and 45 dies in 1886. It is likely that about 75 undated Type I dies were made in early 1885, with only 44 dated 1885. The remaining 30 or so undated dies would then have been dated and used when production started up again in late 1886. Then, to satisfy the demand from the coining department, the Mint made 15 or so more dies of the new design. Both designs could have been struck at the same time.

Survivability: These cents have survived as well as any other date of the 1880s. There was no added collector demand for the date until many years after they were mostly all worn down. Any survivors exist strictly by chance.

Collecting Challenges: These are slightly scarcer than the 1885 issue. Most are well struck. Search for problem-free examples with good eye appeal. Extra effort should be placed in searching for the Type I. Typically, the higher value for the Type II will bring more examples on the market than Type I pieces.

Collecting Circulated Pieces: The Optimal Collecting Grade is AU-50. Beware of cleaned and corroded coins. Choice chocolate-brown coins are very difficult to find.

Collecting Mint State Pieces: The Optimal Collecting Grade is MS-64RB. These are only slightly scarcer than the 1885 issue. Survivors mainly come from the chance find, rather than old-time collector accumulations. Most are well struck with sharp dies. Full red gems are very difficult to find. These are usually similarly priced to the 1885, but in practice are slightly scarcer.

Collecting Proof Issues: The estimated breakdown of the mintage figures between the two types is not known from Mint records. The estimate is based on observed survivors rather than actual production. As one of the highest-mintage dates overall, it would be expected that these would be widely available. This is true only in red-brown grades. Full red examples are rare, with cameo examples very difficult. The planchets for some of this issue come a lighter tan-gold color.

Varieties: Some minor repunched dates are known. None are of any substantial interest. Listings of the Snow variety numbers include the design type as part of the variety identification (*1886 Type I Snow-3*, for example).

1886, Type II Indian Head Cent

CIRCULATION MINTAGE:
EST. 3,650,000 TYPE II CENTS
(OF 17,654,290 TOTAL)

PROOF MINTAGE:
EST. 1,750 TYPE II CENTS (OF 4,290 TOTAL)

Enlarged 1.5x—Actual Size: 19mm

Market Values • Circulation Strikes and Proof Strikes

G-4	VG-8	F-12	VF-20	EF-40	AU-50	MS-60BN	MS-63RB	MS-64RB	MS-64RD
$7.50	$12	$25	$75	$190	$220	$325	$475	$1,100	$5,000

MS-65RB	MS-65RD	MS-66RD	PF-60RB	PF-63RB	PF-64RB	PF-64RD	PF-65RB	PF-65RD	PF-66RD
$4,000	$18,500	$35,000	$200	$350	$950	$5,500	$2,500	$25,000	$40,000

Certified Populations

G - VF	EF-40	EF-45	AU-50	AU-53	AU-55	AU-58	MS-60	MS-61	MS-62	MS-63	MS-64	MS-65	MS-66	MS-67	MS-68	MS-69	MS-70
31	58	39	51	10	43	63	36	23	96	775	1,428	822	84	5	0	0	0

<PF-60	PF-60	PF-61	PF-62	PF-63	PF-64	PF-65	PF-66	PF-67	PF-68	PF-69	PF-70
0	0	0	0	60	130	121	90	20	0	0	0

Field populations: Circulation strike (<MS-60), 80,000; circulation strike (MS-60+), 2,500; Proof, 400.

1886, Type II Cent Production: It is not known when the Mint produced the new obverse master die by Charles Barber, although it was probably made during the hiatus of cent and nickel production early in the year. If so, then the estimated 15 Type II dies dated 1886 would have struck coins at the same time as older Type I dies when coinage resumed. A larger number of coins from the Type II dies show extreme die wear. Perhaps near the end of the year the Mint chose to stretch the life of the dies rather than make more. Dies used to strike Proofs were also put into service to strike regular issues.

Survivability: There was no special significance placed on the Type II style early on, as it was a relatively minor alteration. It was only after 1954 that collectors started to collect these coins as separate entities. As a result, nearly the entire mintage went into circulation and stayed there until they were well worn. The survival of any examples is based on chance rather than from collector hoards. A roll of 50 coins from the same dies appeared in Superior Galleries' section of Auction '81, bringing $30,000. While the

1886, Type I
The last feather points between the I and C in AMERICA.

1886, Type II
The last feather points between the C and A .

appearance of a roll like this greatly altered the relative rarity of this date, it did little to lower the prices. It just made more coins available to collectors.

Collecting Challenges: Quality is quite poor on most of the pieces encountered. Search out pieces struck from an early-die-state die. These will have crisp details and flat fields. Many have been chemically altered by dishonest people seeking to capture the high prices asked for high-grade pieces.

Collecting Circulated Pieces: The Optimal Collecting Grade is EF-40. Select coins with attractive original surfaces. Target this date early on in your collecting, as it will take a while to find an attractive example.

Collecting Mint State Pieces: The Optimal Collecting Grade is MS-63RB. This is one of the tougher dates in all grades. However, as small groups have come to light its rarity has lessened slightly. It is believed that the 50 pieces that came from the Auction '81 roll were mostly full red and all from the same die. These were all later-die-state coins, which have a look likened to melted butterscotch. Another group of 32 1886 Type II pieces was found in 1994 in a bottle buried in Connecticut. Later, they were placed in the Bowers & Merena "Boys Town" sale in March 1998 (lots 353 to 363) where they were graded MS-61RB to MS-64RB. Among these pieces, 18 were of the same variety, Snow-7.

Full red gems are still very rare. Prices for MS-64RD and MS-65RD certified coins have climbed to levels seen only for the top three or four dates in the series.

Collecting Proof Issues: The mintage is estimated from the quantity of known survivors. No official figures break down the division between the two types. The 1886 Type II Proof is prohibitively rare in full red gem condition. Cameo examples are nearly impossible to find. Most available examples are red-brown or totally brown, sometimes with vivid blue toning. The limited quantity of full red coins is curious. Many original coins exhibit a tan-golden color which grading services may find unusual. Perhaps the majority of remaining Proofs at the end of the year were Type II pieces. If so, they may have been purchased by dealers, as was most of the leftover Proof minor coinage. If this is the case, then these would have sat for extended periods in their Mint wrappers, slowly toning to purple or brown.

Some of the five known die pairs used for Proof production were later used on regular coinage.

Varieties: There are a few minor repunched dates. The Snow variety listings must show the design type as well as the variety number (*1886 Type II Snow-3*, for example).

A SNAPSHOT OF THE YEAR 1887

On February 4, 1887, Congress established the Interstate Commerce Commission, making railroads the first industry subject to federal regulation. A related act of Congress, passed in response to public demand, required "just and reasonable" rate changes.

The Pratt Institute opened in Brooklyn, New York (it would go on to train many artists), and the Marine Biological Laboratory was established in Woods Hole, Massachusetts.

In Argonia, Kansas, voters elected Susanna M. Salter as the first female mayor in the United States. A leader in the local Woman's Christian Temperance Union, her nomination was meant to embarrass the organization just weeks after Kansas granted suffrage to women in local elections. The plan backfired and Salter served her term without incident, receiving the sum of one dollar for her service. She declined to run for re-election.

Chester Greenwood of Maine patented an improved version of the earmuffs he had created when he was 15. The inventor went on to patent more than 100 items, including a mechanical mousetrap and a spring steel rake—one of America's 15 Outstanding Inventors, according to the Smithsonian Institution.

By the end of the year there were 200,000 telephone subscribers in America.

A statue of Abraham Lincoln was completed by sculptor Augustus Saint-Gaudens, for Lincoln Park, Chicago. Decades later, millions of Americans would see the artist's dramatic rendition of Miss Liberty on the $20 gold piece struck from 1907 to 1933.

Thomas Edison
Visionary Thomas Edison opened a new laboratory in West Orange, New Jersey, in 1887. He designed and built the facility himself for the quick and economical development of his inventions.

1887 INDIAN HEAD CENT

Enlarged 1.5x—Actual Size: 19mm

CIRCULATION MINTAGE:
45,223,523

PROOF MINTAGE:
2,960

Market Values • Circulation Strikes and Proof Strikes

G-4	VG-8	F-12	VF-20	EF-40	AU-50	MS-60BN	MS-63RB	MS-64RB	MS-64RD
$3	$4	$5	$7	$18	$27.50	$55	$80	$175	$350
MS-65RB	MS-65RD	MS-66RD	PF-60RB	PF-63RB	PF-64RB	PF-64RD	PF-65RB	PF-65RD	PF-66RD
$400	$1,250	$6,000	$250	$325	$400	$2,000	$500	$6,500	$12,500

Certified Populations

G - VF	EF-40	EF-45	AU-50	AU-53	AU-55	AU-58	MS-60	MS-61	MS-62	MS-63	MS-64	MS-65	MS-66	MS-67	MS-68	MS-69	MS-70
59	36	10	30	1	25	34	53	23	113	838	2,064	926	103	22	0	0	0
<PF-60	PF-60	PF-61	PF-62	PF-63	PF-64	PF-65	PF-66	PF-67	PF-68	PF-69	PF-70						
2	11	11	26	342	880	1,049	299	40	0	0	0						

Field populations: Circulation strike (<MS-60), 350,000; circulation strike (MS-60+), 5,000; Proof, 1,000.

1887 Cent Production: Planchets this year and 1888 were supplied by Joseph Wharton's firm. With full-time production restored, the mintage for the year rivaled the record levels of the early 1880s.

Survivability: Cents of 1887 circulated widely and are usually found in medium circulated grades. They are more readily available than dates with similar mintages in the earlier 1880s. Perhaps as more and more cents were struck there was less reason to constantly empty the "penny jar." Regardless of the reason, many more of these later-date cents have survived.

Collecting Challenges: Search out problem-free examples. These tend to be well struck, but many were struck from later-die-state dies. These will be mushy with wavy fields. Die state is not typically a factor in setting the price of a coin, so searching for early-die-state pieces should only cost you extra time.

Collecting Circulated Pieces: The Optimal Collecting Grade is AU-50. Select problem-free examples with original chocolate-brown color.

Collecting Mint State Pieces: The Optimal Collecting Grade is MS-65RB or MS-64RD, which are generally priced similarly. Avoid coins with blotchy or strange toning. Search for full strikes and early die states. Full gems in both red-brown and red are scarce. Full red coins sometimes have a pale tan-golden color (as do some 1886 pieces).

Collecting Proof Issues: The mintage dipped slightly this year, but this does little to change the rarity rating compared to other dates in the 1880s. Many 1887 cents are found with pale tan-golden planchets. Many others have toned to brown, sometimes with vivid iridescent blue toning, which is worth a significant premium. Perhaps many of the issue were left over at the end of the year and were purchased by dealers such as David Proskey, who had been accumulating leftover minor Proof coinage for later sale.

Due to all these factors this date is difficult to find graded full red. Sometimes these are found singly struck, which may hinder the resulting coins from reaching the higher grades. This is one of the toughest dates for collectors of PF-65RD coins. Examples with cameo contrast are exceedingly rare.

Varieties: The Snow-1 doubled die is one of the top 10 varieties of the series. This variety has significant doubling on the right obverse. The doubling is mostly on the central veins of the feathers and OF AMERICA.

1887 Snow-1 (Doubled Die)

A SNAPSHOT OF THE YEAR 1888

In the United States 1888 was long remembered for the Blizzard of '88, which dumped many feet of snow on the Northeast, isolating numerous homes and communities for a week or more. Across the Atlantic, the year was marked by a series of murders in London's Whitechapel district. The crimes of Jack the Ripper presented a mystery that fascinated Americans and was covered by U.S. newspapers.

Post-dedication work on the Washington Monument was completed in Washington, DC, in 1888. Work on this phase of the monument included installation of the iron stairway, a passenger elevator, and windows of the pyramidion (capstone).

The first successful electric trolley cars (their power taken from overhead wires) were introduced for public transportation, in Richmond, Virginia.

National Geographic Magazine was first published in 1888, from there going on to become an American institution. Edward Bellamy's novel *Looking Backward, 2000–1887* envisioned a utopian America, with wealth distributed evenly and citizens enjoying themselves in all pursuits of life. "Casey at the Bat," a poem by Ernest Lawrence Thayer, was printed in the *San Francisco Examiner* on June 3, concluding with its famous line, "There is no joy in Mudville—mighty Casey has struck out."

In 1888 George Eastman introduced the Kodak box camera, an invention that made it possible for amateurs to take photographs. For $25 a shutterbug could buy a Kodak camera loaded with enough film to take 100 snapshots. After sending the camera and film to Kodak headquarters in Rochester, New York, along with $10, the photographer would get the camera back with a new roll of film, plus the developed prints.

In November, Republican Benjamin Harrison was elected president with 233 votes of the Electoral College, compared to 168 for his opponent, Democrat Grover Cleveland. Harrison had taken the lead in primaries held in Maine weeks before the national election, giving rise to the saying, "As Maine goes, so goes the nation."

Benjamin Harrison

Harrison—the grandson of President William Henry Harrison—was elected to the presidency even though he won 100,000 fewer popular votes than Grover Cleveland.

1888, 8 OVER 7 INDIAN HEAD CENT

CIRCULATION MINTAGE:
UNKNOWN; FEWER THAN
30 PIECES ARE KNOWN TO EXIST.

PROOF MINTAGE:
NOT MADE IN PROOF FORMAT

Enlarged 1.5x—Actual Size: 19mm

Market Values • Circulation Strikes

G-4	VG-8	F-12	VF-20	EF-40	AU-50	MS-60BN	MS-63RB	MS-64RB	MS-64RD
$1,000	$1,300	$1,600	$3,200	$6,500	$16,000	$22,000	$27,500	$85,000	—
MS-65RB	MS-65RD	MS-66RD	PF-60RB	PF-63RB	PF-64RB	PF-64RD	PF-65RB	PF-65RD	PF-66RD
—	—	—							

Certified Populations

G - VF	EF-40	EF-45	AU-50	AU-53	AU-55	AU-58	MS-60	MS-61	MS-62	MS-63	MS-64	MS-65	MS-66	MS-67	MS-68	MS-69	MS-70
25	0	0	2	1	1	5	0	0	0	2	21	0	0	0	0	0	0
<PF-60	PF-60	PF-61	PF-62	PF-63	PF-64	PF-65	PF-66	PF-67	PF-68	PF-69	PF-70						

Field populations: Circulation strike (<MS-60), 25; circulation strike (MS-60+), 5.

1888, 8 Over 7 Cent Production: Apparently, one of the 1887 dies was repunched with an 1888 four-digit punch and put into service. The die developed a die break early on and possibly did not last too long, as specimens known from this die are extremely rare today.

Overdates garner much greater collector interest more than other varieties because they are generally collected as part of the regular date series. James F. Ruddy announced the discovered of this variety in the February 11, 1970, issue of *Coin World*. Two examples of the new variety, both Uncirculated, turned up in a small group of Indian Head cents in the attic of a mansion in Virginia. The obvious blob under the last 8 was determined to be the remnant of a 7, and a private search was launched for additional examples. After a few months, the discovery of this variety was announced in the hobby press since no one came forth with additional examples. The editors of *The Numismatist* billed the find as the one of the most important numismatic discoveries of the decade (April 1970, p. 531).

The extensive publicity brought out only one more example (graded Good) within the following year. Confident that this was a very rare variety, the two discovery pieces were offered for $4,950 each in 1971. This was an enormous premium at the time. By comparison, Bowers & Ruddy Galleries offered an 1885 Proof $20 double eagle (worth at least $30,000 today) in the same price list as the 1888/7 cents for $4,295. Eventually dealer Julian Leidman and collector Robert Marks purchased the two discovery pieces.

Survivability: Presently, fewer than 30 examples are known, mostly in low grades. This remains the most coveted variety in the Indian Head cent series and one of the hottest "cherrypicks" for collectors to find in unchecked accumulations.

This variety is so interesting, I will indulge my readers here with some personal experiences with the issue. The present tally of known specimens is as follows:

1. MS-65RD. Reported by Sam Lukes. This piece remains uncertified and last sold for $43,000 in 1991.

168

2. **MS-64RB PCGS. Dr. Thomas Fore Collection.** This example is a beautiful semi-prooflike coin with lots of original red and a contact hit on the cheek. This coin was featured on the cover of the May 1999 issue of *Longacre's Ledger*. Opinions on the effect that the hit has on the grade have differed over time. Prior to 1995, the coin was graded MS-62RB by ANACS. Eagle Eye Rare Coins, my firm (with Brian Wagner as a partner at the time) then purchased the coin from dealership J.J. Teaparty of Boston, for $10,000. Brian and I thought that the coin was certainly undergraded, possibly by as much as two grades. Rather than resubmit it, we quickly sold the coin to a New England collector for $15,000, which was $3,000 below what we thought an MS-63RB was then worth. The deal with the purchaser was that he should submit the coin himself and when it graded MS-63 he could sell it back to us for $18,000 and make $3,000 profit. The first time he submitted it, it graded MS-63RB by PCGS. About a year later he offered the coin to us for $22,500. We were disappointed that he did not offer it for $18,000, but it was his coin, so he had the privilege of setting the price. I said I'd make some phone calls, and in about an hour I pre-sold the coin to another New England collector, Michael (Mick) Arconti, for $25,000. About five minutes after closing the deal, the owner of the coin called up and said that he felt bad about raising the price to me, so he said we could have it for $18,000.

Mick Arconti is one of the many collector friends I've met in this business. He built a beautiful MS-65RD collection of Indian Head cents through my firm during the early 1990s. When he sold his collection, the 1888/7 was one of his real winners. We bought the coin for $35,000 and sold it for $40,000 to Juan X. Suros, who was building a collection of every overdate in the U.S. series. Superior Galleries, in February 1999, auctioned the Suros collection. In that sale, this coin was described as one of the discovery specimens, which it certainly wasn't. It realized $40,250 in the sale and was purchased by Las Vegas dealer David Schweitz. Dave has one of the best eyes in the business and felt, as I had earlier, that it was still undergraded. Upon resubmission it graded MS-64RB by PCGS and was sold into the Dr. Tim Larson collection, perhaps the top Indian Head cent collection ever assembled if one judges by scope as well as high condition.

When Eagle Eye Rare Coins sold the Dr. Larson collection in 2005, the 1888/7 cent set a record by selling for $85,000. It was sold to Dr. Thomas Fore, most likely the top collector of Flying Eagle and Indian Head cent varieties. The Fore Collection boasts the finest die-variety set of Flying Eagle cents, including most all the 1856 cents in top condition.

3. **MS-63BN PCGS.** This coin has a small X-shaped scratch over the first two feathers. It was discovered in Stack's inventory and placed in their Albert W. Savage sale in October 1997 (lot 130). I made a special cross-country trip especially to buy this coin. I conservatively graded it MS-63, but it was all in how severely you judge the small scratch. Bidding opened at an astoundingly low $500 and progressed back and forth in small increments between dealer Anthony Terranova (who was bidding for another dealer in the room) and myself. I finally gave up at $33,000, at which point the room was all abuzz at the hammer price, considering its opening price. The coin graded MS-64BN at NGC and was later offered in Superior Galleries' Pre-Long Beach sale in February 2000. It was later sold into the Thomas Fore collection of Indian Head

cents. Tom downgraded it back to an MS-63 PCGS so he could list it in his registry collection, and also to match the holder with the rest of his collection. He submitted the coin to PCGS with instructions to put whatever grade they felt was appropriate. Given the rarity of the coin, a lower grade was not seen as detrimental to its value—it was still the #3 coin!

4. MS-63RB. One of the two discovery coins, this was sold to Robert Marks in 1971. It was offered in a number of Bowers & Ruddy Auctions in 1972 through 1974. Its whereabouts are presently unknown. It is possibly the ANACS example graded MS-61RB.

5. MS-63RB. This is the second discovery coin. It was sold to dealer Julian Leidman, per Dave Bowers's recollection.

6. AU-58BN PCGS. This was described to me by Bruce Longyear as the most memorable coin he has handled while working for J.J. Teaparty of Boston. He always regretted selling it for only $1,500 in the early 1980s. Brian Wagner and I bought it in 1998 and sold it into the Margene Heathgate collection, which was an outstanding Proof Indian Head cent collection. Ira and Larry Goldberg sold the Heathgate Collection with part of the Benson I Collection in February 2001. The coin sold for $18,400 to a San Francisco Bay area collector, who has one of the top collections as of this writing.

7. AU-58 PCGS. American Numismatic Rarities sale, 2005. This went into a complete AU-58 PCGS collection put together by Chris Lane. The grade of AU-58 is perhaps the most challenging to collect as a set.

8. MS-60 ANACS "Cleaned Net AU-55." This coin has light weakness on the feather tips. It was cherrypicked by large cent specialist Doug Bird in March 1999. It was sold, through Eagle Eye, into the Heathgate Collection for $15,000, but was later traded out for the coin listed above as number 6. It was sold on eBay by Eagle Eye for $10,000 to a Tennessee collector.

9.–13. Five other examples have been reported in About Uncirculated grade.

14.–15. One example known is Extremely Fine. Another, slightly pitted, sold in American Numismatic Rarities' December 2005 Old Colony Sale.

16.–25. An additional 10 examples have been reported in the Good to Very Fine grades.

Collecting Challenges: Obviously this is a rare coin. Only a few collectors are lucky enough to include a decent-grade example in their collection. One must decide if a medium-grade coin is worth the acquisition cost, even if an example becomes available. Due to its rarity, most collectors will have to omit the coin from their collection.

Collecting Circulated Pieces: Examples in Good or Very Good are occasionally available. Be certain the coin is genuine. Many worn 1888 cents with crud on the date look like a phantom 1888/7. See the attribution information below.

Collecting Mint State Pieces: These are seldom available.

Attribution: Most, but not all, 1888/7 cents show a cud (an unstruck area of the coin, where part of the die broke away) in the denticles, about the size of three denticles, at the 9 o'clock position on the obverse. This can be diagnostic and makes for quick attribution at arm's length—very important for cherrypickers to know. Most dealers will get slightly upset if you go through all their 1888 coins with a magnifying glass (they might get even more upset if they find you cherrypicked them!).

One example graded G-4 by PCGS is not the overdate. This is the plate coin in my *Flying Eagle and Indian Cents* (1992), as Snow-3. It was questionable then and has been delisted since. (See "The Continuing Story of the Mis-attributed 1888/7," Richard Snow, *Longacre's Ledger*, Vol. 11.4, December 2001.)

1888/7 Snow-1 (Obverse)
Enlarged 2x—Actual Size: 19mm

1888/7 Snow-1 (Reverse)
Enlarged 2x—Actual Size: 19mm

1888/7 Snow-1 (Detail)

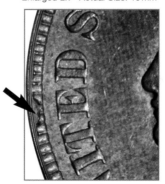

**1888/7 Snow-1
(Cud at 9 o'Clock)**

1888 Indian Head Cent

Enlarged 1.5x—Actual Size: 19mm

CIRCULATION MINTAGE:
37,489,832

PROOF MINTAGE:
4,582

Market Values • Circulation Strikes and Proof Strikes

G-4	VG-8	F-12	VF-20	EF-40	AU-50	MS-60BN	MS-63RB	MS-64RB	MS-64RD
$3	$3.50	$5	$7.50	$22	$27	$65	$125	$300	$1,000

MS-65RB	MS-65RD	MS-66RD	PF-60RB	PF-63RB	PF-64RB	PF-64RD	PF-65RB	PF-65RD	PF-66RD
$950	$3,750	$10,000	$250	$325	$400	$2,000	$525	$6,500	$10,000

Certified Populations

G - VF	EF-40	EF-45	AU-50	AU-53	AU-55	AU-58	MS-60	MS-61	MS-62	MS-63	MS-64	MS-65	MS-66	MS-67	MS-68	MS-69	MS-70
148	36	28	41	2	36	47	42	26	116	1,083	2,470	1,079	92	1	0	0	0

<PF-60	PF-60	PF-61	PF-62	PF-63	PF-64	PF-65	PF-66	PF-67	PF-68	PF-69	PF-70
9	22	13	44	455	874	711	154	41	0	0	0

Field populations: Circulation strike (<MS-60), 200,000; circulation strike (MS-60+), 4,000; Proof, 1,200.

1888 Cent Production: Production remained steady this year. One of the dies had its date repunched over an 1887 die (see 1888, 8 Over 7).

Survivability: There was no incentive for collectors to save this date, so most of the issue went into circulation and remained there until well worn.

Collecting Challenges: This date comes with an average strike, so it would be beneficial to take extra time to find a well-struck example. As with all other later-date Indian Head cents, average-quality specimens are widely available. You should make the extra effort to locate an example with a superior strike.

Collecting Circulated Pieces: The Optimal Collecting Grade is AU-50. Select problem-free examples with exceptional eye appeal.

Collecting Mint State Pieces: The Optimal Collecting Grade is MS-64RB. The rarity of higher-grade Indian Head cents of this era depends on the chance survival of small groups of choice coins. If no original rolls are found then the date becomes rarer in higher grades. Likely, that is what happened to this date. True gems are very tough to find, regardless of the color designation. Full red examples are, of course, even tougher. This date will require extra effort to find nice, high-grade coins.

Collecting Proof Issues: Although this is one of the higher-mintage Proof dates, it remains slightly elusive in high grades. This date is very tough in full red, especially in gem. Cameos are very rare. Some of these come with golden-tan planchets. Most pieces are mostly brown or totally brown. Occasionally, some of these coins graded with the BN (for brown) color designation have vivid blue and purple colors. These are highly desired by collectors. Prices vary widely for these vividly toned coins. Sometimes, in an auction setting, prices for outstanding specimens can skyrocket to many multiples of the prices the typical BN designation warrants.

Many coins of this year are singly struck. This causes the coins to be less than what we expect for Proof issues of the era. Sometimes the feather tips or some of the denticles may show weakness, and rough planchet marks might not get totally struck out. The edge, which is usually sharp, will be highly beveled on singly struck coins. Sometimes singly struck examples with medium mirrors might be mistaken for prooflike circulation-strike coins. Typically, Proofs are double struck at slower speeds to bring out the design to its fullest. This takes time, and one might not be too surprised if the Mint, when producing 4,000+ coins, introduced some time-saving measure at the expense of quality. Perhaps a Mint employee at the time asked himself, "Who would care; after all, they are only pennies!"

Varieties: Aside from the ultra-rare 1888/7 Snow-1, the top variety is the 1888 Snow-2, which is known to numismatists as 1888/7 Die #2, FF 010.7. Noted numismatic author Bill Fivaz discovered the variety in July 1990. It was confirmed at the time and included in my *Flying Eagle and Indian Cents* (1992) as 1888 Snow-2.

1888/888 Snow-2

In 2000 the overdate status was questioned by one of the top collector-specialists, Dr. Tim Larson, in the pages of *Longacre's Ledger* (the publication of the Fly-In Club, the specialty club devoted to this series). Tim convincingly questioned the status of the overdate using overlay photos. It appears that the overdate is most likely just a repunched date: 1888/888. There is a vertical line in the upper loop of

Full-Date 1888 Snow-2

the 8 on this variety, and that did not match up to date overlays that Tim prepared. He suggested that the line was a die scratch. This is still a neat variety with a misplaced digit in the first pearl. Because overdates carry a much higher premium, the label should be placed only on varieties that can be certainly shown to be overdates. (See "1888/7 S2—Is it an Overdate?", Tim Larson, *Longacre's Ledger*, Vol. 10.2, June 2000.)

An example of the 1888 Snow-2 cent is known struck in copper-nickel! The coin is graded by PCGS as a nickel die trial. The coin showed up in 1997 during the ANA Summer Seminar, which I happened to be attending as an instructor. (This is a very worthwhile way to spend a week in the cool Colorado summer sun.) After finishing my class, I sat in with my good friends, J.P. Martin and Bob Campbell, who were teaching the Counterfeit Detection class. They were demonstrating the use of the scanning electron microscope to extract alloy information of coins using x-ray spectroscopy. One of the coins to be tested was an 1888 cent that looked like it was copper-nickel. Sure enough, it tested 25% nickel and 75% copper. After the test I examined the coin and discovered the variety. Everyone was thrilled—and so, I guess, was the owner. Unfortunately the ANA did not tell the owner about the variety. He discovered it independently later. I subsequently found out that East Coast dealer George Maroskos owned the coin. He offered it to me but I declined at the time. I asked to photograph it, and it was put on the cover of *Longacre's Ledger*, Vol. 9.3, August 1999.

The question remains: how did this coin come to be? The firm of Joseph Wharton sold both three-cent and five-cent nickel planchets to the Mint, along with cent planchets. Perhaps three-cent nickel stock was put in the cent blanking press and a few of these odd planchets found their way to the cent press just when the 1888 Snow-2 pieces were being struck. If this is the case, then perhaps there are other pieces yet to be discovered!

It's a new day at ANACS.

ANACS, America's oldest grading service, has undergone some exciting and new changes. We have redesigned our holder to be sleek, stylish, and Crystal Clear™. In addition, we have added new superstar graders to our grading team. In the coming months, be on the lookout for more exciting news from the company you know and trust. It's the dawn of a new day at ANACS.

- The sleek, state-of-the art holder is Crystal Clear™ and durable. It also offers you the unique ability to view the edge of the coin.

- ANACS graders have encyclopedic knowledge of coins backed by more than 125 years of combined grading experience.

- ANACS is The Collector's Choice® because we know what counts: knowledge, integrity, service, and trust. How much we value coin collecting is evident in our work.

A SNAPSHOT OF THE YEAR 1889

At noon on April 22, President Benjamin Harrison opened almost two million acres of former Indian lands in the Oklahoma Territory to white homesteaders. By morning many who arrived earlier—*sooners*, as they were called—had already staked their claims, and by nightfall communities were established at Guthrie, Oklahoma City, and elsewhere.

North Dakota, South Dakota, Montana, and Washington were admitted to the Union this year.

On May 31, a dirt dam burst above the community of Johnstown, Pennsylvania, and in the resulting flood more than 2,000 people were killed. The Johnstown Flood is remembered as one of the worst American disasters of the era, along with the 1871 Chicago fire and San Francisco's 1906 earthquake.

Nellie Bly (Elizabeth Cochrane Seaman), a reporter for Joseph Pulitzer's New York *World*, began her famous quest to beat Jules Verne's fictional character Phileas Fogg's record of traveling around the world in 80 days. She beat the mark by more than a week.

The Wall Street Journal began publication on July 8 as an expansion of a daily financial newsletter issued by Dow Jones & Company. Theodore Roosevelt published the first two volumes of his *Winning of the West*. Roosevelt, a prolific researcher and writer, had a passion for the outdoor life and the American West. Also published in 1889: *A Connecticut Yankee in King Arthur's Court*, by Mark Twain.

The Chicago Auditorium opened on December 9, with President Harrison among those attending. The world's most acclaimed diva, Adelina Patti, sang *Home Sweet Home* as the featured soloist. On another musical note, John Philip Sousa, America's march king, wrote the *Washington Post March* in 1889, naming it after a District of Columbia newspaper.

1889-CC Morgan Dollar
In 1889 the Carson City Mint in Nevada, which had last struck coins in 1885, reopened on July 1 to resume striking gold and silver pieces

1889 INDIAN HEAD CENT

Enlarged 1.5x—Actual Size: 19mm

CIRCULATION MINTAGE:
48,866,025

PROOF MINTAGE:
3,336

Market Values • Circulation Strikes and Proof Strikes

G-4	VG-8	F-12	VF-20	EF-40	AU-50	MS-60BN	MS-63RB	MS-64RB	MS-64RD
$3	$3.50	$5	$7	$20	$25	$60	$80	$175	$600

MS-65RB	MS-65RD	MS-66RD	PF-60RB	PF-63RB	PF-64RB	PF-64RD	PF-65RB	PF-65RD	PF-66RD
$400	$3,500	$8,500	$250	$325	$375	$950	$500	$3,500	$7,000

Certified Populations

G - VF	EF-40	EF-45	AU-50	AU-53	AU-55	AU-58	MS-60	MS-61	MS-62	MS-63	MS-64	MS-65	MS-66	MS-67	MS-68	MS-69	MS-70
25	24	26	44	2	28	25	66	22	100	958	2,816	1,469	88	0	0	0	0

<PF-60	PF-60	PF-61	PF-62	PF-63	PF-64	PF-65	PF-66	PF-67	PF-68	PF-69	PF-70
2	20	7	24	350	885	701	296	1	0	0	0

Field populations: Circulation strike (<MS-60), 300,000; circulation strike (MS-60+), 5,000; Proof, 900.

1889 Cent Production: Mintages start to climb during this era. Planchets this year were purchased from Merchant & Company of Philadelphia. Merchant won the contract with a bid of 26¢ per pound. A slight difference is noticeable in the color of full red examples, which tend to be a bit paler than those of other years.

Survivability: As with the other dates of this era, these were workhorse coins that stayed in circulation long after the design was changed in 1909. High-grade examples survived only by chance.

Collecting Challenges: Select eye-appealing examples without problems, compared to ordinary coins. These mostly come well struck, but with odd or uneven toning.

Collecting Circulated Pieces: The Optimal Collecting Grade is AU-50. Select problem-free examples with exceptional eye appeal. Many collections of circulated Indian Head cents start off from an accumulation, possibly plucked from circulation generations ago. Collections like these tend to start as a hole-filling exercise, which is fun as the set becomes complete. However, a much more rewarding collecting experience comes when a collection is upgraded from average circulated coins to choice circulated examples in the Extremely Fine to About Uncirculated grade range. The object is to search out the ideal coin for each date, taking into account color, strike, and overall quality in addition to the technical grade. In most cases, money spent on carefully selected coins will not be money lost.

Collecting Mint State Pieces: The Optimal Collecting Grade is MS-65RB or MS-64RD. Full reds are scarce, so a 64RD will likely cost more than a 65RB. Gem MS-65RD examples are quite rare. Most have a pale color. Woodgrain toning is prevalent for this issue—a type of toning caused by improperly mixed alloy. (When the planchet strip is rolled out to the correct thickness the pockets of tin and zinc alloy become stretched into streaks.) It will be harder for coins struck from these types of planchets to retain their full red color, so these are usually given a red-brown color designation.

Collecting Proof Issues: These are of average quality, with full red examples very difficult to find. Full red coins are sometimes found with a pale gold color. Full cameo examples are very rare. Curiously, one of the two known die pairs has clashed dies. Clashed dies are caused when the obverse and reverse dies make contact and impart the outline of their designs on each other. Although clashed dies do not alter the desirability of the resulting coins, it is unusual to find them on Proof coins. Many 1889 Proof cents are singly struck. Perhaps quality control was lacking at the Mint this year.

Varieties: Presently 33 different die varieties of interest are known. The best is Snow-1, which has a bold doubled die visible on the right wreath and shield on the reverse. Snow-31 has multiple off-center die clash marks. These show up as a series of dashes (transferred from the denticles of another die) through the O in ONE and C in CENT. Another series of dashes is visible to the left of the E in ONE. The remaining varieties are mostly repunched dates.

A SNAPSHOT OF THE YEAR 1890

In 1890 the federal census made its first use of a computer. Inventor Herman Hollerith, following principles employed in the player piano, Jacquard loom, and other mechanical devices, constructed a machine to process card-punched information.

The census reported the national population at 62,947,714, with two-thirds of Americans living in rural areas. Los Angeles had boomed since 1880, its population growing from roughly 11,000 to 50,000. The richest 1% of Americans earned more income than the poorest 50%. Of the 12 million families in the country, nearly half owned no tangible property. The literacy rate was 87%.

In this year Congress passed the Sherman Anti-Trust Act to curtail "restraint of trade or commerce" and limit the powers of monopolies, which at the time had a stranglehold on certain sectors of the American economy. (Vigorous "trust busting" would not take place until the first decade of the 20th century.) The Sherman Silver Purchase Act set new guidelines for government purchase of silver. William Jennings Bryan won election as a congressman from Nebraska, his first public office. Known as "the silver-tongued orator of the Platte," he would seek and receive the Democratic presidential nomination in 1896, 1900, and 1908. Each bid would be unsuccessful.

1890 Morgan Silver Dollar
The Sherman Act of 1890 replaced the Bland-Allison Act of 1878. Both were essentially government subsidies to silver mining interests. Together, the two acts added some 570 million silver dollars to the nation's holdings.

In November the London banking firm of Baring Brothers failed, pushing British investors to liquidate many of their American securities. Across the Great Pond this caused a short-lived panic on Wall Street; the British were America's dominant foreign investors. (During the 1890s they would capitalize much of the mining in Colorado's Cripple Creek District.)

In 1890 Wyoming joined the Union as the 44th state.

In South Dakota the one-sided Battle of Wounded Knee saw more than 350 Sioux Indians killed by nearly 500 federal soldiers. Their defeat effectively ended Native American resistance to white encroachments.

Charles Dana Gibson, who became America's pre-eminent illustrator of women during the 1890s and early 1900s, created the Gibson Girl, who made her debut in *Life* magazine. Said to personify the ideal "American Girl," she sparked a national craze for illustrations of pretty women.

1890 INDIAN HEAD CENT

CIRCULATION MINTAGE:
57,180,114

PROOF MINTAGE:
2,740

Enlarged 1.5x—Actual Size: 19mm

Market Values • Circulation Strikes and Proof Strikes

G-4	VG-8	F-12	VF-20	EF-40	AU-50	MS-60BN	MS-63RB	MS-64RB	MS-64RD
$3	$3.50	$5	$7	$22	$27	$60	$80	$175	$450
MS-65RB	MS-65RD	MS-66RD	PF-60RB	PF-63RB	PF-64RB	PF-64RD	PF-65RB	PF-65RD	PF-66RD
$400	$1,400	$5,000	$250	$325	$375	$950	$550	$3,500	$5,500

Certified Populations

G - VF	EF-40	EF-45	AU-50	AU-53	AU-55	AU-58	MS-60	MS-61	MS-62	MS-63	MS-64	MS-65	MS-66	MS-67	MS-68	MS-69	MS-70
20	30	26	44	8	29	42	46	19	106	962	2,784	1,069	39	0	0	0	0
<PF-60	PF-60	PF-61	PF-62	PF-63	PF-64	PF-65	PF-66	PF-67	PF-68	PF-69	PF-70						
9	11	11	44	420	1,230	544	43	0	0	0	0						

Field populations: Circulation strike (<MS-60), 375,000; circulation strike (MS-60+), 7,500; Proof, 1,000.

1890 Cent Production: Scovill Manufacturing Company of Waterbury, Connecticut, supplied planchets to the Mint this year. Scovill won the contract with a 20¢-per-pound bid for 500,000 pounds of planchets, which was much lower than the amount that won the contract the year before. One hundred cent blanks weigh one pound, so the contract supplied blanks for about 50 million cents.

Survivability: These coins saw extensive circulation, but enough survived that examples are plentiful in all grades.

Collecting Challenges: Select attractive, problem-free examples. This issue is usually missing some details on the first three feather tips. Otherwise, they are well struck.

Collecting Circulated Pieces: The Optimal Collecting Grade is AU-50. Usually, collectors try to match the color throughout their set. Chocolate brown is the preferred color of circulated coins. In the later years it is easier to find choice-quality coins. Many of these may have a red-brown color. Many collectors include Mint State coins as well.

Collecting Mint State Pieces: The Optimal Collecting Grade is MS-65RB or MS-64RD. Select eye-appealing coins with few problems. Many coins have toned unevenly or were once cleaned.

Collecting Proof Issues: This date is readily available in most grades except in full red. The number of Proofs minted during the 1890s slides to new lows. Collectors mistakenly equate the more common dates struck for circulation as being common in Proof as well. The truth is that many of the dates in the 1890s and 1900s are very tough to find in gem Proof.

Varieties: Snow-1 is an interesting variety and is described as a *quadrupled die*. It shows four distinct outlines on the outer edges of the legend. The Snow-3 has the base of a numeral 1 sticking out of the neck just above the necklace. A total of 16 varieties of interest are presently known, mostly repunched dates.

A Snapshot of the Year 1891

David Kalakaua, king of Hawaii, died on January 20. His portrait had appeared on the famous 1883 Hawaiian silver coins struck at the San Francisco Mint. The king would be succeeded by his sister, Queen Lydia Liliuokalani.

The People's Party, also known as the Populist Party, began in Cincinnati, advocating free and unlimited coinage of silver. Throughout the decade, the "silver question" would be America's most burning political issue.

Thomas Alva Edison filed patents for the radio and a motion picture camera in 1891. Various claimants to the invention of the motion picture, mostly French, predated Edison's American patent, and the precise origin of the medium is still uncertain. Edison would later use strong-arm tactics to discourage independent firms from entering the field.

Carnegie Hall opened in New York City on May 5, the gift of steel baron Andrew Carnegie, who would fund public libraries and other institutions with tens of millions of dollars. Its initial program was music of Tchaikovsky conducted by the composer.

In Springfield, Massachusetts, physical education instructor James Naismith invented basketball—a sport to fill the season between football and baseball.

The Wrigley Company was founded in Chicago, and Stanford University in California opened its doors.

R.I.P The King of Hawaii
David Kalakaua died in 1891. The Hawaiian monarchy would survive only another two years.

The American Numismatic Association was founded in Chicago in October, when a small group of collectors met at the urging of Dr. George F. Heath of Michigan, publisher of *The Numismatist*. The ANA would develop into the world's largest non-profit coin collecting group.

◆

1891 Cent Production: As the mintage indicates, these were produced in lower quantities than cents of 1890.

Survivability: The dates 1889 to 1893 are all of the same basic rarity. These coins circulated extensively for decades, and higher-grade survivors exist mainly by chance. Still, they are fairly common. In Uncirculated grades, the survival of a small hoard of, say, 50 coins (original roll quantity) can alter the availability significantly for a while. Prices usually do not go *down* with the discovery of an original roll, as collector demand will eventually absorb the coins. Many darkly toned coins of this date in MS-63 and MS-64 grades came from a hoard that entered the market in the early 1990s. They seemed to be everywhere for a while, but today the general rarity of this date is still on par with other dates.

1891 INDIAN HEAD CENT

CIRCULATION MINTAGE:
47,070,000

PROOF MINTAGE:
2,350

Enlarged 1.5x—Actual Size: 19mm

Market Values • Circulation Strikes and Proof Strikes

G-4	VG-8	F-12	VF-20	EF-40	AU-50	MS-60BN	MS-63RB	MS-64RB	MS-64RD
$3	$3.50	$5	$7	$22	$27	$60	$80	$175	$450

MS-65RB	MS-65RD	MS-66RD	PF-60RB	PF-63RB	PF-64RB	PF-64RD	PF-65RB	PF-65RD	PF-66RD
$400	$1,250	$5,000	$250	$325	$375	$950	$550	$3,500	$5,500

Certified Populations

G - VF	EF-40	EF-45	AU-50	AU-53	AU-55	AU-58	MS-60	MS-61	MS-62	MS-63	MS-64	MS-65	MS-66	MS-67	MS-68	MS-69	MS-70
45	26	24	41	5	32	28	71	20	108	1,171	2,959	1,282	106	0	0	0	0
<PF-60	PF-60	PF-61	PF-62	PF-63	PF-64	PF-65	PF-66	PF-67	PF-68	PF-69	PF-70						
2	13	8	36	372	1,151	657	136	10	0	0	0						

Field populations: Circulation strike (<MS-60), 350,000; circulation strike (MS-60+), 7,500; Proof, 900.

Collecting Challenges: Select eye-appealing coins with attractive luster. The percentage of red found on Mint State coins may also be a factor, if it fits your goal.

Collecting Circulated Pieces: The Optimal Collecting Grade is AU-50 to MS-63RB. Usually the availability and lower cost of Mint State pieces attract demand from collectors of circulated coins.

Collecting Mint State Pieces: The Optimal Collecting Grade is MS-65RB or MS-64RD. This date is widely available in most grades, including gem full red. Most have an average strike; look for full feather tips.

Collecting Proof Issues: This issue is slightly scarce in high grades. Full red gems are very tough to locate. Many come singly struck with beveled edges. Many come darkly toned with a small percentage of these having vivid purple toning, which is highly desired. Cameo gems are rare.

Varieties: The best variety of this year is the Snow-1 doubled die with strong doubling on the OF and LIBERTY. This variety was discovered in 1990, and very few have been discovered since. Twenty or so other varieties are known, mostly repunched dates, but there are a few doubled-die reverses known. These typically show doubling on the central veins of the wreath, not on the outside edges of the wreath.

1891 Snow-1

A Snapshot of the Year 1892

January 1, 1892, saw the opening of the immigration facility on Ellis Island in New York Harbor. For the next 60 years, 20 million immigrants would pass through its "Golden Door."

The Sherman Anti-Trust Act of 1890 made the Standard Oil Trust illegal, but soon the oil trust continued with a new company, Standard Oil of New Jersey, chartered under liberal state laws. In Pennsylvania a Carnegie Steel Company plant was the scene of a bitter strike and conflict between management and union; in an ensuing fight more than a dozen people were killed.

In Chicago, William Wrigley Jr. began selling chewing gum, and budding architect Frank Lloyd Wright drew up the plans for Charnley House, the first of many houses he would design.

In this year scientific genius Nikola Tesla developed the first practical alternating current motor, and financier J. Pierpont Morgan arranged the formation of the General Electric Company.

Lizzie Borden's father and stepmother were found brutally murdered in their home in Fall River, Massachusetts. Though immortalized in rhyme as a psychopathic killer, Borden would be acquitted at trial.

After a four-year interruption by Benjamin Harrison, Grover Cleveland, running on the Democratic ticket, retook the White House in 1892. Harrison lost re-election because of widespread dissatisfaction with the economy.

In 1892 a ceremony was held for the World's Columbian Exposition, scheduled to open in Chicago to mark the 400th anniversary of Columbus' arrival in America. The Expo itself, however, was delayed until 1893. The first United States commemorative coin, a half dollar, was issued as part of the celebrations.

John Muir on the California State Quarter
In 1892 the conservationist established the Sierra Club.

1892 World's Columbian Expo Half Dollar
The coin would be issued again in 1893.

Charles Barber's New Coins
Amidst the hoopla of the new commemorative half dollar, Barber's 1892 coinage redesign garnered little attention from numismatists.

1892 Indian Head Cent

CIRCULATION MINTAGE:
37,647,087

PROOF MINTAGE:
2,745

Enlarged 1.5x—Actual Size: 19mm

Market Values • Circulation Strikes and Proof Strikes

G-4	VG-8	F-12	VF-20	EF-40	AU-50	MS-60BN	MS-63RB	MS-64RB	MS-64RD
$3	$3.50	$5	$7	$22	$27	$60	$80	$175	$450
MS-65RB	MS-65RD	MS-66RD	PF-60RB	PF-63RB	PF-64RB	PF-64RD	PF-65RB	PF-65RD	PF-66RD
$400	$1,250	$3,500	$250	$325	$375	$600	$550	$1,350	$3,500

Certified Populations

G - VF	EF-40	EF-45	AU-50	AU-53	AU-55	AU-58	MS-60	MS-61	MS-62	MS-63	MS-64	MS-65	MS-66	MS-67	MS-68	MS-69	MS-70
15	27	12	26	4	35	26	45	18	104	1,009	2,718	1,128	112	1	0	0	0

<PF-60	PF-60	PF-61	PF-62	PF-63	PF-64	PF-65	PF-66	PF-67	PF-68	PF-69	PF-70
1	4	10	36	256	1,180	903	287	62	0	0	0

Field populations: Circulation strike (<MS-60), 350,000; circulation strike (MS-60+), 6,000; Proof, 900.

1892 Cent Production: The slightly lower mintage this year is due to a problem in planchet procurement. Earlier, the winning low bid from planchet suppliers was around 20¢ per pound. This year's bids were significantly higher. Scovill Manufacturing was low bidder with a price just under 28¢. Two other bids received were slightly more than 28¢. Mint Director Edward Leach recognized that it was "a put up job" and recommended that all bids be rejected. The Mint struck cents from planchets that were on hand, with additional bronze coming from the melting of older cents and two-cent pieces. Director Leach also recommended that the Mint should start making its own planchets for minor coins.

Survivability: Coins this year survived in roughly the same quantities as those of the previous few years. True gem examples are quite tough to find.

Collecting Challenges: This date comes fairly well struck. Select coins with even color and attractive eye appeal.

Collecting Circulated Pieces: The Optimal Collecting Grade is AU-50 to MS-63RB. Avoid problem coins.

Collecting Mint State Pieces: The Optimal Collecting Grade is MS-65RB to MS-64RD, which should be similarly priced. Certified populations for MS-65RB examples are very low, currently far under the quantity of MS-65RD pieces graded. Perhaps this shows that the source of most high-quality Mint State pieces is perhaps from the chance discovery of one or two original rolls rather than from average accumulations, such as generation-old "penny jars."

Collecting Proof Issues: This date is much more readily available than other dates of the era. Perhaps a select quantity was saved in gem condition, whereas in other years they toned down to brown. We can only guess why. Cameo examples are more readily available than other years, although still scarce.

Varieties: Most of the 13 or so known varieties are fairly minor repunched dates. A few minor reverse doubled dies are known.

A Snapshot of the Year 1893

The Panic of '93 was brought about by continuing poor conditions in American financial markets. The stock market saw a sharp drop on May 5, and collapsed a few weeks later in June. By the end of the year, the resulting depression saw the failure of more than 500 banks, the bankruptcy of 74 railroads, and closing of 15,000 businesses.

The government ended its subsidy to silver, and prices fell. "Free and unlimited coinage of silver" became the rallying cry of politicians who felt that a stronger silver market would help miners, farmers, and other Americans.

Meanwhile, 30-year-old Henry Ford tested his first gasoline-powered automobile, and in Salt Lake City the immense Mormon Tabernacle was dedicated. A six-million-acre tract of land bought by the government from the Cherokees was opened to homesteaders. It was estimated that fewer than 1,100 bison still roamed the United States, a shadow of the countless millions of a few decades earlier. A hurricane hit Savannah, Charleston, and the Sea Islands, leaving 1,000 to 2,000 people dead. The Hawaiian Islands were declared a protectorate of the United States and their queen deposed. In Colorado, women won the right the vote.

A year behind schedule, the World's Columbian Exposition was finally thrown open to the public in 1893. More than 27 million people came to ride the Ferris Wheel, to see the risqué Little Egypt, and to revel in other attractions, including musicals staged by Florenz Ziegfeld, who later created the famous Ziegfeld Follies.

The first to widely publicize the importance Western expansion had on American life was historian Frederick Jackson Turner, who presented his findings to a convention at the Columbian Exposition. Turner suggested that the challenges of the frontier were responsible for developing the American spirit of self-reliance, energy, inventiveness, and realism.

1893 Isabella Quarter Dollar
The country's first and only commemorative quarter was issued for the World's Columbian Exposition. Its obverse honored the Spanish queen who sponsored Christopher Columbus. Its reverse symbolized the industry and creativity of American women.

1893 INDIAN HEAD CENT

CIRCULATION MINTAGE:
46,640,000

PROOF MINTAGE:
2,195

Enlarged 1.5x—Actual Size: 19mm

Market Values • Circulation Strikes and Proof Strikes

G-4	VG-8	F-12	VF-20	EF-40	AU-50	MS-60BN	MS-63RB	MS-64RB	MS-64RD
$3	$3.50	$5	$7	$22	$27	$60	$80	$175	$350
MS-65RB	MS-65RD	MS-66RD	PF-60RB	PF-63RB	PF-64RB	PF-64RD	PF-65RB	PF-65RD	PF-66RD
$350	$800	$3,000	$250	$325	$375	$600	$550	$1,750	$3,500

Certified Populations

G - VF	EF-40	EF-45	AU-50	AU-53	AU-55	AU-58	MS-60	MS-61	MS-62	MS-63	MS-64	MS-65	MS-66	MS-67	MS-68	MS-69	MS-70
7	35	12	26	2	33	26	58	19	92	1,104	3,048	1,925	314	12	0	0	0

<PF-60	PF-60	PF-61	PF-62	PF-63	PF-64	PF-65	PF-66	PF-67	PF-68	PF-69	PF-70
7	8	5	29	453	943	548	248	23	0	0	0

Field populations: Circulation strike (<MS-60), 400,000; circulation strike (MS-60+), 8,000; Proof, 800.

1893 Cent Production: These were made from recoined cents and two-cent pieces. Their quality is average. Many are seen with strike-through depressions caused by some substance on the planchets at the time of striking. Strike-through depressions caused by machine oil or water will leave differing types of depressions, depending on the location of the design elements. A liquid strike-through on the field leaves a small, bright, circular area. If it is on the portrait then the liquid can migrate to the extremities of the design, like the bust point or feather tips. This will show up as weakness with bright luster, but will not be weakly struck, per se.

Survivability: These are about as plentiful as other dates in the era. There was no special reason to save these for many generations after they were struck.

Collecting Challenges: Select problem-free examples with superior eye appeal.

Collecting Circulated Pieces: The Optimal Collecting Grade is AU-50 to MS-63RB. These are plentiful enough that finding a problem-free example should be no problem.

Collecting Mint State Pieces: These are widely available in MS-64RB but much more difficult in MS-65RB, at least for certified examples. A few original rolls turned up in the early 1990s. The average quality of these rolls was MS-64RD, and they tended to have lots of liquid strike-though depressions (see Production notes, above).

Collecting Proof Issues: These are a little scarcer than the common dates, but presently are priced as if they were the commonest date. Gem full red pieces are scarce, as are cameo examples. Vivid purple-toned examples exist and are highly desired by collectors even though they typically are graded "brown."

Varieties: 17 varieties are known, but are mostly minor repunched dates.

A SNAPSHOT OF THE YEAR 1894

On January 8, 1894, a raging fire destroyed many of the abandoned buildings on the Chicago site of the 1893 World's Columbian Exposition.

The nation's financial slump continued, and unemployment and business failures were the news of the day. The decade saw many labor union strikes. On June 18, Congress established the first Monday of every September as Labor Day.

Coca-Cola was sold in bottles for the first time, and Milton S. Hershey marketed his Hershey Bar, launching a reputation that would label Hershey, Pennsylvania as "Chocolate Town, U.S.A." Wilhelm Conrad Roentgen discovered the x-ray, leading to a revolution in medical treatment.

Rudyard Kipling
The author's *Jungle Book*, published in 1894, was a collection of adventurous children's stories set in British-ruled India.

Popular songs and melodies of the day included Popular songs and melodies of the day included "Humoresque," "Sidewalks of New York," and "I've Been Working on the Railroad" (first called the "Levee Song"). Englishman Rudyard Kipling, who at the time was in residence in Brattleboro, Vermont, saw publication of his *Jungle Book*. William Sydney Porter (later known by his nom de plume, O. Henry) published *The Iconoclast*, changing its name to *The Rolling Stone* with the April 28 issue.

At the San Francisco Mint, only 24 dimes were struck this year, creating a numismatic rarity.

1894 Indian Head Cent

Circulation Mintage:
16,749,500

Proof Mintage:
2,632

Enlarged 1.5x—Actual Size: 19mm

1894 • Market Values • Circulation Strikes and Proof Strikes

G-4	VG-8	F-12	VF-20	EF-40	AU-50	MS-60BN	MS-63RB	MS-64RB	MS-64RD
$5	$6	$10	$15	$45	$55	$85	$115	$195	$375
MS-65RB	**MS-65RD**	**PF-66RD**	**PF-60RB**	**PF-63RB**	**PF-64RB**	**PF-64RD**	**PF-65RB**	**PF-65RD**	**PF-66RD**
$375	$800	$3,500	$250	$325	$400	$600	$550	$1,750	$3,500

Certified Populations

G - VF	EF-40	EF-45	AU-50	AU-53	AU-55	AU-58	MS-60	MS-61	MS-62	MS-63	MS-64	MS-65	MS-66	MS-67	MS-68	MS-69	MS-70
13	31	27	33	7	20	39	35	29	85	885	2,466	1,218	174	10	0	0	0

<PF-60	PF-60	PF-61	PF-62	PF-63	PF-64	PF-65	PF-66	PF-67	PF-68	PF-69	PF-70
3	8	9	32	371	1,127	609	221	10	0	0	0

Field populations: Circulation strike (<MS-60), 300,000; circulation strike (MS-60+), 6,000; Proof, 800.

1894 Cent Production: Mintage levels dropped this year to a low for the decade. In 1893 and 1894 an economic depression caused many coins from previous years to be brought out of hiding and into circulation. This caused a glut of cents and nickel five-cent pieces. As a result, coining operations for these denominations ceased in April and did not resume for many months.

Survivability: As the low-mintage date for the 1890s, these are more coveted by collectors, but in reality are not much scarcer than other dates of the era, except in very low grade. Most of the coins of this era stayed in circulation and were saved in higher grades by accident in the same average amounts each year.

Collecting Challenges: Search out problem-free examples with attractive eye appeal. These usually come well struck.

Collecting Circulated Pieces: The Optimal Collecting Grade is AU-50 to MS-63RB. These are popular as a lower-mintage date. This may be a bit tougher date to find for lower-grade Good to VG collections. Check each example for the Snow-1 repunched date (see page 188).

Collecting Mint State Pieces: The Optimal Collecting Grade is MS-65RB or MS-64RD. This is a popular date, and it brings a slight premium above other dates of the era. Most are moderate grades, MS-64RB being widely available, though no more than any other date of this era. Full red examples tend to be an orange-gold. Gems are available and are no rarer than other years of the decade.

Collecting Proof Issues: These come with good mirrors and usually have a good amount of red. Vivid purple-toned examples are slightly tougher to locate than in other dates. Gems are available, and are quite rare with cameo contrast.

Varieties: The Snow-1 repunched date (1894/1894) is one of the top varieties of the Indian Head cent series. Many advanced collectors collect it as part of the regular date set, an honor only given to only a few varieties (the 1867/67, 1869/69, and 1873 Doubled LIBERTY being other examples). This variety is an easily seen repunched date, so examples are easily discovered in low grades. These are usually well struck. A half-roll quantity came on the market in the early 1990s. Most of these pieces were of high quality although they may have numerous little carbon spots.

1894/1894 Snow-1

1894/1894 (S-1) • Market Values • Circulation Strikes

G-4	VG-8	F-12	VF-20	EF-40	AU-50	MS-60BN	MS-63RB	MS-64RB	MS-64RD
$30	$40	$65	$130	$225	$350	$550	$950	$2,000	$6,500
MS-65RB	MS-65RD	MS-66RD	PF-60RB	PF-63RB	PF-64RB	PF-64RD	PF-65RB	PF-65RD	PF-66RD
$4,500	$15,000	—							

A Snapshot of the Year 1895

In 1895 the country's economic health remained poor, with funds in the United States Treasury reserves falling to $41 million. In an effort to ease the nation's problems, bankers J.P. Morgan and August Belmont loaned the government $62 million in gold, against bonds at an attractive rate. Exportation and hoarding made gold somewhat scarce. Gatherings were staged by advocates of free and unlimited coinage of silver to support the diminishing market. In the meantime, gold discoveries in the Cripple Creek District of Colorado brought new supplies of the yellow metal onto the market.

During this year, an estimated 750,000 workers walked off their jobs, demanding higher wages, shorter hours, or both. Coxey's Army, a rag-tag mélange of unemployed laborers, traveled from Ohio to Washington, DC. Although unsuccessful in their attempt to petition Congress, Coxey and his followers garnered much publicity and earned themselves a place in history books.

On May 20, in a converted store at 153 Broadway in New York, an audience is said to have viewed a four-minute film of a boxing match—possibly the first motion picture projected to a paying audience. Many historians, however, contend that this distinction belongs to a film showed in Paris in December.

Elsewhere in New York City, the American Bowling Congress was founded to organize the popular sport, also called box ball. The coming years would bring energized interest and standardized rules. And in another arena, the first professional football game was played in Latrobe, Pennsylvania. The Latrobe YMCA defeated the Jeannette Athletic Club, 12 to 0.

Stephen Crane's Civil War novel, *The Red Badge of Courage*, saw print this year. In a lighter vein, the four-line poem, "The Purple Cow," by Gelett Burgess, was published. "America the Beautiful," by Katherine Lee Bates, made its debut.

"He Had Burned Several Times to Enlist...."
"He had read of marches, sieges, conflicts, and he had longed to see it all. His busy mind had drawn for him large pictures extravagant in color, lurid with breathless deeds." (*The Red Badge of Courage*, published 1895)

1895 INDIAN HEAD CENT

CIRCULATION MINTAGE:
38,341,574

PROOF MINTAGE:
2,062

Enlarged 1.5x—Actual Size: 19mm

Market Values • Circulation Strikes and Proof Strikes

G-4	VG-8	F-12	VF-20	EF-40	AU-50	MS-60BN	MS-63RB	MS-64RB	MS-64RD
$3	$4	$5	$7	$15	$25	$40	$65	$125	$250
MS-65RB	MS-65RD	MS-66RD	PF-60RB	PF-63RB	PF-64RB	PF-64RD	PF-65RB	PF-65RD	PF-66RD
$225	$750	$2,500	$250	$325	$400	$600	$550	$1,350	$3,500

Certified Populations

G - VF	EF-40	EF-45	AU-50	AU-53	AU-55	AU-58	MS-60	MS-61	MS-62	MS-63	MS-64	MS-65	MS-66	MS-67	MS-68	MS-69	MS-70
14	21	9	37	6	27	34	50	24	76	766	2,781	2,040	242	11	0	0	0
<PF-60	PF-60	PF-61	PF-62	PF-63	PF-64	PF-65	PF-66	PF-67	PF-68	PF-69	PF-70						
2	6	5	29	225	802	879	317	24	0	0	0						

Field populations: Circulation strike (<MS-60), 400,000; circulation strike (MS-60+), 8,000; Proof, 750.

1895 Cent Production: Mintages rose this year, and would remain high until the last year of Indian Head cent coinage in 1909.

Survivability: Cents of this year are widely available. As the series drew to a close in the next 14 years, the coins saved from circulation tend to be of a higher quality.

Collecting Challenges: These come well struck and are easily located in most grades.

Collecting Circulated Pieces: The Optimal Collecting Grade is AU-50 to MS-63RB. These are easily found in all grades. Search out a problem-free example. A common problem with all Indian Head cents is cleaning. In years past, when "Brilliant Uncirculated" meant "bright red," many examples were harshly cleaned to meet the expectations of beginner collectors. A quality-conscious collector should get a feel for how an original Uncirculated coin looks—and avoid harshly cleaned pieces, which have little resale value.

Collecting Mint State Pieces: The Optimal Collecting Grade is MS-64RD or MS-65RB. This date is widely available in low grades. Collectors should be cautioned that small imperfections on high-grade coins could hurt their desirability. Collectors impatient to search for high-quality coins should perhaps stick with MS-64RB graded coins.

Collecting Proof Issues: This is a relatively common date even though the mintage is much lower than those of earlier dates. These come with attractive eye appeal more often than other dates. Full red gems are as readily available as those of most other dates, but cameo examples are quite scarce. Of the five Proof die pairs of this year, three of them have repunched dates of varying boldness. Proof collectors tend to be interested strictly in date sets, not varieties, so these do not tend to bring much of a premium.

Varieties: Presently 30 varieties are known; most of these are repunched dates.

A Snapshot of the Year 1896

In 1896 the Supreme Court upheld a Louisiana law furthering racial segregation, and decided that states could provide blacks with "separate but equal" education, transportation, and other public services. Despite Justice John Harlan protesting that "the Constitution is color-blind," the doctrine would not be overturned until 1954.

Utah was admitted to the Union as the 45th state.

In his famous "Cross of Gold" speech, July 8, William Jennings Bryan warned that if cities were torn down they would spring up again as if by magic, but if farms failed, grass would grow in the city streets. Riding on a platform of free and unlimited coinage of silver, Bryan won his first Democratic nomination for president. He would be defeated by William McKinley, governor of Ohio.

In mid-August, gold was discovered in Alaska's Klondike region. A new gold rush would erupt early the following year, with Seattle, Washington the main staging area for entrepreneurs going north.

Charles Dow published the first edition of the Dow Jones Industrial Average on May 26.

In 1896 Burt L. Standish published his first Frank Merriwell novel, *Frank Merriwell, or First Days at Farwell*. Eventually these popular adventure stories would sell 125,000 copies per week, mostly to boys eager for each installment.

1896 was a banner year for the American with a sweet tooth. Confectioner Leo Hirschfield marketed paper-wrapped Tootsie Rolls, named after his young daughter Clara (nicknamed Tootsie). In Chicago, Cracker Jack was introduced, soon to be immortalized in the song "Take Me Out to the Ball Game."

"Buy Me Some Peanuts and Cracker Jack..."
The new confection would soon be connected forever to the great American pastime.

1896 Indian Head Cent

Enlarged 1.5x—Actual Size: 19mm

CIRCULATION MINTAGE:
39,055,431

PROOF MINTAGE:
1,862

Market Values • Circulation Strikes and Proof Strikes

G-4	VG-8	F-12	VF-20	EF-40	AU-50	MS-60BN	MS-63RB	MS-64RB	MS-64RD
$3	$4	$5	$7	$15	$25	$40	$65	$125	$250
MS-65RB	MS-65RD	MS-66RD	PF-60RB	PF-63RB	PF-64RB	PF-64RD	PF-65RB	PF-65RD	PF-66RD
$250	$950	$2,000	$250	$325	$400	$800	$550	$2,500	$5,500

Certified Populations

G - VF	EF-40	EF-45	AU-50	AU-53	AU-55	AU-58	MS-60	MS-61	MS-62	MS-63	MS-64	MS-65	MS-66	MS-67	MS-68	MS-69	MS-70
15	22	15	30	3	28	20	53	13	66	740	2,453	1,413	120	11	10	0	0
<PF-60	PF-60	PF-61	PF-62	PF-63	PF-64	PF-65	PF-66	PF-67	PF-68	PF-69	PF-70						
3	3	5	18	218	812	690	129	1	0	0	0						

Field populations: Circulation strike (<MS-60), 500,000; circulation strike (MS-60+), 8,000; Proof, 700.

1896 Cent Production: As the country began to recover from the depression of 1893, businesses began to feel strong growth, justifying the need for more coins. The Mint experienced strong demand for cents and thus devoted much energy to increasing output this year and for the years to follow.

Survivability: The coins of this issue were put into circulation and stayed there for at least a generation.

Collecting Challenges: These are widely available in most all grades except in gem condition. Select eye-appealing coins with good strikes and no problems.

Collecting Circulated Pieces: The Optimal Collecting Grade is AU-50 to MS-63RB. These should be easy to find without any problems.

Collecting Mint State Pieces: The Optimal Collecting Grade is MS-65RB or MS-64RD. These are a bit scarcer than other dates in the later 1890s, although this is not currently reflected in the price. Full red gems are surprisingly scarce. These tend to be a bit bright pale-gold, rather than the red-gold of other dates. Perhaps this makes them harder to be accepted as true gems.

Collecting Proof Issues: The mintage for this issue dips below the 2,000 mark for the first time since 1877. Mintages from here until the end of the series will remain at these lower levels. This date is very tough with full red color, especially in PF-65RD or higher grades. Many of the high-end examples will get the cameo designation.

Varieties: Presently 16 varieties are known, mostly minor repunched dates.

A SNAPSHOT OF THE YEAR 1897

In reaction to the 1896 Klondike gold discovery, thousands of gold seekers headed north through Chilkoot Pass to Dawson and other outposts. By the end of 1897, the region's haul was estimated at $22 million. Among those joining in the Klondike gold rush was Jack London, who penned his first successful stories there. The economic depression of recent years was eased in part by optimism from the Klondike and Cripple Creek gold strikes.

In Carson City Robert Fitzsimmons won the world heavyweight boxing title, beating "Gentleman Jim" Corbett on March 17. The match was filmed by motion picture camera, and in the ensuing years various companies would compete for the rights to film such contests. The losers would sometimes re-enact the bout using actors (with the audience not informed). "Movies," as they came to be known, were shown not in motion picture theaters (as today), but in connection with vaudeville shows or in arcades.

In Washington, the Library of Congress was completed across the street from the Capitol Building, which had served as the nation's book repository since 1851.

In the fields of science and medicine, the discovery was made that malaria—a centuries-old scourge of mankind—is carried by the common mosquito; the American Osteopathic Association was founded; and in Chicago, the Yerkes Observatory was opened. The latter would soon make contributions to spectroscopy and studies of the Milky Way, among other disciplines in astronomy.

In 1897 the first North American subway opened in Boston.

Francis Church, editor of the *New York Sun*, famously responded to a young reader's letter with, "Yes, Virginia, there is a Santa Claus." John Philip Sousa, America's March King, performed for the first time his rousing *Stars and Stripes Forever*, and armchair adventurers were treated to Rudyard Kipling's *Captains Courageous* and Richard Harding Davis' *Soldiers of Fortune*.

"Yes, Virginia, There Is A Santa Claus."
In 1897 Francis Church would pen his famous reply to an eight-year-old girl's question. (Illustration by Thomas Nast in *Harper's Weekly*, January 1, 1881)

At Coney Island, New York, George C. Tilyou opened Steeplechase Park, part of what would become America's largest and most famous amusement park. Gustav Walter established the Orpheum Circuit of theaters this year, building on his first Orpheum Theatre, opened in San Francisco in 1887.

1897 INDIAN HEAD CENT

CIRCULATION MINTAGE:
50,464,392

PROOF MINTAGE:
1,938

Enlarged 1.5x—Actual Size: 19mm

Market Values • Circulation Strikes and Proof Strikes

G-4	VG-8	F-12	VF-20	EF-40	AU-50	MS-60BN	MS-63RB	MS-64RB	MS-64RD
$3	$4	$5	$7	$15	$25	$40	$65	$125	$250
MS-65RB	MS-65RD	MS-66RD	PF-60RB	PF-63RB	PF-64RB	PF-64RD	PF-65RB	PF-65RD	PF-66RD
$225	$700	$2,000	$250	$325	$400	$800	$525	$1,950	$5,000

Certified Populations

G - VF	EF-40	EF-45	AU-50	AU-53	AU-55	AU-58	MS-60	MS-61	MS-62	MS-63	MS-64	MS-65	MS-66	MS-67	MS-68	MS-69	MS-70
85	33	20	40	4	45	30	45	17	84	929	2,811	1,580	293	31	0	0	0
<PF-60	PF-60	PF-61	PF-62	PF-63	PF-64	PF-65	PF-66	PF-67	PF-68	PF-69	PF-70						
2	7	8	20	284	693	775	340	49	0	0	0						

Field populations: Circulation strike (<MS-60), 650,000; circulation strike (MS-60+), 12,000; Proof, 750.

1897 Cent Production: This is a larger-mintage date. This and other dates of this era circulated extensively without any reason to be saved for 50 years. By the end of World War II they were curiosities of a distant age, saved by non-collectors (or future collectors) only because they were different.

Survivability: These are found in all grades easily, although most are worn down to Good condition.

Collecting Challenges: Select problem-free examples with attractive eye appeal.

Collecting Circulated Pieces: The Optimal Collecting Grade in AU-50 to MS-63RB. Find problem-free examples. Avoid cleaned coins.

Collecting Mint State Pieces: The Optimal Collecting Grade is MS-65RB or MS-64RD. These are well struck and are easily found in most grades except for MS-65RD or higher. The lack of the survival of gem full red coins is quite interesting. The entire amount of all gem survivors of any date in the late 1890s could be the result of only two to five original rolls. The quality of these rolls will also dictate how rare the date will be in gem condition. Were they spotted, mildewed, water damaged? Or is the roll full of pristine gems of the highest order? These are the things that dictate the rarity of Indian Head cents in high grade.

Collecting Proof Issues: This is another lower-mintage issue, although they tend to be as readily available as other dates in the late 1890s. 1897 Proofs are a bit difficult to find in gem full red. However, some of the prettiest examples of Proof Indian Head cents are known for this year. Super-deep-mirror cameo gems are known for this date. The deep mirror cameo Proofs are the first coins made from new dies. In addition to a frosted design, these coins typically have a mirrored surface that is not smooth— it appears to be crystallized and is commonly referred to as *orange peel fields*. This happens because the die is initially polished while it is soft. During the hardening process the steel contacts slightly. This forces the fields to buckle slightly. Orange peel fields are highly desired by collectors.

Varieties: One of the most popular misplaced digit varieties of the series is the Snow-1 "1 in the Neck." It shows a bold base of a numeral 1 sticking out of the neck midway between the chin and pearls. It is a fairly scarce variety in high grades, but more readily available in low grades. This is due to the ease by which this variety can be seen in low grades—what is known as a *naked-eye variety*. These are surprisingly rare in gem and full red condition. Only an MS-63RD is presently known in full red and there are no MS-65RB pieces known. This variety is labeled on the holder by ANACS and PCGS, the authentication and certification attesting to it being a genuine variety, which, in turn, increases its desirability among collectors.

1897 Snow-1 ("1 in the Neck")

A Snapshot of the Year 1898

In February 1898 smoldering tensions in Cuba were ignited by the sinking of the U.S. battleship *Maine* in Havana's harbor. The ship's explosion and the resulting 260 deaths were blamed on Spain, which was trying to bring its colony under control. Americans already had an anti-Spain bias, and sided with Cubans who wanted independence from the old empire. The previous year, William Randolph Hearst's *New York Journal* had printed a letter (stolen from the mail in Havana) in which the Spanish minister to the United States lampooned President McKinley as a weakling and a vote-panderer. In 1897 Hearst had sent artist Frederic Remington to Cuba to paint scenes of Spanish atrocities; Remington is said to have observed that all was quiet and there would be no war. Legend has it Hearst cabled him: "You furnish the pictures and I'll furnish the war." With the sinking of the *Maine*, Hearst finally had the spark he needed. His warmongering now included the rallying cry, "Remember the *Maine*. To hell with Spain!" Other publishers took up this strident theme in order to sell their own newspapers.

A United States gunboat captured the Spanish *Buena Ventura* on April 22. Spain declared war two days later, and the U.S. followed suit. In the 112-day Spanish-American War, Commodore George Dewey emerged as an American hero. His flagship, the *Olympia*, led the victors in the Battle of Manila Bay, conquering the Spanish navy in a single day. Dewey's portrait would be featured on countless consumer products: cigar labels, pinback buttons, music boxes, slot machines, souvenir spoons. Theodore Roosevelt also won fame in the war, with the famous charge of his Rough Riders in the Battle of San Juan Hill.

Careful research over the years would fail to decisively pin the *Maine*'s destruction on the Spanish. Various theories would instead link it to a boiler explosion, or even to sabotage by American newspaper agents eager to bring the Cuban situation to a dramatic head.

In 1898 the United States annexed Hawaii.

New York City absorbed land and comprised the five boroughs of Manhattan, Brooklyn, Queens, the Bronx, and Staten Island. On Broadway, Victor Herbert's musical *The Fortune Teller* opened on Broadway, featuring the "Gypsy Love Song."

Caleb Bradham came up with the moniker *Pepsi-Cola* for his soft drink.

This was the birth year of William H. Sheldon, who would grow up to be a coin collector specializing in large cents, and the inventor of the Sheldon rarity scale and 70-point numerical grading system.

Commodore George Dewey

"You may fire when you are ready, Gridley." (Dewey to the captain of the *Olympia*, May 1, 1898)

1898 INDIAN HEAD CENT

CIRCULATION MINTAGE:
49,821,284

PROOF MINTAGE:
1,795

Enlarged 1.5x—Actual Size: 19mm

Market Values • Circulation Strikes and Proof Strikes

G-4	VG-8	F-12	VF-20	EF-40	AU-50	MS-60BN	MS-63RB	MS-64RB	MS-64RD
$3	$4	$5	$7	$15	$25	$40	$65	$125	$225
MS-65RB	MS-65RD	MS-66RD	PF-60RB	PF-63RB	PF-64RB	PF-64RD	PF-65RB	PF-65RD	PF-66RD
$200	$600	$2,000	$250	$325	$400	$600	$500	$1,500	$4,500

Certified Populations

G - VF	EF-40	EF-45	AU-50	AU-53	AU-55	AU-58	MS-60	MS-61	MS-62	MS-63	MS-64	MS-65	MS-66	MS-67	MS-68	MS-69	MS-70
87	33	21	42	4	45	32	45	17	84	949	2,841	1,600	293	31	0	0	0
<PF-60	PF-60	PF-61	PF-62	PF-63	PF-64	PF-65	PF-66	PF-67	PF-68	PF-69	PF-70						
4	8	4	16	153	810	896	365	61	0	0	0						

Field populations: Circulation strike (<MS-60), 1,000,000; circulation strike (MS-60+), 15,000; Proof, 750.

1898 Cent Production: This issue is similar in mintage to the cent of 1897. The cent was by far the most abundant coin in the country. It was probably the most useful coin at the time to the average American. This was the era when the novelty games in penny arcades actually cost a cent.

Survivability: These coins circulated to a great extent and served the nation for at least 50 years. Examples are readily available in all grades except full red gem.

Collecting Challenges: Search out an attractive problem-free example.

Collecting Circulated Pieces: The Optimal Collecting Grade is AU-50 to MS-63RB. The only challenge should be to find the best coin to match the other coins in your collection. The colors of bronze coins vary so much that matching a certain shade of red-brown, if desired, can be very difficult.

Collecting Mint State Pieces: The Optimal Collecting Grade is MS-65RD. Search out well-struck, problem-free examples. All gem full red Indian Head cents are scarce.

Collecting Proof Issues: Although this is another lower-mintage Proof issue, 1898 Proofs exist in average to higher-than-average quantities, so there should be little problem in finding an attractive specimen. Some of the prettiest gem cameo coins are found for this date; extra care must have been taken in their production. (In fact, all denominations of this year can be found with outstanding cameo contrast.)

Varieties: 36 varieties of specialist interest are known for this year. These are mostly repunched dates, none of which are particularly dramatic.

A SNAPSHOT OF THE YEAR 1899

On February 10 President McKinley signed a peace treaty with Spain, officially ending the Spanish-American War. Under its terms, the United States acquired Guam and Puerto Rico, and paid $20 million for certain rights in the Philippines. Cuba, the flashpoint of the conflict, won independence from the defeated empire.

On February 14, Congress authorized the use of voting machines rather than older non-mechanical systems, if individual states desired them for their election processes.

In May a conference was held at The Hague, the Netherlands. Two dozen delegates met to discuss warfare limitations, disarmament, and the arbitration of international disputes.

On October 14, the *Literary Digest* stated, "The ordinary horseless carriage is at present a luxury for the wealthy; and although its price will probably fall in the future, it will never, of course, come into as common use as the bicycle." Earlier that summer, President William McKinley had become the first American president to ride in an automobile when he took a spin in a Stanley Steamer at his Canton, Ohio home.

Popular songs of the day included "My Wild Irish Rose" and "A Bird in a Gilded Cage." Scott Joplin's "Maple Leaf Rag" was published by John Stark, of St. Louis. An immediate hit, Joplin's tune joined a roster of popular ragtime and cakewalk numbers of the 1890s, including "At a Georgia Camp Meeting" and "Smoky Mokes."

President William McKinley
In 1899 the president signed a treaty ending the United States' war with Spain.

1899 Cent Production: Mintages in the mid- to late 1890s crept up higher and higher each year.

Survivability: This date is a bit more common than most of the dates that follow. Perhaps more examples were saved over the years because of it being the last date in the 1800s (although it is not the last date in the 19th century).

Collecting Challenges: These are widely available and will be fairly easy to locate in all grades except full red gem.

Collecting Circulated Pieces: The Optimal Collecting Grade is AU-50 to MS-63RB. Locate problem-free original coins with attractive eye appeal.

1899 INDIAN HEAD CENT

CIRCULATION MINTAGE:
53,598,000

PROOF MINTAGE:
2,031

Enlarged 1.5x—Actual Size: 19mm

Market Values • Circulation Strikes and Proof Strikes

G-4	VG-8	F-12	VF-20	EF-40	AU-50	MS-60BN	MS-63RB	MS-64RB	MS-64RD
$3	$4	$5	$7	$15	$25	$30	$50	$100	$200
MS-65RB	**MS-65RD**	**MS-66RD**	**PF-60RB**	**PF-63RB**	**PF-64RB**	**PF-64RD**	**PF-65RB**	**PF-65RD**	**PF-66RD**
$175	$500	$1,750	$250	$325	$400	$600	$500	$1,350	$3,500

Certified Populations

G - VF	EF-40	EF-45	AU-50	AU-53	AU-55	AU-58	MS-60	MS-61	MS-62	MS-63	MS-64	MS-65	MS-66	MS-67	MS-68	MS-69	MS-70
66	30	20	34	3	32	26	49	21	79	824	2,880	2,035	540	77	1	0	0
<PF-60	**PF-60**	**PF-61**	**PF-62**	**PF-63**	**PF-64**	**PF-65**	**PF-66**	**PF-67**	**PF-68**	**PF-69**	**PF-70**						
0	4	6	15	203	721	946	380	74	0	0	0						

Field populations: Circulation strike (<MS-60), 1,500,000; circulation strike (MS-60+), 18,000; Proof, 800.

Collecting Mint State Pieces: The Optimal Collecting Grade is MS-65RD. These are widely available in all grades. MS-65RD and better pieces are a bit tougher, but such examples are among the easiest to find of the era (only 1909 is easier).

An example of this date, graded MS-68RD by PCGS, is the finest graded coin of the entire Indian Head cent series. It sold for an astounding $69,000 when it was auctioned as part of the Joseph P. Gorrell collection by Heritage at the Florida United Numismatists (FUN) show in January 2003. Earlier, it was in the Dr. Alan Epstein collection, which was the finest Indian Head cent collection ever assembled. When my firm, Eagle Eye Rare Coins, purchased the Dr. Epstein collection in 1996, this particular coin was so special to its previous owner that it was repurchased at the full asking price of $13,500. A bit later Dr. Epstein resold it though Eagle Eye into the Gorrell collection, for $14,500. Nobody could have guessed the astounding price it would command a few years later.

Collecting Proof Issues: Although this date has a lower Proof mintage than some others, examples seem to have survived a bit better than earlier years. Very high-quality examples are readily available. Beware of spotted coins, as the exquisite beauty of a gem Proof can be greatly diminished by the existence of an obvious dark spot.

Varieties: There are 22 varieties known for this date. Most are minor repunched dates. Snow-13 is a so-called "overdate" 1899/7. It was listed as such in *Walter Breen's Complete Encyclopedia of U.S. and Colonial Coins,* but what appears to be an overdate is nothing more than a die chip inside the last 9. This is still a popular variety, though.

A Snapshot of the Year 1900

In 1900 the nation's population was just shy of 76 million; in the preceding decade nearly 3.7 million immigrants had journeyed to America's shores. The country's literacy rate reached a new high of 89.3%.

In March gold was finally and conclusively enthroned as the financial standard of the United States. Congress passed an act making it the measure against which other monetary units, including currency, would be valued. The long-running argument over the gold-to-silver ratio was ended.

On June 14, Hawaii became a territory of the United States.

In Kansas, Carry Nation and her band of prohibition advocates took axes to saloons and other liquor-serving establishments and publicly destroyed their intoxicating wares.

Technology continued apace in 1900. There was one roughly telephone for every 55 men, women, and children in the country. About 8,000 automobiles were on the registration rolls, and 4,000 were produced that year. (The nation had about 10 miles of paved roads.) Orville and Wilbur Wright manufactured a glider that incorporated some of their theories on flight.

1900 Lafayette Dollar (Reverse)

Social reformer Jacob A. Riis observed that the average work-at-home garment industry employee earned 30¢ per day. The typical American laborer's week was 70 hours long.

William Jennings Bryan again ran for president— the 1900 campaign would be his second of three attempts. This year he had the blessings of the Democratic and Populist parties as he ran against Republican incumbent William McKinley. The latter, promising "a full dinner pail" to his fellow citizens, won overwhelmingly with 292 electoral votes to Bryan's 155. His running mate was the governor of New York, author and Spanish-American War hero Theodore Roosevelt.

The Act of March 14 authorized the Treasury to melt and recoin all worn and non-current coins that were received then and in the future, and to pay for them at par, with any loss to be absorbed by the government. This thinned the herd of worn-down coins that circulated in commerce and rested in Treasury vaults, including earlier-dated pieces that had returned from Latin America in the late 1870s (although most such coins had already disappeared). For the price of $2 per coin, collectors were treated to the country's first commemorative dollar, honoring the French general Lafayette. The coins were dated 1900, but had actually been struck on December 14 the previous year. Eventually about 36,000 coins (of the 50,000 struck) were sold.

1900 INDIAN HEAD CENT

CIRCULATION MINTAGE:
66,831,502

PROOF MINTAGE:
2,262

Enlarged 1.5x—Actual Size: 19mm

Market Values • Circulation Strikes and Proof Strikes

G-4	VG-8	F-12	VF-20	EF-40	AU-50	MS-60BN	MS-63RB	MS-64RB	MS-64RD
$2	$3	$4	$5	$10	$20	$35	$55	$110	$225
MS-65RB	**MS-65RD**	**MS-66RD**	**PF-60RB**	**PF-63RB**	**PF-64RB**	**PF-64RD**	**PF-65RB**	**PF-65RD**	**PF-66RD**
$190	$800	$2,500	$225	$300	$375	$600	$525	$1,500	$4,500

Certified Populations

G - VF	EF-40	EF-45	AU-50	AU-53	AU-55	AU-58	MS-60	MS-61	MS-62	MS-63	MS-64	MS-65	MS-66	MS-67	MS-68	MS-69	MS-70
24	38	22	44	5	38	28	72	28	89	770	2,787	2,099	474	46	0	0	0
<PF-60	**PF-60**	**PF-61**	**PF-62**	**PF-63**	**PF-64**	**PF-65**	**PF-66**	**PF-67**	**PF-68**	**PF-69**	**PF-70**						
3	6	3	23	170	833	696	392	80	10	0	0						

Field populations: Circulation strike (<MS-60), 1,000,000; circulation strike (MS-60+), 12,500; Proof, 800.

1900 Cent Production: A record number of cents was produced this year, although this is one of the lower-mintage dates of the 1900s. Mint Director George E. Roberts began to call for the striking of Indian Head cents at the branch mints of San Francisco and New Orleans.

Survivability: These were not saved from circulation early on, and most examples are well circulated. Enough are available to satisfy collector demand in all grades except MS-65RD and higher.

Collecting Challenges: Select eye-appealing coins with few problems.

Collecting Circulated Pieces: The Optimal Collecting Grade is AU-50 to MS-63RB. There is no particular difficulty in finding this date in an attractive grade.

Collecting Mint State Pieces: The Optimal Collecting Grade is MS-65RD. This date is very hard to find in gem condition, at least in relation to other dates in the 1900s.

Collecting Proof Issues: These are about as readily available as other dates in the era. This is a popular date to collect as part of a turn-of-the-century Proof set. Gem full red examples are scarce, but only in the context of some of the more common dates of the 1880s. Cameos are available, although few have graded as such.

Varieties: There are 23 collectible varieties. Most are minor repunched dates. Three examples of this date are known struck in gold, and at least one example in silver. The reason for the existence of these coins is a mystery. The gold examples weigh 4.26 to 4.35 grams, which is slightly more than the official 4.18-gram weight of a quarter eagle planchet, so they are probably not accidental off-metal errors. Both the silver and gold examples are struck from the same dies, with light roughness on the reverse die, probably from die rust. These were likely struck outside the knowledge of Mint officers. When they show up in auctions they always generate extremely high interest.

A Snapshot of the Year 1901

January of this year saw the state of Texas established as a center of oil production, with the Spindletop reserve in Beaumont gushing 110,000 barrels per day for nine days before it was capped.

British-Americans paused to honor the memory of Queen Victoria, who died on January 22, 1901. The long-seated monarch had reigned over the United Kingdom since 1837.

In March 1900 the first Mercedes motorcar was built, and in Detroit that August the Cadillac motor company was founded. In December King Camp Gillette announced his plans to market a disposable razor.

On September 6 President William McKinley visited the Pan-American Exposition in Buffalo, New York. As he met well-wishers in a greeting line, McKinley was shot twice by a Polish anarchist. The president died from his wounds eight days later—his assassin would be executed within two months—and was succeeded by Vice President Theodore Roosevelt. "TR" inherited from his predecessor an established world power with an overseas empire. As a member of the reform wing of the Republican party, Roosevelt saw his role as being the nation's moral leader and a protector against business interests that sought to prey on the American people.

In November, the United States and Great Britain signed the Hay-Pauncefote Treaty, which gave British consent to U.S. control of a canal to be built across the Isthmus of Panama to join the Atlantic and Pacific oceans.

In Philadelphia, a new minting facility opened for business, in the third building since 1792 to house the nation's main mint.

McKinley at the Hall of Martyrs
The nation would mourn when the president joined Lincoln and Garfield in 1901. (Illustration from *Harper's Weekly*, September 14, 1901)

◆

1901 Cent Production: In 1901 the Mint again set a production record, breaking the previous year's record. This is technically the first issue of the 20th century, but collectors prefer to group the 20th-century issues as all the coins dated "19—." The third Philadelphia Mint opened for production this year. The building had a classical Roman temple façade. Massive Ionic columns led to a lobby with vaulted ceilings that were bejeweled with seven Tiffany glass mosaics. Today the building houses Philadelphia Community College. This improved facility allowed for a much higher production of cents.

1901 INDIAN HEAD CENT

CIRCULATION MINTAGE:
79,609,158

PROOF MINTAGE:
1,985

Enlarged 1.5x—Actual Size: 19mm

Market Values • Circulation Strikes and Proof Strikes

G-4	VG-8	F-12	VF-20	EF-40	AU-50	MS-60BN	MS-63RB	MS-64RB	MS-64RD
$2	$3	$4	$5	$10	$20	$35	$55	$100	$200
MS-65RB	MS-65RD	MS-66RD	PF-60RB	PF-63RB	PF-64RB	PF-64RD	PF-65RB	PF-65RD	PF-66RD
$175	$500	$2,000	$200	$300	$325	$600	$500	$1,500	$4,000

Certified Populations

G - VF	EF-40	EF-45	AU-50	AU-53	AU-55	AU-58	MS-60	MS-61	MS-62	MS-63	MS-64	MS-65	MS-66	MS-67	MS-68	MS-69	MS-70
26	47	23	81	7	49	43	90	33	161	1,641	5,249	3,377	606	52	0	0	0
<PF-60	PF-60	PF-61	PF-62	PF-63	PF-64	PF-65	PF-66	PF-67	PF-68	PF-69	PF-70						
1	7	2	12	243	810	923	492	121	20	0	0						

Field populations: Circulation strike (<MS-60), 1,250,000; circulation strike (MS-60+), 18,000; Proof, 800.

Survivability: Very few coins were saved at the time of issue. A popular souvenir item that sold at events such as the 1901 Pan American Exposition (in Buffalo, New York) were newly issued cents encased in aluminum advertising cards. These came in a variety of styles and sayings, such as "Keep me for good luck." These *encased coins* are collected quite actively today, and the encasements are worth much more with the original coins intact. Many times, though, the temptation to remove high-grade examples of Indian Head cents from these holders is too much for their owners. A coin, when removed from such a holder, is usually found to be slightly damaged from the encasing process. Part of an advertising design may be impressed into the rim of the coin, or it may be slightly bent.

Collecting Challenges: Search for problem-free examples. These are found with average to full strikes. Avoid coins damaged from being inserted in aluminum encasements.

Collecting Circulated Pieces: The Optimal Collecting Grade is AU-50 to MS-63RB. These, like other issues of the 1900s, are widely available.

Collecting Mint State Pieces: Available in most grades, the Optimal Collecting Grade for the 1901 cent is MS-65RD. However, finding a problem free MS-65RD example may require some patience.

Collecting Proof Issues: These are available with some searching. Full red gems are scarce, as with all Proofs of this era. Cameos are available, but are very tough to find.

Many early-die-state examples from this date onward until 1907 show fine die-polishing lines across the whole face of the die, including the portrait. When the coin is turned in the light it will appear as if the coin has been wiped with an abrasive rag. As the coin is turned further the lines disappear and the coin shows very deep mirror fields. These are actually lines on the die that are transferred to the coin, and are desirable as the earliest die state of the dies. Most cameos will show these lines.

Varieties: There are 20 varieties listed. Most are minor repunched dates.

A SNAPSHOT OF THE YEAR 1902

On January 1, 1902, in Pasadena, California, the first Tournament of Roses Association football game was held, with Michigan besting Stanford 49–0. (In 1923 the contest would become known as the Rose Bowl.)

Technology continued to grow. In April this year the Texas Oil Company (Texaco) was founded, built on that state's recent petroleum discoveries. A traveler on the New York Central Railroad could leave New York and arrive in Chicago just 20 hours later.

The teddy bear entered American life in 1902, created by a candy store owner inspired by a cartoon in the November 18 issue of the *Washington Evening Star*. The cartoon showed President "Teddy" Roosevelt refusing to shoot a tethered bear cub while on a hunting trip. The president was famous for his interest in protecting natural resources; during his term, the nation would add nearly 150 million acres to its reserves, mostly in the West. The Department of the Interior was established this year.

Meanwhile, business trusts were becoming an increasing concern, and President Roosevelt took action. On March 10 he announced the government's proceedings, under the Sherman Anti-Trust Act, against the J.P. Morgan–controlled National Securities Company. Still the mergers and monopolies continued. The American International Harvester Company was incorporated in New Jersey on August 12, capitalized with $120 million and controlling the output of 85% of the nation's farm machinery. A merger of the Canadian Copper Company and the Orford Copper Company, arranged by J.P. Morgan and others, created the International Nickel Company.

On June 28 Congress passed the Isthmian Canal Act, authorizing the construction of a canal across Panama—or an alternative route across Nicaragua if arrangements could not be made with Columbia (which controlled the proposed construction area) and the Panama Canal Company of France (which held the concession). The French were paid $40 million, and the Columbia question was settled by a coup of railroad workers, barmen, and militia members—supported by the fire brigade and by American adventurers, and encouraged by U.S. navy ships in the area—who proclaimed independence from Columbia in 1903. Their new republic of Panama was quickly given official recognition by the State Department, and, equally quickly, it leased to the United States a strip 10 miles wide for the canal.

A Man, A Plan, A Canal: Panama
The famous palindrome (read the same backward as forward) describes Roosevelt's ambition in Central America. (Cartoon from *Puck*, August 24, 1904)

The average wage of a shop girl in Boston this year was about $5 to $6 per week, with New England mill workers earning about the same. On May 12, nearly 150,000 members of the United Mine Workers went on strike in the anthracite coal mines. The cost of coal rose from $5 in May to about $30 in October, and many schools were closed because of the high winter fuel costs.

1902 INDIAN HEAD CENT

CIRCULATION MINTAGE:
87,374,704

PROOF MINTAGE:
2,018

Enlarged 1.5x—Actual Size: 19mm

Market Values • Circulation Strikes and Proof Strikes

G-4	VG-8	F-12	VF-20	EF-40	AU-50	MS-60BN	MS-63RB	MS-64RB	MS-64RD
$2	$3	$4	$5	$10	$20	$35	$55	$100	$200
MS-65RB	MS-65RD	MS-66RD	PF-60RB	PF-63RB	PF-64RB	PF-64RD	PF-65RB	PF-65RD	PF-66RD
$175	$500	$1,750	$200	$300	$325	$600	$500	$1,350	$3,500

Certified Populations

G - VF	EF-40	EF-45	AU-50	AU-53	AU-55	AU-58	MS-60	MS-61	MS-62	MS-63	MS-64	MS-65	MS-66	MS-67	MS-68	MS-69	MS-70
41	55	35	72	6	47	53	85	40	154	1,554	4,674	3,025	1,257	178	10	0	0
<PF-60		PF-60		PF-61		PF-62		PF-63		PF-64		PF-65		PF-66		PF-67	
0		4		3		22		218		968		844		440		59	
PF-68		PF-69		PF-70													
10		0		0													

Field populations: Circulation strike (<MS-60), 1,500,000; circulation strike (MS-60+), 15,000; Proof, 750.

1902 Cent Production: This was another record year of production. Possibly in an effort to extend the die life, the gap between the dies was set a bit wider. Cents of this date show weakness in the feather tips and bust point a bit more often than other dates. The shield and denticles are also typically weak. Some of the dies have the design sunk slightly deeper, which also contributed to the weakness encountered on this year's coinage.

Survivability: These circulated widely and were not plucked from circulation until the late 1940s.

Collecting Challenges: Choose problem-free examples with exceptional eye appeal.

Collecting Circulated Pieces: The Optimal Collecting Grade is AU-50 to MS-63RB. This date is common in the context of the later Indian Head cents. Search for well-struck examples with full details on the shield.

Collecting Mint State Pieces: The Optimal Collecting Grade is MS-65RD. These are available in all grades. MS-65RD and higher grades are difficult to find. One roll, possibly two, showed up in the late 1990s, with many coins graded MS-65RD, but with numerous light carbon spots.

Collecting Proof Issues: The 1902 Proof comes very attractive and is one of the most common dates in the series in gem condition. This is due to the chance survival of a few exceptional coins, as the mintage is fairly low for the series. Early-die-state coins come with fine die-polishing lines. During this year, and the next two, a change in die preparation eliminated the cameo contrast on most denominations. Only the first couple of coins minted from a die will have any contrast between the devices and field. Coins of this date designated as cameos are very rare.

Varieties: 14 varieties are presently known, mostly repunched dates. Snow-4 has a dramatic die gouge by the eye on the portrait. It is very similar to the 1890-CC "Tail Bar" Morgan silver dollar.

A SNAPSHOT OF THE YEAR 1903

Motorized transportation continued to capture the American imagination in 1903, the year Henry Ford founded the Ford Motor Company. On May 23 the first transcontinental automobile trip began, with two adventurers driving a 20-horsepower Winton touring car from San Francisco to New York. Never mind that there were no gas stations at the time, and fewer than 150 miles of paved roads—they wheeled into the Big Apple on July 26. The Harley-Davidson motorcycle roared onto the scene this year, and a week before Christmas, brothers Orville and Wilbur Wright made their pioneering flights in a heavier-than-air self-propelled machine.

King Edward VII
The British monarch sent greetings to the United States by wireless radio. (Commemorative medal of the Corporation of Rochester, England, 1902)

On January 19 Guglielmo Marconi sent a wireless radio message from President Theodore Roosevelt to Britain's King Edward VII, transmitting from four 250-foot wooden towers at South Wellfleet, Massachusetts.

> His Majesty, Edward VII.
> London, Eng.
>
> In taking advantage of the wonderful triumph of scientific research and ingenuity which has been achieved in perfecting a system of wireless telegraphy, I extend on behalf of the American People most cordial greetings and good wishes to you and to all the people of the British Empire.
>
> THEODORE ROOSEVELT
> Wellfleet, Mass., Jan. 19, 1903

The king's reply came back from England:

> Sandringham, January 19, 1903
> The President,
> White House, Washington, America
>
> I thank you most sincerely for the kind message which I have just received from you, through Marconi's trans-Atlantic wireless telegraphy. I sincerely reciprocate in the name of the British Empire the cordial greetings and friendly sentiment expressed by you on behalf of the American Nation, I heartily wish you and your country every possible prosperity.
>
> EDWARD R. and I.

In November the first World Series game was played when the American League and National League champions met in a post-season playoff in a best-of-nine contest. The winners were the Boston Red Sox. The World Series would not be held the next year due to a feud between the manager of the New York Giants (champions of the National League) and the president of the American League. After that hiatus the World Series would take place every year, from 1905 onward.

1903 Indian Head Cent

Circulation Mintage:
85,092,703

Proof Mintage:
1,790

Enlarged 1.5x—Actual Size: 19mm

Market Values • Circulation Strikes and Proof Strikes

G-4	VG-8	F-12	VF-20	EF-40	AU-50	MS-60BN	MS-63RB	MS-64RB	MS-64RD
$2	$3	$4	$5	$10	$20	$35	$55	$100	$200
MS-65RB	MS-65RD	MS-66RD	PF-60RB	PF-63RB	PF-64RB	PF-64RD	PF-65RB	PF-65RD	PF-66RD
$175	$500	$1,750	$200	$300	$325	$600	$525	$1,350	$3,500

Certified Populations

G - VF	EF-40	EF-45	AU-50	AU-53	AU-55	AU-58	MS-60	MS-61	MS-62	MS-63	MS-64	MS-65	MS-66	MS-67	MS-68	MS-69	MS-70
50	48	28	68	5	46	51	99	24	117	1,143	4,983	3,203	543	57	0	0	0
<PF-60	PF-60	PF-61	PF-62	PF-63	PF-64	PF-65	PF-66	PF-67	PF-68	PF-69	PF-70						
9	10	2	24	265	951	637	346	78	0	0	0						

Field populations: Circulation strike (<MS-60), 1,750,000; circulation strike (MS-60+), 16,000; Proof, 750.

1903 Cent Production: 1903 is another high-mintage date.

Survivability: These circulated extensively and today are available in all grades.

Collecting Challenges: As with other dates, select problem-free original examples.

Collecting Circulated Pieces: The Optimal Collecting Grade is AU-50 to MS-63RB. Beware of cleaned coins, as they have a limited resale value.

Collecting Mint State Pieces: The Optimal Collecting Grade is MS-65RD. These come well struck with good luster. Regardless that this date (as well as others of the 1900s) is considered common, collectors should exert the same amount of care as they would if they were buying a coin worth 10 times as much. To many collectors, the thrill is in the chase and capture of the one prized example that "speaks" to them stronger than any other.

Collecting Proof Issues: Although this is a lower-mintage date, there tends to be enough high-grade examples available. PF-65RD examples and higher tend to be no rarer than most other dates in the late-date set, which traditionally covers 1879 to 1909. This date, as is seen in 1902, does not come with any appreciable cameo contrast. Most early-die-state examples have die polishing lines which appear when the coin is turned a certain way in the light, and then disappear when the coin is turned further. The die polishing lines may look like hairlines on the coin to the uninitiated. In the past, I have been able to buy superb uncertified gem Proofs of this date for PR-63 or lower prices from dealers who do not handle enough of these coins to know about the die polishing.

Varieties: There are 23 or so known varieties. These are mostly minor repunched dates.

A SNAPSHOT OF THE YEAR 1904

On January 4, the Supreme Court ruled that citizens of Puerto Rico could freely come to the mainland United States—not as aliens, but also not as U.S. citizens. (Full citizenship would come in 1917.) In February the U.S. ended its occupation of Cuba.

A raging fire in downtown Baltimore, Maryland, destroyed more than 2,600 buildings in early February—the largest urban conflagration since the Chicago fire of 1871. Losses were estimated at $80 million. Among the numismatic losses were medals and other items from the T. Harrison Garrett estate, kept in Baltimore while the main collection was exhibited at Princeton University.

Ida M. Tarbell's book *The History of the Standard Oil Company* was published, a pivotal study that inspired future business reforms. It painted a disturbing picture of profits made by the Rockefeller family at the expense of the rest of America. Tarbell's readers learned that John D. Rockefeller had a personal annual income of $45 million and that his firms controlled 90% of the oil business in America. The book helped arouse passions against monopolies, trusts, and big business in general. On March 14, the Supreme Court ordered that the Northern Securities Company, a railroad holding company, be dissolved.

The Rockefellers weren't the only ones living well. Businessman W.A. Clark, who made millions of dollars mining copper in Montana, moved into his 130-room mansion at Fifth Avenue and 77th Street in New York, setting a new standard for domestic opulence.

Elsewhere in New York, the first section of the city's subway system was opened in late October. It consisted of a conduit extending north from the Brooklyn Bridge to 145th Street and Broadway.

Held a year too late to celebrate the 1803–1903 centennial, the 1904 Louisiana Purchase Exposition brought visitors to St. Louis from around the world. It was arguably the most successful such event since the World's Columbian Exposition of 1893. Attractions included the diesel engine (designed by Rudolf Diesel) and the Ferris wheel—the latter a popular ride from the World's Columbian Exposition. The Inside Inn, with its 2,257 rooms, was a stunning success at the fair, netting a $300,000 profit for its owner, Ellsworth M. Statler, who would later build a chain of hotels with its flagship facility in Buffalo, New York.

The year's presidential campaign saw incumbent President Theodore Roosevelt soundly winning against Democratic candidate Alton B. Parker—even though they differed little on the issues.

Teddy Roosevelt
Roosevelt had the unchallenged support of the Republican party in the 1904 election. By 1912 he would swing away from the conservatism of the Republicans and accept the nomination of the Progressive party, nicknamed the "Bull Moose Party."

1904 INDIAN HEAD CENT

CIRCULATION MINTAGE:
61,326,198

PROOF MINTAGE:
1,817

Enlarged 1.5x—Actual Size: 19mm

Market Values • Circulation Strikes and Proof Strikes

G-4	VG-8	F-12	VF-20	EF-40	AU-50	MS-60BN	MS-63RB	MS-64RB	MS-64RD
$2	$3	$4	$5	$10	$20	$35	$55	$100	$200
MS-65RB	MS-65RD	MS-66RD	PF-60RB	PF-63RB	PF-64RB	PF-64RD	PF-65RB	PF-65RD	PF-66RD
$175	$500	$1,750	$200	$300	$325	$600	$550	$1,500	$5,500

Certified Populations

G - VF	EF-40	EF-45	AU-50	AU-53	AU-55	AU-58	MS-60	MS-61	MS-62	MS-63	MS-64	MS-65	MS-66	MS-67	MS-68	MS-69	MS-70
29	52	21	48	5	32	46	74	22	106	1,000	4,172	2,439	466	25	0	0	0

<PF-60	PF-60	PF-61	PF-62	PF-63	PF-64	PF-65	PF-66	PF-67	PF-68	PF-69	PF-70
1	12	12	35	381	827	616	131	31	0	0	0

Field populations: Circulation strike (<MS-60), 2,000,000; circulation strike (MS-60+), 15,000; Proof, 700.

1904 Cent Production: This is another higher-mintage date, although slightly fewer coins were minted compared to other dates of the 1900s.

Survivability: Although produced in lower quantities than most other dates of the era, there appears to be about the same number of surviving 1904 cents. This date is no more scarce than any other of the 1900s. The chance survival of only a few original rolls can alter the rarity of the high-end examples in the collector market. In the 1990s and beyond, the discovery of original rolls has been a very rare occurrence.

Collecting Challenges: Select problem-free examples with attractive eye appeal.

Collecting Circulated Pieces: The Optimal Collecting Grade is AU-50 to MS-63RB. These tend to come well struck and attractive.

Collecting Mint State Pieces: The Optimal Collecting Grade is MS-65RD. Select eye-appealing coins with no problems. All brown and red-brown coins graded MS-65 or higher, and all red coins, should be purchased certified. Grade certification is not a cure-all, as the coins still need to be looked at for strike, problems, and eye appeal, but it is a good starting point. At least the *worst* cleaned and altered coins will be eliminated from the selection of contenders for your collection.

Collecting Proof Issues: This is a lower-mintage date in Proof. Early-die-state pieces hardly ever come with a cameo contrast, but do have the die-polishing lines seen on other issues from 1901 to 1907. True full red gems are very scarce and hotly contested. The prices for many later-date Proofs in gem condition are presently deceptively low compared to more common earlier dates. Collectors and price-guide writers both typically equate the scarcer Proof dates in the 1900s with the common circulation strikes.

Varieties: Only 12 varieties are known for this year. These are mostly minor re-punched dates.

A Snapshot of the Year 1905

In 1905 the average life expectancy for an American was 47 years. The typical American worker made between $200 and $400 per year, and 14 percent of United States homes had a bathtub. Boasting a population of only 1.4 million people, California was the 21st most populous state in the Union. Meanwhile, the population of Las Vegas, Nevada—established that year as a railroad town—was 30.

May of 1905 saw the last epidemic of yellow fever in the United States. In Louisiana, Dr. Rudolph Matas urged the Orleans Parish Medical Society to pinpoint the geographical distribution of the mosquitoes carrying the disease. The Society would advocate for screens on windows and cisterns, and urge that swamps be drained to eliminate breeding grounds. Although 456 people would die in this final epidemic, the New Orleans yachting and opera seasons would go on as scheduled, and in October, despite his advisers' warnings, President Roosevelt would accept an invitation to visit the city.

On July 16 Commander Robert Peary of the United States Navy set sail on his second expedition to the North Pole. This venture would prove unsuccessful, but he would finally reach his goal in another attempt in 1909.

Russian and Japanese delegates met in the United States on August 29 to agree to terms of peace for their recent war in Korea and Manchuria, arranging an armistice for August 31. On September 5 the skirmish fought between the two nations ended with the signature of a peace treaty at Portsmouth, New Hampshire. Stung by defeat, by late October Czar Nicholas would issue an imperial manifesto intended to quell unrest by transforming Russia from an absolute autocracy to a semi-constitutional monarchy. The experiment would prove a failure.

On October 5 the Wright brothers made their longest flight yet: 38 minutes and three seconds.

Robert Peary
The explorer studied tides for the Coast and Geodetic Survey during his North Pole expeditions.

1905 INDIAN HEAD CENT

CIRCULATION MINTAGE:
80,717,011

PROOF MINTAGE:
2,152

Enlarged 1.5x—Actual Size: 19mm

Market Values • Circulation Strikes and Proof Strikes

G-4	VG-8	F-12	VF-20	EF-40	AU-50	MS-60BN	MS-63RB	MS-64RB	MS-64RD
$2	$3	$4	$5	$10	$20	$35	$55	$100	$200
MS-65RB	MS-65RD	MS-66RD	PF-60RB	PF-63RB	PF-64RB	PF-64RD	PF-65RB	PF-65RD	PF-66RD
$175	$500	$2,000	$200	$300	$325	$650	$550	$1,350	$4,000

Certified Populations

G - VF	EF-40	EF-45	AU-50	AU-53	AU-55	AU-58	MS-60	MS-61	MS-62	MS-63	MS-64	MS-65	MS-66	MS-67	MS-68	MS-69	MS-70
46	51	28	64	7	47	51	96	27	140	1,326	4,878	3,522	756	40	0	0	0
<PF-60	PF-60	PF-61	PF-62	PF-63	PF-64	PF-65	PF-66	PF-67	PF-68	PF-69	PF-70						
1	8	11	27	336	814	644	285	94	0	0	0						

Field populations: Circulation strike (<MS-60), 2,250,000; circulation strike (MS-60+), 17,500; Proof, 750.

1905 Cent Production: Cent mintage climbed back up to a near-record level this year.

Survivability: A good estimate of the survivors in various grades might show the high degree of attrition these coins suffered over the years. Each year, between one million and five million cents of earlier years were deemed unfit for circulation, melted by the Mint, and recoined into new cents. My own estimate of surviving coins of this year breaks down roughly, by grade, as: Poor to Very Good, 2,000,000; Fine to About Uncirculated, 50,000; Mint State, Red-Brown, 15,000; Mint State, Full Red, 1,000.

Collecting Challenges: Find an eye-appealing example with a good strike and no problems. While strike is not a common problem with this date, it is worthwhile to search out the best coins you can find for whatever grade level you desire.

Collecting Circulated Pieces: The Optimal Collecting Grade is AU-50 to MS-63RB. Buy only problem-free examples. The major problems to avoid are cleaning, scratches, rim hits, corrosion, and spotting.

Collecting Mint State Pieces: The Optimal Collecting Grade is MS-65RD. Cents of this date are easily found in all grades except MS-65RD and higher. Fully struck pieces are harder to find than weakly struck. The common weak area is the feather tips.

Collecting Proof Issues: 1905 was not a particularly low-mintage year. Many of the coins, especially early-die-state coins, come with the die-polishing lines commonly found on 1901 to 1907 issues. These do not affect the grade of the coin, or at least they shouldn't. It seems that many coins that warrant a PF-65 grade or higher are only graded PF-64 because of these die-polishing lines. Typically these coins were graded early in the history of the grading services. Today's more experienced grader knows not to equate the presence or lack of die-polishing lines into the grade.

Varieties: There presently are 27 varieties, mostly minor repunched dates. Three varieties are known with doubled-die reverses.

A SNAPSHOT OF THE YEAR 1906

On February 23, saloonkeeper Johann Koch, known as the "Bluebeard of Chicago," was executed for murdering at least one of his 40+ wives. When he was arrested, police discovered in his room a loaded revolver, $625 in cash, several wedding rings with their inscriptions filed off, and a fountain pen holding 58 grams of arsenic.

In New York on March 28, the State Meteorological Office announced that the science of predicting the weather was "within our grasp."

On April 18 a major earthquake destroyed most of San Francisco, California, killing more than a thousand people. Shock waves continued on the 19th, and raging fires threatened the devastated city, including the fashionable Nob Hill district. Firefighters, frustrated by the destruction of water mains in the first temblor, took to using dynamite to try to defeat the infernos. To stop looters and control the disorder of thousands of people fleeing the city, martial law was declared and the Army was mobilized to assist local police.

On September 28, Secretary of War William Howard Taft declared himself provisional governor of Cuba after the resignation of President Eric Parma, under threat from anti-Yankee rebel forces led by Jose Gomez. In early October Taft would send the first of 5,500 soldiers to the island—ostensibly to supervise the disarming of both sides, but actually to suppress the liberal revolution.

San Francisco, 1906
The earthquake and fires of April 1906 rendered 225,000 citizens (of 400,000) homeless, destroyed 28,000 buildings, and wreaked more than $400 million in property damage.

1906 Indian Head Cent

CIRCULATION MINTAGE:
96,020,530

PROOF MINTAGE:
1,725

Enlarged 1.5x—Actual Size: 19mm

Market Values • Circulation Strikes and Proof Strikes

G-4	VG-8	F-12	VF-20	EF-40	AU-50	MS-60BN	MS-63RB	MS-64RB	MS-64RD
$2	$3	$4	$5	$10	$20	$35	$55	$100	$200
MS-65RB	MS-65RD	MS-66RD	PF-60RB	PF-63RB	PF-64RB	PF-64RD	PF-65RB	PF-65RD	PF-66RD
$175	$500	$2,500	$200	$300	$325	$650	$550	$1,350	$4,000

Certified Populations

G - VF	EF-40	EF-45	AU-50	AU-53	AU-55	AU-58	MS-60	MS-61	MS-62	MS-63	MS-64	MS-65	MS-66	MS-67	MS-68	MS-69	MS-70
54	72	46	80	2	73	61	82	39	159	1,430	5,877	3,417	535	21	0	0	0

<PF-60	PF-60	PF-61	PF-62	PF-63	PF-64	PF-65	PF-66	PF-67	PF-68	PF-69	PF-70
2	4	1	28	219	781	569	238	45	0	0	0

Field populations: Circulation strike (<MS-60), 2,500,000; circulation strike (MS-60+), 15,000; Proof, 650.

1906 Cent Production: The Mint produced a record number of cents this year.

Survivability: These coins circulated widely, and were not saved for numismatic purposes until the late 1940s. Original-roll quantities were occasionally discovered as late as the 1960s. Since the advent of third-party certification, any original roll that still exists does not stand much chance of staying intact. For protection purposes alone, certification offers many benefits. A gem full red Indian Head cent that has existed in a roll for 100 years will certainly stay that way even longer if nothing gets on its surface. The chance slip of a finger to the surface of a coin may leave skin oils that will turn into a fingerprint in the future. Also, someone coughing or speaking carelessly in the vicinity of an exposed coin may lead to ugly spotting over time.

Collecting Challenges: This date is usually found fully struck. Search out eye-appealing coins.

Collecting Circulated Pieces: The Optimal Collecting Grade is AU-50 to MS-63RB. This is one of the most plentiful dates in average circulated grades.

Collecting Mint State Pieces: The Optimal Collecting Grade is MS-65RD. Select problem-free examples with attractive eye appeal.

Collecting Proof Issues: This is a lower-mintage date in the late-date series, 1879 to 1909. These coins are fairly difficult to locate in all grades except PF-64RB. Gem full red examples are difficult, but some exceptional pieces are seen from time to time. Cameos are available for this date more frequently than for previous dates.

Varieties: There are more than 40 varieties recorded for this date. Most are minor repunched dates. Three dies are known with minor doubled dies. An example struck on a gold quarter-eagle planchet is known. It is graded AU-58 by NGC. Unlike the 1900 gold Indian Head cent, this appears to be a true wrong-metal planchet error.

A Snapshot of the Year 1907

In January 1907 Charles Curtis of Kansas became the first Native American senator in the United States. He would later serve as vice president under Herbert Hoover.

Early in the year, President Theodore Roosevelt put the United States Army in charge of building the Panama Canal, overseen by Colonel George Washington Goethals as chief engineer.

In May an outbreak of bubonic plague hit San Francisco, California, still recovering from the earthquake and fires of the previous year. The city's Health Department would eventually offer 5¢ for every rat delivered, dead or alive, to its offices, in an attempt to control the spread of the disease. (One ad recommended using tongs and dropping the dead rats into kerosene for an hour, going on to state, "They must be delivered to the stations in tightly covered cans labeled so as to show in what neighborhood they have been caught.")

S.S. Ancon in the Panama Canal
The first ship to transit the canal would be the *S.S. Ancon*, in August 1914—just days after World War I erupted in Europe.

Local newspapers suppressed news of the plague, fearing that it would scare off Eastern investors whose money was needed to rebuild the shattered city.

American advocates of women's suffrage were encouraged by developments in Europe in 1907: in Finland the first women were elected to the national parliament, and in Norway the right to vote was granted to women of a certain income bracket. (Britain would not be so accommodating, with dozens of women arrested in London for demanding suffrage.)

In late October a major banking panic was halted when J.P. Morgan, Henry Clay Frick, E.H. Harriman, James Stillman, and other financiers pooled $25 million to invest in the crashing New York Stock Exchange and bail out struggling banks.

The new state of Oklahoma was admitted to the Union in November, combined from the old Indian and Oklahoma territories.

1907 INDIAN HEAD CENT

CIRCULATION MINTAGE:
108,137,143

PROOF MINTAGE:
1,475

Enlarged 1.5x—Actual Size: 19mm

Market Values • Circulation Strikes and Proof Strikes

G-4	VG-8	F-12	VF-20	EF-40	AU-50	MS-60BN	MS-63RB	MS-64RB	MS-64RD
$2	$3	$4	$5	$10	$20	$35	$55	$100	$200
MS-65RB	MS-65RD	MS-66RD	PF-60RB	PF-63RB	PF-64RB	PF-64RD	PF-65RB	PF-65RD	PF-66RD
$175	$500	$2,000	$200	$300	$350	$950	$550	$1,750	$4,000

Certified Populations

G - VF	EF-40	EF-45	AU-50	AU-53	AU-55	AU-58	MS-60	MS-61	MS-62	MS-63	MS-64	MS-65	MS-66	MS-67	MS-68	MS-69	MS-70
92	88	59	105	10	70	80	112	49	188	1,949	6,260	3,291	242	14	0	0	0
<PF-60	PF-60		PF-61	PF-62		PF-63	PF-64		PF-65	PF-66		PF-67	PF-68		PF-69		PF-70
5	3		6	24		262	753		487	270		33	0		0		0

Field populations: Circulation strike (<MS-60), 3,000,000; circulation strike (MS-60+), 18,000; Proof, 650.

1907 Cent Production: This date holds the record for production of any coin minted by the United States up until this time. The Mint would break this production record again in 1909, but that year's mintage is divided between Indian Head cents and those of the new Lincoln design.

Late in 1907 the country saw a financial panic due to the failure of a few large businesses. Stock prices crashed and nearly started an economic meltdown. Financier J.P. Morgan and a group of bank executives temporarily supported the failing banks and restored stability to the market. The resulting inquiry resulted in the beginnings of what would become the Federal Reserve System.

Survivability: Cents of 1907 circulated widely and are the most commonly found in average circulated condition. Even if only 5% of the mintage were saved, which is likely, there would be enough coins to satisfy demand from collectors. Even so, examples in Good condition sell today for at least 100 times their face value! This is a testament to both the collector demand for Indian Head cents and the shrinking value printed on their face.

Collecting Challenges: Select problem-free coins. These are plentiful enough that a quality example should be easy to acquire.

Collecting Circulated Pieces: The Optimal Collecting Grade is AU-50 to MS-63RB. Avoid problems and take extra care to find the coin that matches your set the best.

Collecting Mint State Pieces: The Optimal Collecting Grade is MS-65RD. Only in lower Mint State grades is this date the most common. In gem condition a 1907 cent is slightly more difficult to find than many other dates. The issue of quality over technical grade is an important concern here. Many 1907 cents do not come with the great eye appeal found on other dates. This is purely a factor of chance survival of a few lesser-quality rolls than anything else. Take extra time to find the real attractive pieces.

Collecting Proof Issues: This is the low-mintage date of the later dates, 1879 to 1909, in Proof format. This is surprising to newer collectors. The Mint did not produce Mint State coins for collectors, and they didn't want to make more Proof issues than they could sell. Coins this year come with die-polishing lines more often than do other dates. True gems are very scarce and command a good premium over other dates. Full cameo examples exist but are scarce.

Varieties: There are 47 varieties of this date currently recorded, more than any other date. Collecting these could be a daunting task. Collections assembled by early variety collectors Joe Haney and Al Mays Sr. were close to complete, and formed the basis of my *Flying Eagle and Indian Cent Attribution Guide, Volume 6, 1900–1909*. Today, at least, collectors have a referral list or attribution guide. Joe Haney had been collecting Indian Head cent varieties long before anyone else thought to look for them. Al Mays Sr. started collecting them in the late 1990s when I decided to add the known varieties to the book that was published in 1992. Al purchased many of the known varieties. The Al Mays collection was auctioned through Heritage Galleries in 2005. Today, collecting later-date Indian Head cents can be a fascinating excursion. There are certainly enough coins to look through. A collector on a modest budget can look through and buy many interesting repunched dates, misplaced dates, and even doubled dies, for small premiums.

A SNAPSHOT OF THE YEAR 1908

January 1, 1908, was marked by the first instance of the ball dropping in Manhattan's Times Square to herald the arrival of the new year.

On February 26 Tex Avery was born. He would grow up to be a cartoonist, animator, writer, and director, most famous for his work at the Warner Bros., Metro-Goldwyn-Mayer, and Hanna-Barbera studios. Avery created Bugs Bunny, Daffy Duck, and Droopy Dog, and influenced generations of animators with his style and creativity. Three months later, on May 30, Mel Blanc would be born—the voice actor who would give vocal expression to many of Avery's famous characters.

On May 21 the first horror movie, *Dr. Jekyll and Mr. Hyde*, premiered in Chicago. The one-reel film was by the Selig Polyscope Company.

On November 3, William Howard Taft, the Republican candidate, was elected 27th president of the United States. Lame-duck president Theodore Roosevelt would visit the city of Panama later in the month—the first president to travel abroad during his term of office.

In December, Texas-born fighter Jack Johnson made boxing history when he knocked out reigning champ Tommy Burns of Canada, becoming the first black man to hold the heavyweight championship of the world. 30-year-old Johnson was the fifth American to hold the title.

William Jennings Bryan and the Gold:Silver Ratio

Bryan had campaigned for the presidency in 1896 on a Free Silver platform. In 1900 he championed anti-imperialism, and in 1908, was strongly anti-trust. He called for Democrats to renounce conservatism, fight monopolies and big banks, and embrace progressive ideals.

1908 INDIAN HEAD CENT

CIRCULATION MINTAGE:
32,326,367

PROOF MINTAGE:
1,620

Enlarged 1.5x—Actual Size: 19mm

Market Values • Circulation Strikes and Proof Strikes

G-4	VG-8	F-12	VF-20	EF-40	AU-50	MS-60BN	MS-63RB	MS-64RB	MS-64RD
$2	$3	$4	$5	$10	$20	$35	$55	$100	$200
MS-65RB	MS-65RD	MS-66RD	PF-60RB	PF-63RB	PF-64RB	PF-64RD	PF-65RB	PF-65RD	PF-66RD
$175	$500	$1,750	$200	$300	$325	$600	$525	$1,350	$3,500

Certified Populations

G - VF	EF-40	EF-45	AU-50	AU-53	AU-55	AU-58	MS-60	MS-61	MS-62	MS-63	MS-64	MS-65	MS-66	MS-67	MS-68	MS-69	MS-70
50	50	22	59	4	35	44	76	24	118	1,392	5,515	3,740	621	20	0	0	0
<PF-60	PF-60	PF-61	PF-62	PF-63	PF-64	PF-65	PF-66	PF-67	PF-68	PF-69	PF-70						
6	5	8	20	207	793	843	391	42	0	0	0						

Field populations: Circulation strike (<MS-60), 2,500,000; circulation strike (MS-60+), 17,500; Proof, 700.

1908 Cent Production: Mintage figures dropped dramatically this year.

Survivability: Although fewer coins were minted in 1908 compared to the previous year, this date is essentially no harder to locate today than any other, except perhaps in low grades.

Collecting Challenges: Examples in every grade are available. Select the most attractive and problem-free coin you can.

Collecting Circulated Pieces: The Optimal Collecting Grade is AU-50 to MS-63RB. Avoid problem pieces. Examples with odd color have usually been cleaned and should be avoided as well. Collecting choice Extremely Fine and About Uncirculated Indian Head cents is a very difficult and challenging pursuit. Many collectors who are very active have said to me that they maintain multiple collections in varying grades. As they upgrade their top set, the duplicates go into secondary collections. Only when collectors need money for a very expensive date will they part with their lowest set.

Collecting Mint State Pieces: The Optimal Collecting Grade is MS-65RD. These come well struck with better-than-average luster. 1908 cents are not any scarcer than those of other dates, although the mintage might suggest otherwise. All Indian Head cents in gem full red condition are difficult to find. Additional effort should be taken to acquire pieces with no major problems such as spots.

Collecting Proof Issues: This is a lower-mintage date within the later-date Proofs. These tend to come with very good mirrors, although deep mirror cameo examples are quite scarce. The Mint's practice of leaving die-polishing lines on the dies seems to have ended, as this date is not usually found with them.

Varieties: 26 varieties are known for this date. About half of these are repunched dates of moderate interest. The remaining varieties are misplaced dates, which are quite prevalent for this year. Misplaced dates are varieties wherein remnants from some of the digits are found in the denticles or areas of the portrait. (They could conceivably be anywhere on the design, but tend to be found in these two areas.) Prevailing opinion is that these digits were intentionally tapped into the dies, perhaps to test their hardness. The digits are usually found only on obverse dies. Collectors pay the highest premiums for the most prominent examples with the errant digit extending into the field area or in some other obvious place. Significant misplaced date varieties are listed in my *Flying Eagle and Indian Cent Attribution Guide, Volume 6, 1900–1909*. Additional examples are listed in *Two Dates are Better Than One, A Collectors Guide to Misplaced Dates*, by Kevin Flynn. One collector-researcher, Marvin Erickson, has assembled an enormous collection of misplaced dates. He began a search for these varieties long before they became well known to the general collecting public.

1908-S INDIAN HEAD CENT

Enlarged 1.5x—Actual Size: 19mm

CIRCULATION MINTAGE:
1,115,000

PROOF MINTAGE:
NOT MADE IN PROOF FORMAT

Market Values • Circulation Strikes

G-4	VG-8	F-12	VF-20	EF-40	AU-50	MS-60BN	MS-63RB	MS-64RB	MS-64RD
$65	$75	$85	$100	$150	$225	$275	$375	$425	$800
MS-65RB	**MS-65RD**	**MS-66RD**	**PF-60RB**	**PF-63RB**	**PF-64RB**	**PF-64RD**	**PF-65RB**	**PF-65RD**	**PF-66RD**
$600	$3,000	$8,000							

Certified Populations

G - VF	EF-40	EF-45	AU-50	AU-53	AU-55	AU-58	MS-60	MS-61	MS-62	MS-63	MS-64	MS-65	MS-66	MS-67	MS-68	MS-69	MS-70
694	337	219	198	37	151	185	76	68	216	1,524	3,782	2,387	333	0	0	0	0
<PF-60	**PF-60**	**PF-61**	**PF-62**	**PF-63**	**PF-64**	**PF-65**	**PF-66**	**PF-67**	**PF-68**	**PF-69**	**PF-70**						

Field populations: Circulation strike (<MS-60), 80,000; circulation strike (MS-60+), 2,500.

1908-S Cent Production: This cent is important as being the first minor coinage struck at a branch mint. The San Francisco Mint, nicknamed *The Granite Lady*, was built in 1874 and had survived the great earthquake of the morning of April 18, 1906, with just slight damage. The fire that raged on all sides of the building later on that day blackened the stone and buckled the heavy iron shutters. The fire destroyed most of the city, but the mint was spared destruction because it had its own well that firefighters could tap into.

In years prior to the earthquake and subsequent economic hardships, gold and silver coins were the only coinage used in the Western states. Transactions were rounded to the nearest 5¢. Now, due to changes in the economy (brought on in part by the relative ease of railroad travel from the East), it was desirable to have the cent denomination available so that prices could be increased in smaller increments. The introduction of a sales tax alone necessitated the use of the cent. In addition, the street-car fare was raised from 5¢ to 6¢.

The Mint delivered the entire mintage of coins on November 27. These were struck on presses used for silver coinage, as the two presses for cent production were not yet delivered. This is the third-lowest mintage of the Indian Head cent series. Planchet stock for this year was often improperly mixed, so the coins vary with either woodgrain toning or a bright golden color.

Survivability: The new cents were certainly a curiosity to the local population, and initially circulated widely. Later, by the time the new Lincoln design became dominant, the general public selectively removed the Indian Head cents from circulation. There seems to have been no initial interest in saving these coins before they entered circulation. Today, the coins are scarce in low grades, but available in mid-range grades, most being Fine to Very Fine. Mint State survivors are very scarce overall. The chance survival of a few roll quantities has made gem full red examples somewhat readily available. Many of these come from a roll that had a filled final A in AMERICA on the obverse.

Collecting Challenges: These cents are scarce and popular, so demand is high. Many come with weak feather tips. Search for fully struck examples.

Collecting Circulated Pieces: The Optimal Collecting Grade is AU-50 to AU-58. There is not a great difference in prices between coins graded Good to Very Fine. For collectors on a budget it is worthwhile to buy the highest grade with the price jumping less than 50%. For example, a Fine coin lists for $85, a Very Fine at $100, and an Extremely Fine at $150. The extra $15 to buy the Very Fine will give you a lot more value for the money than would the extra $50 to buy the Extremely Fine. On the other hand, the best advice is always to buy the best coin you can afford that fits your collection.

Collecting Mint State Pieces: The Optimal Collecting Grade is MS-65RB or MS-64RD. It might be difficult to find coins with full feather tips. Take extra time to search these out. These come with woodgrain toning, which is acceptable for red-brown graded coins. Full red coins should be struck on evenly colored planchets. Many full red coins are of a lighter golden color. Some original coins might easily be mistaken as being cleaned if compared to their Philadelphia Mint contemporaries. Occasionally prooflike examples are available. These are highly desired and are worth an additional premium.

Varieties: A repunched mintmark, Snow-1, is known for this date. The repunching is to the south and is visible in the upper part of the S. Many other repunched dates have been reported but all others have turned out to be caused by strike doubling. When the lower die (anvil die) is loose in the press it can move slightly when the coin is struck. This action leaves a microscopic outline on the design elements in one direction. (The clue to detecting strike doubling: the doubling is seen on the mintmark as well as on some of the surrounding design elements. Since the mintmark is added to the die separately from the design element, it cannot be a repunched mintmark.)

1908-S/S Snow-1

A Snapshot of the Year 1909

A war was raging in the United States in 1909: a battle waged against alcohol by prohibitionists, with women at the forefront. Carry Nation now had 500 followers, an "army" that organized destructive raids on saloons. She vowed to keep fighting as long as "there are yet some hell-holes" in Kansas—"Then I will organize a band of women who will smash all of the saloons in the world." In New York State 315 townships banned drinking establishments, as did 48 towns in Colorado; in Ohio, 57 of the state's 66 counties shut down their bars. In Tennessee it was an offense to manufacture or sell liquor.

Carry Nation
She believed that alcohol destroyed families—so she was determined to destroy alcohol. The famous prohibitionist collapsed on stage during a speech in 1911. Her final words: "I have done what I could." (Illustration by political cartoonist Albert T. Reid, 1901)

On January 27 the U.S. governor of Cuba left the island and Jose Gomez was sworn in as president of the republic. Later in the year the United States would ouster the Liberal dictator of Nicaragua.

Commander Robert Peary of the United States Navy is credited as the first person to reach the North Pole, on April 6, 1909. He had sailed to Greenland in the *Roosevelt* and then traveled to the pole in a 90-mile, 36-day trek. Peary's claim would be contested by a Brooklyn doctor, Frederick Cook, who insisted he'd reached the pole in 1908, accompanied by two Eskimos. In December 1909 a committee dismissed Cook's claim and conclusively announced Peary's accomplishment. (Congress would recognize Peary in 1911 with its official thanks for his achievement, but research years later would suggest that he might have missed the pole by as much as 30 miles.)

On November 14 President William Taft announced that a naval base would be built at Pearl Harbor in Hawaii, to protect the United States from Japanese attack.

New York City played host to Sergei Rachmaninov on November 28, as he presented the world premier of his third piano concerto.

In 1909 the Indian Head cent was consigned to history: the Lincoln cent, issued to commemorate the centennial of the Great Emancipator's birth, would take its place on the numismatic scene.

1909 INDIAN HEAD CENT

CIRCULATION MINTAGE:
14,368,470

PROOF MINTAGE:
2,175

Enlarged 1.5x—Actual Size: 19mm

Market Values • Circulation Strikes and Proof Strikes

G-4	VG-8	F-12	VF-20	EF-40	AU-50	MS-60BN	MS-63RB	MS-64RB	MS-64RD
$3.50	$4	$5	$6	$18	$22	$37	$60	$100	$200
MS-65RB	MS-65RD	MS-66RD	PF-60RB	PF-63RB	PF-64RB	PF-64RD	PF-65RB	PF-65RD	PF-66RD
$175	$500	$1,750	$200	$300	$375	$600	$525	$1,350	$3,500

Certified Populations

G - VF	EF-40	EF-45	AU-50	AU-53	AU-55	AU-58	MS-60	MS-61	MS-62	MS-63	MS-64	MS-65	MS-66	MS-67	MS-68	MS-69	MS-70
26	41	15	47	2	37	25	87	44	192	2,057	7,531	5,407	670	14	0	0	0

<PF-60	PF-60	PF-61	PF-62	PF-63	PF-64	PF-65	PF-66	PF-67	PF-68	PF-69	PF-70
4	7	3	22	249	845	789	415	32	0	0	0

Field populations: Circulation strike (<MS-60), 1,500,000; circulation strike (MS-60+), 20,000; Proof, 800.

1909 Cent Production: The Mint changed its procedure for making cent dies this year. For this date only, and continuing on all Lincoln cents, the entire design with the date was sunk into the die at one time. Prior to this year the procedure was to add the date after the obverse die was sunk with the design and legend. This change eliminated the possibility of a repunched date. Every cent with doubling on the date from this year onward is called a *doubled die*, rather than a *repunched date.*

Up until this time, many of the planchets used were purchased by contract from manufacturing companies. This year the Mint crafted its own planchets for the entire mintage.

Coinage of Indian Head cents ceased mid-year, awaiting the new Lincoln design by Victor D. Brenner to be finished. The 1909 mintage is the lowest since 1885.

Survivability: As the last Indian Head cent, many people put away examples of this date. Many roll quantities existed, making this the most common date in gem full red condition. However, most of the 1909 cents put away were the new Lincoln design with the designer's initials V.D.B. on the reverse, which are today on the order of 100 times more common than the 1909 Indian Head cent. In lower grades the coin is as common as any other, although catalogers tend to price it a bit higher than earlier dates. Only in Good and Very Good is it slightly scarcer, but not enough to warrant paying more.

Collecting Challenges: Search out exceptional pieces. Try not to pay a large premium over other common dates.

Collecting Circulated Pieces: The Optimal Collecting Grade is AU-50 to MS-63RB. These come well struck, so buy the most attractive coin available.

Collecting Mint State Pieces: The Optimal Collecting Grade is MS-65RD. This is the most readily available date in the series in high grade. Select eye-appealing examples.

Collecting Proof Issues: 1909 Proofs tend to be available with good eye appeal. Gem full red examples are difficult to find. Mirrors tend to be moderate, with cameo examples being fairly scarce. As a year with three designs (Indian Head, Lincoln with V.D.B., and Lincoln without V.D.B.), there is slightly higher demand for this date over others.

Varieties: No repunched dates are possible, as the date was added to the hub instead of to coinage dies starting this year. At least two dies are known with doubling on the designer's initial L. This is a minor doubled die and is relatively common.

1909-S INDIAN HEAD CENT

CIRCULATION MINTAGE:
309,000

PROOF MINTAGE:
NOT MADE IN PROOF FORMAT

Enlarged 1.5x—Actual Size: 19mm

Market Values • Circulation Strikes

G-4	VG-8	F-12	VF-20	EF-40	AU-50	MS-60BN	MS-63RB	MS-64RB	MS-64RD
$350	$400	$435	$450	$500	$600	$700	$800	$1,250	$2,500
MS-65RB	MS-65RD	MS-66RD	PF-60RB	PF-63RB	PF-64RB	PF-64RD	PF-65RB	PF-65RD	PF-66RD
$1,750	$5,500	$17,500							

Certified Populations

G - VF	EF-40	EF-45	AU-50	AU-53	AU-55	AU-58	MS-60	MS-61	MS-62	MS-63	MS-64	MS-65	MS-66	MS-67	MS-68	MS-69	MS-70
1,740	390	277	174	47	141	165	73	51	163	1,499	3,451	1,885	142	1	0	0	0
<PF-60	PF-60	PF-61	PF-62	PF-63	PF-64	PF-65	PF-66	PF-67	PF-68	PF-69	PF-70						

Field populations: Circulation strike (<MS-60), 25,000; circulation strike (MS-60+), 3,500.

1909-S Cent Production: This is the lowest-mintage cent of the entire series. Its dies, produced in Philadelphia, were completely hubbed with the date incorporated. As a result, there are no positional variations for the date. The obverse dies always show slight weakness on the first feather tip. Collectors should rely on a full shield and bust point to confirm a full strike, as all 1909-S cents will show this feather-tip weakness. In fact, any example with full feather tips should be checked for an added mintmark. The mintmark is slightly larger than the one used for the new Lincoln design. Planchets tend to be a bit lighter than their Philadelphia Mint counterparts. They tend to be a straw-golden color.

Survivability: These coins were saved as the last of their issue. Non-collectors saved them as the last of the design, and numismatists pulled them quickly from circulation due to their known low mintage. The rarity is much lower than the low-mintage coins of earlier years because of this higher survival rate.

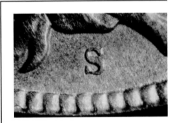

1909-S Mintmark

This date is very rare in low grades, so prices for grades below Very Fine tend to be very similar. Most examples grade Very Fine to About Uncirculated. In Mint State, the coins are fairly scarce. Full red examples are very difficult to locate.

Collecting Challenges: Avoid problem pieces. Don't expect to find any bargain-priced examples unless the coins are cleaned or have had some other indignity performed on them.

Collecting Circulated Pieces: The Optimal Collecting Grade is EF-40. Overgrading is a problem because dealers believe there is not a big enough spread between grades to make their profit margin. I argue that the ease of selling these at present levels *should* equate to lower margins.

Collecting Mint State Pieces: The Optimal Collecting Grade is MS-64RB. The certified populations on this date are similar in most grades to many of the semi-common dates. This may be the case, but most 1909-S cents are submitted for certification and the more common dates of Indian Head cents are often not submitted. The 1909-S is a very popular cent and should be compared to another coin of similar mintage that is usually always submitted for certification, the 1909-S V.D.B. Lincoln cent. In MS-65RB and MS-65RD, the number of 1909-S V.D.B. coins graded by ANACS, NGC, and PCGS is 10 times what is shown for the 1909-S Indian Head cent.

Varieties: No varieties are known for the 1909-S cent.

Counterfeits: Many counterfeits exist for this coin. Some are false-die counterfeits. These tend to have very sharp, flat edges, whereas the genuine 1909-S issue has a beveled edge. Most numerous are Philadelphia Mint 1909 cents with an added mint-mark. These will usually have a very sharp first feather tip. Since all authentic 1909-S coins have a slight weakness on this point, a sharp feather tip might give away a suspicious offering. Certification and a written bill of sale from a reputable dealer will greatly decrease your chance of purchasing a counterfeit.

For more on counterfeit and altered cents, see appendix B.

APPENDIX A: THE LIFE OF JAMES B. LONGACRE

The Longacre family of Delaware County, Pennsylvania, had immigrated to the area from Sweden well before the establishment of the colony. James Barton Longacre was born on August 11, 1794, into a rural agrarian life. His mother died early in his life, and after his father remarried, young Longacre found the situation intolerable. At the age of 12, he ran away from his home for the city life of Philadelphia.

LONGACRE'S EARLY LIFE

Longacre's first apprenticeship was in a bookstore owned by John F. Watson. He worked diligently for Watson for many years, learning the skills that he lacked from his early departure from home life. It was apparent to Watson that Longacre's talent was as a portrait artist. Watson gave James his leave in 1813 so that he could learn engraving from George Murray of Philadelphia. Teacher and apprentice remained close friends for many years, and Watson was later helpful in promoting Longacre's private works.

Longacre indentured himself with Murray as an apprentice. The contract held Longacre for a period of no fewer than three years and 10 months. At the time, George Murray was a partner in Murray, Draper, Fairman & Co., a banknote-engraving firm acquired in 1810 from the demise of the engraving business started by Mint Engraver Robert Scot in 1795.

At the time, before the age of photography, the only way to mass produce any artistic work on the printed page was to have an engraving made in either wood or, preferably, copper or steel. Longacre proved a very capable artist in this process. Among his published works from this period were the portraits of Washington, Jefferson, and Hancock on a facsimile of the Declaration of Independence, published by John Binns in 1818. This plate was the largest engraving ever made up to that time in the United States. It measured 35" by 25" and cost the publishers $9,000. From this work and subsequent engravings, Longacre gained a very fine reputation for transferring other artist's portraiture to steel engravings. In 1819 he left Murray and set up his own business at 230 Pine Street in Philadelphia.

The young engraver's first contract came from brothers John and Joseph Sanderson, who were assembling a collection of biographies entitled *Biography of the Signers to the Declaration of Independence*. This work was published in nine volumes from 1820 through 1827. Almost immediately problems began with the project, primarily focusing on the writing (by John Sanderson), which suffered from a lack of proper editorial finishing. Also, accusations of plagiarism were thrown at them in the press, and ultimately, the Sanderson brothers quit the venture in 1822, after publishing only two of the nine volumes. The project, being underfinanced from the start, had not been producing satisfactory revenue. However, the first two volumes sold well enough that a continuation of the project was feasible. Also a new writer, Robert Waln Jr., and a new publisher, Ralph Pomeroy, were hired on. The time-consuming task of engraving the portraits continued to be done by Longacre, who produced nearly all of the 30-plus engravings.

It must have been evident to Longacre that the quality of his engravings was the main reason for the continued sales of this work. Unfortunately, he was still under contract, so he reaped no additional reward for the success of the books. During this time he also produced a set of engravings featuring actors in their character roles for *The American Theatre* (1826).

After the Sanderson-Pomeroy series ended, Longacre began the planning stages of his own biographical series of engravings. His idea was to make engravings from life of prominent persons, accompanied by brief biographical

James B. Longacre at 41

sketches. He weighed the good and bad from the *Biography of the Signers to the Declaration of Independence* and decided to place the emphasis on the portrait itself and not the biography. By 1831 publishing contracts were signed, subscriptions were issued, and sales agents were contacted. Longacre invested $1,000 of his own money to procure all the necessary equipment for the project, which was to be called *The American Portrait Gallery*.

Longacre's dream of producing a great portrait series was about to become a reality in 1831 when, to his great surprise, he discovered the existence of a rival project! He learned of it that February from an advertisement in a Washington newspaper, proclaiming the future publication of *An American Portrait Gallery*, which was to be issued by the summer of 1832 by James Herring of New York. Longacre must have been stunned by the appearance of a competing project. He quickly contacted Herring in October to strike a deal to collaborate on these identical projects.

John Herring was, at the time, secretary of the American Academy of Fine Arts. Although an artist, his business acumen was much more developed than Longacre's. One need only look as far as their engravings: Herring's invariably come with a copyright, while Longacre omitted this feature, as he would later regret. Herring's ideas for the series differed from Longacre's in that he was including all great Americans, not just living ones, and was giving each a lengthy biography.

Having learned many of the hardships associated with a project of this nature from his experiences with the Sanderson-Pomeroy series, Longacre showed Herring and the Academy that collaboration was essential to its success. The Academy accepted Longacre's contributions, and since they had already drawn up a plan, Longacre had to modify his own plans to fit theirs. He was really in no position to continue on his own, having sold only 20 or so subscriptions. The collaboration looked as if it would benefit all parties involved.

The project became *The National Portrait Gallery of Distinguished Americans*. This monumental work was published in four volumes between 1834 and 1839. It was in these works that Longacre began to show his own talent as an original portrait artist. The series contained 144 plates by 26 engravers. Longacre traveled extensively to fulfill his desire to make his engravings from life portraits. He would make a watercolor drawing from life, from which he would make his engraving plate. Among his original drawings are fine portraits of President Madison at age 82, and President Jackson, both completed from life in July of 1833.

Longacre made quite a name for himself with the political leaders of the day, many of whom were extremely flattered by his fine portraits. One of these individuals, former vice president John C. Calhoun, would later help Longacre secure the position of engraver at the Mint.

James Longacre also built a fine family during these years, marrying Eliza Stiles in 1827. They had five children: Sarah in 1828, Andrew in 1831, James Madison in 1833, Eliza Huldah in 1837, and Orleans in 1840. The memories of his own disadvantaged and fractured childhood motivated James Longacre to create a sound environment for his children.

Lagging sales of *The Gallery* (due in part to the depression of 1837) forced Longacre to declare bankruptcy. To pay back

Eliza Stiles Longacre, 1835

his debts, he traveled to the South and Western Reserve states peddling his works from town to town. His wife, Eliza, and young daughter, Sarah, managed the business of shipping and accounting back in Philadelphia. Later that year, Longacre formed a banknote-engraving company, Toppan, Draper, Longacre & Co., with Charles Toppan and William Draper. Longacre, who by this time had gained a reputation as the best engraver in the country, had known William Draper since his time as an apprentice.

THE MINT HIRES LONGACRE

Director of the Mint Robert M. Patterson appointed Longacre to be chief engraver on September 16, 1844, after more than a month-long search following the death of the previous chief engraver, Christian Gobrecht.

The talents associated with engraving steel printing plates are quite different from those needed for the arts of coin design, hub and punch making, and die sinking. Longacre was not entirely trained in any of these talents. He was not under pressure to produce for the first five years of his work at the Mint, as all that was required during this time was die manufacture.

Many die errors occurred during Longacre's early years at the Mint. Examples of these early blunders are evident on the 1844/81 and 1851/81 cents, where the "18" date-punch was inadvertently used upside down. All 1851 half cents show an extra 1 to the right of the date. Some 1846 half dollars show the last 6 punched into the die lying horizontally, and then corrected. Double eagles of 1850 to 1858 indicate that LIBERTY (on the headband) was originally started as LLI, and then corrected.

Longacre Shortly After Joining the Mint

It is unlikely that many of these errors should be attributed to Longacre himself. Engravers by the very nature of their work tend to develop the traits of a perfectionist. Moreover, the die shop was under the control of the chief coiner—at this time, Franklin Peale.

Franklin Peale (one of 17 children of famed artist/inventor Charles Willson Peale) was a gifted mechanical engineer, and was instrumental in upgrading the Mint's antiquated equipment. He brought the portrait lathe and steam coining press to the Mint from his travels to Europe. Peale had over the years become very comfortable in his position at the Mint, to the point that he considered himself to be irreplaceable. He had built a side business making hubs and dies for medals for special clients. Additionally, Peale and Mint Director Robert M. Patterson had been systematically skimming profits off of bullion deposits.

There were growing internal tensions between Longacre and Mint Director Patterson and his loyal chief coiner. Having an ethical chief engraver threatened their sideline. Peale used every opportunity to meddle in Longacre's work. The ultimate goal was the latter's replacement.

The attacks came to a head when the new denominations of the gold dollar and double eagle were called for in 1849. It began as a clash over the use of the Contamin portrait lathe, the single piece of machinery the two men used for die production. While Peale was dominating the machine, Longacre complained. Peale sabotaged many of Longacre's projects.

The development of the first double eagle was done in the midst of the battle between the two men. Peter F. Cross, a part-time assistant to Longacre from New York, made the first obverse die for the coin between November 6 and December 20, 1849. Longacre produced the reverse die at the same time. When the first 1849 double eagle was made on December 22, Longacre noted in his diary, "The work did not come up as well as expected." Longacre reworked the obverse design and finished it on January 11, 1850. The die trial was left undated.

On January 26, 1850, several gold specimens were struck to test the dies. Peale complained about the new dies, declaring that the design was too deep to strike up correctly. Longacre needed one of the gold specimens to correct the problem, but Peale blocked their use, citing accounting problems, and had them melted. Longacre believed that this was an attack on his authority. Peale relented and allowed a piece in silver to be struck.

The conspiracy against Longacre also included Mint Director Patterson. Patterson had, on Christmas Day, 1849, gone so far as to secretly give a promise of appointment to Charles Cushing Wright, effective on the day Longacre was ousted. This promise was carried out in early February 1850. Longacre later related the matter in a deposition against Peale:

> [The Director} called on me privately in my room, when he stated that he had the painful intelligence to communicate to me that my removal from office had been determined on by the government, and advised me rather urgently to send in my resignation without delay. I was surprised and troubled at this communication, because it was, under the circumstances, a mortifying termination to a severe and painful effort to sustain, single handed, the arduous requirements of my office. I knew that I had labored faithfully, and I had never known my character as an artist to be seriously assailed. In the absence of positive information, these incidents were of a character to excite the suspicion of secret and unfriendly interference. I resolved not to use haste that was recommended in throwing up my commission, but first to seek an interview with the Secretary of the Treasury, who was Mr. Meridith of this city, and with whom, from my previous acquaintance, I had not the slightest cause to apprehend an unfriendly purpose.

Longacre went to Washington on February 12, 1850, to save his job. While there, he learned that all of the incriminating information that was given to Treasury Secretary Meridith was totally fabricated by Patterson and Peale. Longacre sought little retribution, satisfied only to continue his work at the Mint unimpaired. Patterson was replaced when the administration changed in 1853, and Peale was fired in 1854.

Longacre's wife, Eliza, died during 1850. This event and the problems at the Mint might have given him reason enough to leave Philadelphia and head for new opportunities in San Francisco, but he chose to stay with the Mint. His most productive years were just ahead.

PIONEER GOLD AND FEDERAL COINS

There is a hypothesis given by some numismatists that Longacre worked on certain private pioneer gold dies. Some interesting entries in his diary during the next few months bring to light new information.

On April 16, 1850, Longacre traveled to New Brunswick, New Jersey, to meet with Peter Y. Cross. On April 17, he wrote: "Gave Mr. Cross the dies (1 pair) with the necessary directions to be made for Dobosq and Co." It is interesting that Longacre was now free to work on a private contract and apparently felt no apprehension to openly do so. Longacre's diary also notes that he used outside sources for various punches. An example of this outside work was detailed as he wrote that William Dougherty made a LIBERTY punch for use on the head of the gold dollar.

Longacre accomplished what his predecessors could not—he was able to add his initials to his new gold dollar and double eagle. His initials, JBL, are located on the truncation of the base of the bust of Liberty on the double eagle. His initial on the gold dollar is a single incuse L. No public objection has ever been noted to the addition of his initials.

During the next 15 years, James Longacre designed more new denominations than at any other time since the early years of the Mint. Among the new coin denominations designed by Longacre are the gold dollar and double eagle (1849), trime or silver three-cent piece (1850), $3 gold piece (1854), small cent (1856), two-cent piece (1864), nickel three-cent piece (1865), and nickel five-cent piece (1866).

Longacre's first designs for the gold dollar and double eagle used features for the head of Liberty that were inspired by a Greco-Roman statue, *Venus Accroupie* or Crouching Venus, which at the time was on display in Philadelphia (and is now located in the Vatican museum).

During the early 1850s, Longacre worked on new ideas for the small cent. Many of the designs for these patterns were utilitarian in their nature, the main emphasis being on the experimental materials used. The first patterns were small coins with center holes to increase the outside diameter. These annular cents contained a small amount of silver to maintain the metal value of the coin. Other small-cent patterns were made using already existing dies. An 1853 cent pattern was made using a current quarter eagle die for the obverse. Another cent pattern die was reduced directly from a silver dollar!

The next new denomination called for was the silver three-cent coin, in 1851. Peale and Longacre again were at odds. Peale created a pattern for the new denomination using a motif originally designed by Christian Gobrecht in 1836. It featured a liberty cap with rays. Longacre used very simple designs of a shield within a star for the obverse and a Roman numeral III encircled by the letter C for the reverse. Longacre's design was accepted. This simple design had to be reformatted more than once because of difficulties in striking it up.

During this time, gold from California was reaching the Mint in record quantities. This oversupply created an imbalance between gold and silver prices. Silver increased in value compared to the weakness in gold. This imbalance drove out of circulation all silver coinage except for the silver three-cent piece, which had less than its face value worth of silver. This problem was temporarily corrected by the Mint Act of February 21, 1853, which slightly reduced the amount of precious metal in the silver coinage from half dollars to half dimes. Longacre was required to show this change by altering the designs. For the quarter and half dollar dies, he made a punch that added rays to the reverse. For the obverse of these and the smaller denominations, he put arrows on either side of the date. The reverse dies with rays tended to crack early in their life, so they were dropped the following year.

The year 1854 brought the introduction of the new $3 coin. Longacre's Liberty Head was crowned with a headdress of feathers inspired by the Indian tribes of northern Mexico, symbolizing the source of the majority of the gold used in the coins. This Indian Princess is of the same head design used later for the Indian Head cent, but with the headdress redesigned. The new reverse design was an innovative wreath balancing the agricultural products of the North and South. Corn and wheat from the North was combined with cotton and tobacco from the South. This wreath has been referred to as the "Agricultural Wreath." This design was also used later for the Flying Eagle cent, in 1856.

The gold dollar was also redesigned to this Indian Princess theme, using the same head but altered by making the headband very wide and shortening the feathers. This design did not strike up well at all, and was redesigned to the same style as the $3 gold piece a few years later. The reverse also carried the new cornucopia wreath.

During 1854 and 1855 the Mint rejected the idea of changing the alloy of the cent and began experiments on a slightly-reduced-size copper large cent. Longacre started using an original design of a Flying Eagle motif on these cent patterns. They proved difficult to strike up fully.

In late 1856 Mint Director Snowden was interested in getting Congress to pass a new cent coin, in a new metal and a new size. Longacre was instructed to create new working designs. The difficulties in striking coins in a harder nickel alloy would require a different design from his earlier Flying Eagle. Rather

Longacre at 61

than devise a new design, he looked back 20 years to the Flying Eagle dollars of Christian Gobrecht. Gobrecht's design had in turn been based on drawings by the artist Titian Peale, brother of Franklin Peale.

On Longacre's original design the eagle is shown flying upwards holding a shield and arrows. This was probably considered a bit too busy for the small coin, and was dropped. On the finished coin the eagle is flying level.

In 1858, alterations were made to both the obverse and reverse designs of the cent to help the longevity of the dies. On the obverse, the eagle's relief was made shallower and the lettering smaller. It is believed that Assistant Engraver Anthony Paquet is responsible for this Small Letters design revision. The font used is very similar to punches used on medals by Paquet. The relief of the reverse was lowered and the design was also changed slightly. These changes did not, however, correct the problem of short die life. The inherent design flaw (having the head and tail of the eagle directly opposite the wreath) could only be solved with a totally different design.

Paquet tried to correct this problem with a modification of the Flying Eagle design. He proposed a new eagle that was bent in such a way that its head and tail would not oppose the wreath on the reverse. Unfortunately, this Small Eagle design looks more like a quail that has just been shot than a symbol of our national spirit.

Longacre's new Indian Head design was also created in 1858. A more accurate name for this design would be "Liberty With Indian Headdress," as the profile used on the Indian Head cent is obviously not a Native American. The source of the profile was borrowed from Longacre's earlier gold coinage designs.

Three new reverse designs were tested also at this time. The choices included a Plain Oak Wreath, an Oak Wreath with an ornamented shield, and a Laurel Wreath. Pattern coinage dated 1858 of all the design combinations were sold to collectors of the day. The Laurel Wreath and the Indian Head were adopted for use the next year with minor modifications.

The Laurel Wreath design is actually an olive wreath, but was dubbed *Laurel* by Mint Director Snowden, and has been know as such ever since. It survived only one year in production. A design with a more national character was desired starting in 1859 with patterns, and in 1860 for general circulation; an Oak Wreath and Shield design was used for the reverse. This design was used on the cent reverse until the change to the Lincoln design in 1909.

**Longacre's
Laurel Wreath Design**
Enlarged 1.5x—Actual Size: 19mm

Longacre's longest-lasting design, however, was not the Indian Head cent, but his new Cereals Wreath design for the reverse of the dime, which was used from 1860 until 1916. The design was also used on the half dime until its demise in 1873.

Work had begun in the last part of 1863 for Longacre's next new project, the two-cent piece. Two original designs were made. The first was a revolutionary design of George Washington, facing right, with a motto GOD AND OUR COUNTRY above. Adoption of this design would have set a precedent of featuring famous Americans on the coinage of the United States.

The other design Longacre put forward was a shield with arrows and a laurel wreath, echoing the wartime posture of the country. Another motto, GOD OUR TRUST, was added to a ribbon above. This was later changed to IN GOD WE TRUST and eventually became a standard motto on all American coinage.

Minor modifications were made in the spring of 1864 to both the two-cent and one-cent pieces. The two-cent coin's motto lettering was made slightly larger and the cent design

**Longacre's
Cereal Wreath Design**
Enlarged 1.5x—Actual Size: 17.9 mm

was changed by sharpening the details. Apparently, Longacre was satisfied with this latest change, as he added his initial L to the ribbon below the head-dress. This would be his last revision on the cent.

In March 1865, the issuance of a nickel three-cent coin was passed through Congress to help redeem the much derided paper Fractional Currency that had clogged up the commerce of the Civil War era. Longacre had not forgotten the dif-ficulty of designing coins for this hard metal. His design incorporated the same head used on all his Liberty and Indian portraits, with the modification of a small coronet in the hair. The reverse was his laurel wreath from the 1859 cent design, with the addition of the Roman numeral III. Nowhere on the coin was the word "Cents."

Longacre's nightmare of preparing dies for striking coins in nickel alloy was only beginning. The next coin to fall to non-precious-metal "token" status was the five-cent piece. Longacre again tried his hand at portraying a famous American for the new nickel coin. This time he featured the recently assassinated and martyred President Lincoln. This was rejected as possibly being destructive to the Reconstruction process. He also resurrected the Washington design from the two-cent pattern of 1864. Various reverses using different wreath styles and lettering were tried. The design eventually settled on used the shield from the two-cent coin, minus the wartime arrows. The reverse was a simple "5" surrounded by 13 "stars and bars."

Longacre's other project for 1866 was the revision of the gold and silver coinage. The Act of March 3, 1865, called for the motto IN GOD WE TRUST to appear on all coinage large enough to permit the addition. Longacre added a scroll above the reverses of all silver coins larger than a dime and all gold coins larger than the $3 piece.

In 1867, with the silver and gold design revisions complete, Longacre began to correct the design of the five-cent coin. His Coronet-style head from the three-cent piece was tested with var-ious wreath styles from the previous year. Another, more intricate, design was made featuring the typ-ical Longacre Liberty Head. The design showed Liberty wearing a headdress of three large feathers and a four-star headband, with a ribbon featuring a new motto, UNION AND LIBERTY. No doubt very proud of this design, he added LONGACRE F. below the truncation of the bust. Although a

It has long been numismatic lore that the model for the Indian Head cent was Longacre's first daughter, Sarah (born 1828, later Sarah Longacre Keen). The story was that as a young girl of 12, Sarah visited her father at the Mint when he was at work designing the new cent. A group of Indians were also visiting the Mint at the time, and the chief let the little girl try on his headgear. The effect was so striking that her father made a quick sketch and submitted it as the new cent design.

Unfortunately, over the years, the story has gotten so distorted that all credi-bility has been argued aside. The fact that Sarah was already 30 years old in 1858 is the first obvious error. The Indian head-dress, Longacre wrote, was inspired by drawings of Indians of the Chippewa nation in the Lake Superior area, and not from any chance encounter at the Mint.

The cute story aside, the Indian Head cent may well carry the profile of Sarah Longacre. A sepia drawing done by Longacre around 1840 of Sarah shows all too well the similarities between her and the Indian princess. A later sketch, made from this earlier drawing, shows up in Longacre's sketchbook that also contains his other small-cent sketches, including the Indian Head cent prototype sketch. The most noticeable feature is the "Longacre nose," whose profile lines run straight from the tip to the forehead. The eyebrows, lips, and chin shape are very similar on all these sketches.

beautiful design, the only change that was made to the five-cent coin was the removal of the rays.

This same year Longacre redesigned the coinage of the Republic of Chile. His "Fine Style" designs were a great improvement over the crude coinage that preceded them. Longacre made these dies apparently on his own account, receiving $2,000 for this service.

Early in 1868, a bill was written that would· make the cent, three-cent, five-cent, and ten-cent coinage all from nickel alloy. The inclusion of the dime to this group seemed to doom yet another denomination to mere token status. Longacre made stereotypical designs, again using the Coronet style and various reverses from earlier designs. A large trial in nickel alloy for the ten-cent size was made using the old large-cent, Coronet-style Liberty. The idea was abandoned when it was decided that the ten-cent coin would be too large for the hard nickel alloy.

1867 Five-Cent Pattern (Judd 561)

Longacre had begun work later in the year on other denominations utilizing the same Coronet design. The $10 piece was one that he had finished by year's end.

THE END OF "A LONG AND USEFUL LIFE"

James B. Longacre died very suddenly on January 1, 1869, at the age of 75. A memorial meeting was held at the Mint on January 5. Eulogies were given by Dr. H.R. Linderman, Charles Barber, and William DuBois. Also in attendance were James Booth, and A. Loudon Snowden, as well as the rest of the Mint staff.

Linderman said of Longacre:

> Mr. Longacre, my friends, was no ordinary man. His talents were of high order, and would, with his industrious and frugal habits, have enabled him to achieve success and distinction in any professional or business career. His refined nature, however, appeared to avoid the sharp conflicts of life, and he sought, in quiet devotion to art, a congenial field exercise of his powers, and in it he achieved a success sufficient to satisfy a reasonable ambition. He reached by merit the honorable position of engraver of the National Mint, and so discharged its duties for a period of a quarter of a century as to command the continued confidence of the government and the public.
>
> Mr. Longacre was a man of strong religious faith, and adorned that faith by his daily walk and conversation. Like all truly great and good men, he was modest in deportment. His official duties were performed with a faithfulness worthy of all commendation; whilst his intercourse with his brother officers and subordinates was characterized by dignity, frankness, and urbanity, and the utmost kindness. After a long and useful life, and with faculties unimpaired, our friend passed peacefully and contented to his rest. Let us ever cherish his memory, and strive to emulate his virtues.

Appendix B: Counterfeit and Altered Coins

Counterfeits were once a great detriment to the enjoyable pursuit of coin collecting. Throughout the 1950s until the mid-1970s, collectors had a good chance of buying a counterfeit if they strayed from traditional sources for their coins. The average collector was mostly ignorant about counterfeit detection, and there was nowhere to turn for protection. Venues not typically known for numismatic expertise (such as flea markets, estate auctions, and garage sales) were places where counterfeits could easily be found. At the typical coin show, counterfeits were offered knowingly by what one might call "fly-by-night" dealers, who gave no invoice and had no permanent place of business. Other established coin dealers may have unknowingly offered counterfeits as well. While the established dealers may have had more regard for their reputation and would probably refund the cost of a counterfeit if asked, it was still up to the collector to discover the counterfeit. It was buyer beware!

In the early 1970s Vigil Hancock, president of the American Numismatic Association from 1975 to 1977, along with noted collector John Jay Pittman and dealer Abe Kosoff, took on the problem of counterfeits in the marketplace. Together they created the ANA Certification Service, with Charles R. Hoskins as director. The sharing of knowledge of counterfeits made collectors aware of the extent of the problems. Coins that were commonly counterfeited were now issued authentication papers from ANACS. This slowed the traffic of counterfeits within the hobby, but they still were easily sold to inexperienced collectors looking for bargains.

The authentication of coins evolved into the certification of grades as well. This change to certified grading, with its automatic guarantee of authenticity, has been the main reason that the coin collecting hobby has grown dramatically over the last decade. Encapsulated grading (commonly called "slabbing" today) in 1986 was the idea that changed the coin hobby forever. Now, in addition to a guarantee of authenticity, there was a tamper-proof holder to ensure the coin's legitimacy. Today's collector who buys certified coins from established dealers or auction companies is assured of protection from buying counterfeits.

Genuine 1856

However, with the advent of Internet auctions, counterfeits are again being sold to the unwary. It is wise to be very cautious when buying uncertified coins from people you may not be able to locate later. If the bargain coin you bought turns out to be fake, there may be little recourse if the seller is in, for example, China.

The following examples are just a sampling of the pieces that have fooled collectors over the years. The Flying Eagle and Indian Cent Collectors Society (the Fly-In Club) maintains a "Counterfeit Library" of many of these coins, available for members to borrow as they would a book from a library.

Altered 1856

Altered Dates (Typically 1856, 1877)

Most counterfeits were made to deceive collectors, so the scarcer dates are usually the target of counterfeiters. Many real coins are altered to look like a more valuable date. A common alteration is made by taking an 1858 Flying Eagle cent and changing the date to look like 1856. This is usually easily detected if you know the diagnostics and features of a real 1856

Altered 1856, Detail

cent. Most alterations are made from lower-grade 1858 cents and may be artificially worn or corroded to hide the alteration work. The majority of 1856 cents grade VF or better, so the offering of a low-grade example is reason enough to be suspicious. Additionally, a quick check to see if the letters in the legend are not of the Small Letters style (used only in 1858) may eliminate an alteration. The digits of the genuine 1856 are much different from the digits on the 1858, especially in the shape of the 5. Genuine 1856 cents show the upright of the 5 pointing directly at the center of the ball at the end of the bottom loop. 1858 cents all have it pointing to the left of the ball.

The 1877 cent is also a target for an alteration from a more common coin, such as an 1879. On the example above, a few things should alert a collector right away. First, the reverse is from the wrong die used for 1877. All Mint State 1877 cents had a Shallow N in ONE. An 1879 cent (from which this piece was altered) always has a Bold N in ONE. Also the base of the digit 1 shows a slight bulge. This is found on all genuine 1879 Indian Head cents, and never on an 1877.

Of course a Bold N on an 1877 does not automatically condemn it as a counterfeit. Pictured is a circulated Proof example. All 1877 Proofs have a Bold N. Only a few dies are known for both the Proof and circulation-strike 1877 Indian Head cent, so basic knowledge of the die diagnostics will help authenticate any 1877.

Spark Erosion Counterfeits (Patterns, Any Flying Eagle Cent, Most Better-Date Indian Head Cents)

A spark erosion counterfeit is made by transferring an image of a real coin to a die, by way of an electric current. The die is immersed in an electrolytic bath with the host coin held a slight distance off its face. As a current is passed between the coin and the die, tiny pits are etched into the die. The die is then polished to remove as much of the pitting as possible. By their nature, these coins are not difficult for moderately experienced collectors to spot. They usually have polished fields, and heavy pitting around and on the devices. The edges are normally very sharp, like those of a Proof issue.

Altered 1877

Altered 1877, Detail

Genuine 1877 Circulated Proof

Spark Erosion 1873

Spark Erosion 1875

Spark Erosion 1878

Spark Erosion 1908-S

Spark Erosion 1909-S

Spark Erosion S Mintmark

Genuine S Mintmark

The 1873 counterfeit on page 236 is a very crudely made piece. Aside from the numerous raised pimples covering the coin, it may be noticed that it has a Shallow N reverse, a feature not known on genuine coins made this year.

The 1875 likewise has a Shallow N. This design is also not known on this date. There are fewer raised pimples on this one; perhaps the counterfeiter took extra care in preparing the die. However, it still has a very sharp edge and the details are very rough.

The 1878 counterfeit also bears telltale signs of the spark erosion process.

The 1908-S and 1909-S counterfeits shown share the same reverse. The dies are very well made. Maybe they would fool many collectors—and even some dealers—especially if they were included in a collection bought casually. The weakness in the denticles and the raised rim are two unusual aspects of these coins.

Transfer Dies (Any Flying Eagle or Better-Date Indian Head Cent)

The transfer die counterfeit is made by creating dies by directly transferring the design from a host coin. This is done by impacting the coin, and destroying it in the process, with a soft metal die. These counterfeits can be quite deceptive, if care is taken in making the dies. Knowledge of the characteristics of genuine coins will help identify possible counterfeits.

If all the details of the host coin get transferred to the die, so will any defects, such as contact marks. These will show up as depressions on all of the counterfeit coins made from this die. Unlike those on genuine coins, the depressions will have the same surface qualities as the surrounding areas of the coin. By noting the position of the depressions on multiple coins, you can identify counterfeits.

Transfer Die 1869

Transfer Die 1873 S-6, Circulated

Transfer Die 1873 S-6, Uncirculated

Genuine 1873 S-6

The 1869 cent above is obviously fake because it has a Bold N reverse, which was not used until the next year. If it were not for this oversight, this coin would probably remain undiscovered in many a collection.

The 1873 counterfeits pictured here are of a known variety: Snow-6, with a numeral 3 punched into the first pearl. Just by chance the counterfeiter used this variety as a host coin. The quality of these counterfeits is so good that they have escaped detection until very recently. Many examples of transfer dies counterfeits are artificially worn, perhaps in a rock tumbler, and recolored to hide much of the counterfeiter's work. The second 1873 cent is an unusual "Mint State" example of the counterfeit. Comparing the images, it may be difficult to say which is the counterfeit. Only careful inspection of the dies reveals the bottom one as the genuine example. Many of the raised pimples do not show up on the genuine example. A large transferred contact mark is visible on the O in ONE on both counterfeits (but not on the genuine).

The 1876 counterfeit pictured is also a very deceptive coin. No genuine 1876 Indian Head cent is known with a Shallow N reverse, so a specialist will immediately recognize it as fake. If this mistake had not been made, the counterfeit probably would have escaped detection for a long time.

The 1877 counterfeit (right) is very close to perfection. The obverse carries all the diagnostics of the genuine Mint State 1877 coin. The reverse features the Bold N, which, as mentioned earlier, is found only on the Proof of this year. Additionally, the reverse is rotated in medal alignment, top to top, rather than the usual coin alignment of top to bottom. While unusual alignments are not immediately

Transfer Die 1876

Transfer Die 1877

Transfer Die 1909-S

Transfer Die S Mintmark   **Genuine S Mintmark**

reason to condemn a coin, on the 1877 cent it definitely cause for concern. Perhaps the counterfeiter lives in Canada, where medal alignment is natural on the coins in circulation.

The 1909-S cent would fool any casual observer. The surfaces look normal and even the mintmark looks right. However, there are numerous spike-like lines around the field just inside the denticles. This is unknown on any genuine 1909-S cent, so it is a dead giveaway that this is a fake.

Added Mintmarks (1908-S and 1909-S)

A common counterfeit is made by adding an S mintmark to the more common 1908 and 1909 Philadelphia Mint coins. While both dates are found with added mintmarks, the 1909 is most commonly faked in this way. Again, by knowing the characteristics of the genuine coins, you can more easily detect counterfeits. For example, it is known by reading this book that all genuine 1909-S Indian Head cents have missing details on the left half of the first feather. This is not from a weak strike; it is part of the design. However, the 1909 cents from Philadelphia show full details on the first feather. If you want to buy a 1909-S with full feather details, be prepared to buy a counterfeit!

Added S Mintmark

Added S Mintmark, Detail   **Genuine S Mintmark**

Plating, Polishing, and Whizzing (Any Coin)

Although not actually counterfeits, coins that were "processed" to simulate a higher grade are as much a problem as the fakes and alterations described. It used to be very common to hear of people engaged in processing coins by the thousands! I hate to imagine how many beautiful VF, EF, and AU Indian Head cents have been ruined for the sake of a quick buck.

The simplest form of coin processing is polishing, illustrated by the 1896 coin below. The luster is gone and what remains is a very smooth surface. Comparison with an original Mint State coin will make a polished coin obvious for what it is. Some polish jobs are more difficult to detect.

The 1868 and 1871 pieces have been electroplated with copper to simulate mint red color. These are usually very bright and unnatural in appearance. If some of the plating wears off, the toned areas will have sharp outlines rather than a normal even shading between red and brown.

Whizzing is a problem that catches collectors all the time. The production and sale of these pieces is, in my opinion, as onerous a practice as selling counterfeits. Whizzed coins have their surfaces wire brushed in such a way as to simulate mint luster. These can be very deceptive, but familiarity with luster patterns of original Mint State coins will help you avoid whizzed pieces. Typically they will show a raised lip on the edge of the letters and devices (caused by the movement of the surface metal).

Polished 1896

Copper-Plated 1868

Copper-Plated 1871

Whizzed 1863

Whizzed 1863, Detail

Contemporary Counterfeits (Any Date)

Very rarely, we can find a fake made to circulate in commerce along with then-current Indian Head cents. These are usually crude pieces artificially worn to increase their acceptability in transactions. The 1891 piece pictured here was made from hand-engraved dies, and is very interesting. Here is one instance where the counterfeit is more interesting than the coin it hopes to mimic.

Contemporary Counterfeit 1891

Some Final Advice

Familiarity with the types of counterfeits will go a long way toward helping you avoid them. Buy from established dealers who will guarantee the authenticity of coins they sell. Learn what an original coin looks like; this will likewise help you avoid being taken by counterfeits and problem coins. If a coin look suspicious in any way, don't buy it. Even if it seems like a bargain and turns out to be genuine, there is no price too cheap for a problem coin!

APPENDIX C: MARKET PRICE HISTORY

MINT STATE COINS, BY DATE

This table shows historical prices for Flying Eagle and Indian Head cents in Mint State. Prices are taken from the *Guide Book of United States Coins* (the "Red Book"), from the *Unc.* listings in the 1947 and 1967 editions, the *MS-60* listings in the 1987 edition, and the *MS-63* listings in the 2007 edition. (Due to "gradeflation," or the relaxation of grading standards over the years, the MS-60 of 1987 is often the MS-63 of today.)

Date	1947 ed.	1967 ed.	1987 ed.	2007 ed.	% Increase
1856	$150.00	$2,600.00	$3,500.00	$18,500.00	12,233%
1857	5.00	100.00	300.00	650.00	12,900%
1858 Large Letters	8.50	147.50	300.00	650.00	7,547%
1858 Small Letters	10.00	147.50	300.00	650.00	6,400%
1858, 8 Over 7	n/a	unpriced	1,000.00	1,000.00	0
1859	4.50	90.00	300.00	500.00	11,011%
1860 Pointed Bust (a)	4.50	70.00	160.00	500.00	11,011%
1860 Round Bust (a)	4.50	70.00	160.00	225.00	4,900%
1861	8.00	100.00	235.00	275.00	3,338%
1862	1.10	35.00	130.00	160.00	14,445%
1863	1.00	30.00	130.00	160.00	15,900%
1864, CN	3.00	65.00	175.00	200.00	6,567%
1864, No L	4.75	66.00	85.00	140.00	2,847%
1864, With L	30.00	300.00	340.00	650.00	2,067%
1865	3.50	45.00	70.00	135.00	3,757%
1866	11.00	150.00	185.00	330.00	2,900%
1867	9.50	145.00	185.00	350.00	3,584%
1868	9.50	160.00	185.00	300.00	3,058%
1869	11.00	370.00	350.00	600.00	5,355%
1870	11.00	175.00	225.00	565.00	5,036%
1871	16.00	220.00	275.00	600.00	3,650%
1872	22.50	300.00	350.00	925.00	4,011%
1873, Close 3 (b)	5.50	92.50	125.00	550.00	9,900%
1873, Doubled LIBERTY	n/a	n/a	1,200.00	13,000.00	983%
1873, Open 3 (b)	5.50	92.50	125.00	325.00	5,809%
1874	5.50	92.50	115.00	250.00	4,445%
1875	6.50	92.50	100.00	250.00	3,746%
1876	6.50	115.00	135.00	380.00	5,746%
1877	37.50	950.00	1,500.00	4,000.00	10,567%
1878	6.50	100.00	135.00	380.00	5,746%
1879	2.75	42.50	55.00	120.00	4,264%
1880	2.50	32.50	45.00	130.00	5,100%
1881	2.75	32.50	45.00	90.00	3,173%
1882	2.00	32.50	45.00	90.00	4,450%
1883	2.00	30.00	45.00	90.00	4,450%
1884	2.50	40.00	55.00	120.00	4,700%
1885	6.50	62.50	75.00	200.00	2,977%
1886, Type I (c)	2.50	45.00	60.00	225.00	8,900%
1886, Type II (c)	2.50	45.00	60.00	475.00	18,900%
1887	1.65	25.00	40.00	80.00	4,748%
1888, 8 Over 7	n/a	n/a	unpriced	27,500.00	—
1888	1.65	30.00	40.00	125.00	7,476%
1889	1.65	25.00	40.00	80.00	4,748%

Date	1947 ed.	1967 ed.	1987 ed.	2007 ed.	% Increase
1890	$1.50	$25.00	$40.00	$80.00	5,233%
1891	1.50	25.00	40.00	80.00	5,233%
1892	2.00	27.50	40.00	80.00	3,900%
1893	1.50	26.00	40.00	80.00	5,233%
1894	3.00	47.50	50.00	115.00	3,733%
1895	1.50	22.50	37.00	65.00	4,233%
1896	3.00	28.50	37.00	65.00	2,067%
1897	3.00	25.00	35.00	65.00	2,067%
1898	2.50	27.50	35.00	65.00	2,500%
1899	3.00	20.00	35.00	65.00	2,067%
1900	1.50	15.00	34.00	55.00	3,567%
1901	1.50	12.50	34.00	55.00	3,567%
1902	0.85	12.50	34.00	55.00	6,371%
1903	1.50	12.50	34.00	55.00	3,567%
1904	1.00	12.50	34.00	55.00	5,400%
1905	1.00	12.50	34.00	55.00	5,400%
1906	1.00	12.50	34.00	55.00	5,400%
1907	2.00	12.50	34.00	55.00	2,700%
1908	1.75	16.00	35.00	55.00	3,043%
1908-S	7.50	140.00	155.00	375.00	4,900%
1909	0.75	17.50	45.00	60.00	7,900%
1909-S	30.00	400.00	400.00	900.00	2,900%

(a) The Pointed Bust and Round Bust varieties of 1860 were differentiated in the Red Book in 1994.
(b) The Close 3 and Open 3 varieties of 1873 were first differentiated by numismatists in the 1960s.
(c) The Type I and Type II varieties of 1886 were differentiated by numismatists in 1954.

MINT STATE COINS, BY TYPE OR VARIETY

This table shows historical prices for Mint State Flying Eagle and Indian Head cents. Prices are taken from the *Guide Book of United States Coins* (the "Red Book"), from the *Unc.* listings in the 1947 and 1967 editions, the *MS-60* listings in the 1987 edition, and the *MS-63* listings in the 2007 edition. Prices given are for the most common coin of each type or variety.

Date	1947 ed.	1967 ed.	1987 ed.	2007 ed.	% Increase
Flying Eagle, 1856	$150.00	$2,600.00	$3,500.00	$18,500.00	12,233%
Flying Eagle, 1857-1858	8.50	147.50	300.00	650.00	7,547%
Indian Head, C-N, 1859	4.50	90.00	300.00	500.00	11,011%
Indian Head, C-N, 1860-1864	1.00	30.00	130.00	160.00	15,900%
Indian Head, 1864-1909	0.75	17.50	45.00	60.00	7,900%

PROOF COINS, BY TYPE OR VARIETY

This table shows historical prices for Proof-format Flying Eagle and Indian Head cents. Prices are taken from the *Guide Book of United States Coins* (the "Red Book"), from the *Proof* listings in the 1947 and 1967 editions, and the *PF-63* listings in the 1987 and 2007 editions. Prices given are for the most common Proof coin of each type or variety.

Date	1947 ed.	1967 ed.	1987 ed.	2007 ed.	% Increase
Flying Eagle, 1856, Proof	$200.00	$3,300.00	$4,000.00	$20,000.00	9,900%
Flying Eagle, 1857-1858, Proof	35.00	1,775.00	3,200.00	8,200.00	23,328%
Indian Head, C-N, 1859 Proof	10.00	600.00	1,500.00	1,600.00	15,900%
Indian Head, C-N, 1860-1864, Proof	10.00	325.00	900.00	700.00	6,900%
Indian Head, 1864-1909, Proof	2.75	55.00	375.00	300.00	10,809%

BIBLIOGRAPHY

Alexander, David T., Thomas K. DeLorey, and Brad Reed. *Coin World Comprehensive Catalog & Encyclopedia of United States Coins*. Sidney, OH: Coin World, 1995.

ANACS Population Report. Columbus, OH: ANACS. Various issues.

Bowers, Q. David. *A Buyer's and Enthusiast's Guide to Flying Eagle and Indian Cents*. Bowers and Merena Galleries, 1996.

Bowers, Q. David, with Douglas Winter. *The United States $3 Gold Piece*. Wolfeboro, NH: American Numismatic Rarities, 2005.

Breen, Walter H. *The United States Minor Coinage 1793–1916*. New York, NY: Wayte Raymond, Inc., 1954.

Breen, Walter H. *The Secret History of the Gobrecht Coinages 1836–1840*. New York, NY: Wayte Raymond, Inc., 1954.

Breen, Walter H. "Blundered Dies of U.S. and Colonial Coins." *Empire Topics*, October 1958. (First publication of the 1873 Doubled LIBERTY cent.)

Breen, Walter H. *Complete Encyclopedia of U.S. and Colonial Proof Coins*. Albertson, NY: F.C.I. Press, 1977.

Breen, Walter H. *Walter Breen's Complete Encyclopedia of U.S. and Colonial Coins*. New York, NY: Doubleday & Co., 1988.

Bressett, Kenneth (editor). *A Guide Book of United States Coins*, 2006 edition. Atlanta, GA: Whitman Publishing, LLC, 2005.

Bressett, Kenneth E., with narrative by Q. David Bowers. *The Official American Numismatic Association Grading Standards for United States Coins*, sixth edition. Atlanta, GA: Whitman Publishing, LLC, 2005.

Carothers, Neil. *Fractional Money*. New York, NY: John Wiley & Sons, Inc., 1930.

Cartwright, Timothy. "The Thrill of Discovering the 1871 S4, Shallow N Reverse." *Longacre's Ledger*, December 1999.

Coin World Almanac. Sidney, OH: Coin World, 1976 and later editions.

Coin World. Sidney, OH: Amos Press. Various issues.

COINage. Ventura, CA: Miller Publications. Various issues.

Coins Magazine. Iola, WI: Krause Publications. Various issues.

Conger, George R. "The Controversial Feathered Headdress." *Longacre's Ledger*, April 1992.

Conger, George R. "An Argument Favoring Sarah as Longacre's Model." *Longacre's Ledger*, July 1992.

DeLorey, Thomas K. "Was Mischief Afoot in 1857 Die Clashes?" "Collectors' Clearinghouse," *Coin World*, July 1, 1977.

DeLorey, Thomas K. "Longacre, Unsung Engraver of the U.S. Mint." *Longacre's Ledger*, January 1992. Reprinted from *The Numismatist*, October 1985.

Eaton, W.C. "The Eagle Cents of 1858." *The Numismatist*, January 1916. Updated in *The Numismatist*, November 1920, and further in *The Numismatist*, March 1921.

Eaton, W.C. "The Eagle Cents of 1857." *The Numismatist*, May 1921. Most research for this article was done by E.R. Alvord.

Fivaz, Bill. "Never In My Wildest Dreams." *Rare Coin Review* No. 62. Description of the discovery of the 1857 Flying Eagle cent with clash marks from a Liberty Seated quarter dollar.

Fivaz, Bill. "Definitely a Difference!" *Longacre's Ledger*, Summer 1994. Description of the differences in the neck feathers on the letter size varieties of the 1858 Flying Eagle cent.

Fivaz, Bill, and J.T. Stanton. *The Cherrypickers' Guide to Rare Die Varieties*, fourth edition, volume 1. Mike Ellis, editor. Savannah, GA: Stanton Books and Supplies, 2000.

Fuld, George and Melvin. *U.S. Civil War Store Cards*. Token and Medal Society, 1972.

Fuld, George and Melvin. *Patriotic Civil War Tokens*, fourth edition. Token and Medal Society, 1982.

Goe, Rusty. *The Mint on Carson Street*. Reno, NV: Southgate Coins and Collectables, 2005.

Hettger, Henry T. "Collusive Bidding on Indian Head Cent Planchets in 1892." *Longacre's Ledger*, October 1991.

Jones, John F. "The 1856 Flying Eagle Cent." *The Numismatist*, April 1944.

Judd, J. Hewitt. *United States Pattern Coins*, 9th edition, edited by Q. David Bowers. Atlanta, GA: Whitman Publishing, LLC, 2005.

Julian, R.W. *Medals of the United States Mint: The First Century 1792–1892*. El Cajon, CA: Token and Medal Society, Inc., 1977.

Julian, R.W. "The Flying Eagle Cent." *COINage*, October 1987.

Julian, R.W. "The Indian Head Cent." *COINage*, May 1988.

Julian, R.W. "The Cent Becomes Bronze: 1864." *FUN-Topics*, Summer 1987.

Julian, R.W. "The 1877 Indian Head Cent." *Coins Magazine*, October 1992.

Kross, Herman E. *Documentary History of Banking and Currency in the United States*. Volumes 1–4. New York, NY: Chelsea House Publishers, 1983.

Larson, Dr. Timothy. "The 1888/7 S2 – Is it an Overdate?" *Longacre's Ledger*, June 2000.

Longacre's Ledger. Journal of the Fly-In Club. Contains much information on die varieties, rarity ratings, etc.

Numismatic Guaranty Corporation of America Census Report. Parsippany, NJ: Numismatic Guaranty Corporation of America. Various issues.

Numismatic News. Iola, WI: Krause Publications. Various issues.

Numismatist, The. Colorado Springs, CO. Various issues.

Pilliod, Chris. "What Error Coins Can Teach Us About Die Settings." *The Numismatist*, April 1996.

Pilliod, Chris. "Can a Two-Headed Cent Really Exist? Yes, But Only in 1859." *Longacre's Ledger*, Dec. 2000.

PCGS Population Report. Newport Beach, CA: Professional Coin Grading Service. Various issues.

Pollock, Andrew W. III. *United States Patterns and Related Issues*. Wolfeboro, NH: Bowers and Merena Galleries, 1994.

Rare Coin Review. Wolfeboro, NH: Bowers and Merena Galleries, Inc. Various issues.

Sebby, Vernon. "A Discussion of High Grade, Mint State Indian Cents," four-part series. *Longacre's Ledger*, 2001–2002.

Sirna, Ronald R. "Collecting Proof Indian Cents for Fun." *Longacre's Ledger*, December 2002.

Snow, Richard. "The Midnight Minter." *Longacre's Ledger*, January 1991.

Snow, Richard. "High Leaves, Low Leaves." *Longacre's Ledger*, April 1991.

Snow, Richard. "The Indian Head Cent of 1877." *The Numismatist*, March 1998.

Snow, Richard. "The Showdown." *Longacre's Ledger*, September 2002.

Snow, Richard. *Flying Eagle and Indian Cents*. Tucson, AZ: Eagle Eye Press, 1992.

Snow, Richard. *Flying Eagle and Indian Cent Attribution Guide, Vol. 1, 1856–1858*, second edition. Tucson, AZ: Eagle Eye Rare Coins Inc., 2001.

Snow, Richard. *Flying Eagle and Indian Cent Attribution Guide, Vol. 1, 1859–1869*, second edition. Tucson, AZ: Eagle Eye Rare Coins Inc., 2003.

Snow, Richard. "Proof Die Identification for Indian Cents." *Longacre's Ledger*, Fall 1994.

Smithsonian Institution, National Portrait Gallery. *American Portrait Prints*. Wendy Wick Reaves, ed. 1984.

Steinberger, Otto C. "Indian Cent Date Varieties." *Numismatic Scrapbook Magazine*. Serial feature commencing with the December 1961 issue, later reprinted as a monograph.

Steve, Larry R. "THE F.IND.ERS REPORT." *Longacre's Ledger*, various issues.

Steve, Larry R. "An Analysis of the 1867 Over 67." *Longacre's Ledger*, June 2001.

Steve, Larry R., and Kevin J. Flynn. *A Comprehensive Guide to Selected Rare Flying Eagle and Indian Cent Varieties*. Jarrettsville, MD: Nuvista Press, 1995.

Taxay, Don. *Counterfeit, Mis-Struck and Unofficial U.S. Coins*. New York, NY: Arco Publishing, 1963.

Taxay, Don. *Scott's Comprehensive Catalogue and Encyclopedia of U.S. Coins*. New York, NY: Scott Publishing, 1971.

Taxay, Don. *U.S. Mint and Coinage*. New York, NY: Arco Publishing, 1966.

Travers, Scott A. *Official Guide to Coin Grading and Counterfeit Detection*, edited by Q. David Bowers. Professional Coin Grading Service, 1997.

Van Ryzin, Robert R. *The Crime of 1873*. Iola, WI: Kruse Publications, 2001.

Vermeule, Cornelius. *Numismatic Art in America*. Cambridge, MA: Belknap Press, 1971.

Wharton, Joseph. "Project for Reorganizing the Small Coinage of the United States of America." April 15, 1864.

Yeoman, R.S. (editor). *A Guide Book of United States Coins*. Kenneth E. Bressett, recent and current editor. Racine, WI; New York, NY; and Atlanta, GA: various editions beginning with 1947.